Behind the Scenes

Covering the JFK Assassination

Darwin Payne

University of North Texas Press
Denton, Texas

Permissions:
University of North Texas Press
1155 Union Circle #311336
Denton, TX 76203-5017

The paper used in this book meets the minimum requirements of the American National Standard for Permanence of Paper for Printed Library Materials, z39.48.1984. Binding materials have been chosen for durability.

Library of Congress Cataloging-in-Publication Data

Names: Payne, Darwin, author.
Title: Behind the scenes : covering the JFK assassination / Darwin Payne.
Other titles: Covering the JFK assassination
Description: Denton, Texas : University of North Texas Press, [2023] |
  Includes bibliographical references and index.
Identifiers: LCCN 2023028668 (print) | LCCN 2023028669 (ebook) | ISBN
  9781574419115 (cloth) | ISBN 9781574419221 (ebook)
Subjects: LCSH: Kennedy, John F. (John Fitzgerald),
  1917-1963--Assassination. | Payne, Darwin. | Presidents--Assassination--
  United States. | Presidents--Assassination--Press coverage--
  Texas--Dallas. | Reporters and reporting--Texas--Biography. | BISAC:
  HISTORY / United States / 20th Century | LANGUAGE ARTS & DISCI-
  PLINES / Journalism | LCGFT: Autobiographies. | Personal narratives.
Classification: LCC E842.9 .P39 2023 (print) | LCC E842.9 (ebook) | DDC
  973.922092 [B]--dc23/eng/20230713
LC record available at https://lccn.loc.gov/2023028668
LC ebook record available at https://lccn.loc.gov/2023028669

The electronic edition of this book was made possible by the support of the Vick Family Foundation.

Typeset by vPrompt eServices.

Contents

Preface

NEARLY SIX DECADES have passed since the assassination in Dallas of our nation's thirty-fifth president, John Fitzgerald Kennedy. How astonishing to realize that eleven additional presidents have held this high office since then. His assassination has taken such a grip on our memory that through coming ages it may rival that of Abraham Lincoln's tragic death. Books, articles, photographs, films, commercials, and wildly improbable conspiracy theories regularly recall the loss suffered when rifle shots ended President Kennedy's life during his first term of office.

Although the youngest person ever elected to the White House, he had served three terms in the US House of Representatives, was twice elected to the US Senate, won the Pulitzer Prize for *Profiles in Courage*, and married a beautiful and adored wife, Jacqueline Bouvier. His vibrant personality, handsome features, and athleticism overshadowed those of his predecessors—lackluster Warren Harding, silent Cal Coolidge, engineer Herbert Hoover, wheelchair-bound Franklin Roosevelt, former haberdasher Harry Truman, and war hero Dwight Eisenhower, then in his early 70s. Kennedy was the dynamic president who promised a brighter future.

Such dreams were shattered in the shocking daytime tragedy on November 22, 1963, followed by unexpected events that could have been imagined only by an untethered novelist. To those of us alive on that fateful day, especially those of us in Dallas, the memories of that and ensuing events can't be erased. We continue to be captivated.

Throughout our nation's nearly 250-year history, we have endured four presidential assassinations. In our histories we deal primarily with the first, that of Lincoln, and the fourth, that of Kennedy. Hardly remembered are those of the second and third victims, James Garfield in 1881 and William McKinley in 1901.

Besides myself, my close relatives—parents, sisters, grandparents, aunts and uncles, cousins, and wife—lived in Dallas. We loved the city. It provided the path for bringing middle-class life to our families and thousands of others who gave up uncertain lives as tenant farmers to earn regular wages in this growing city. But many citizens elsewhere felt otherwise about the city after the assassination. For them, and for some in Dallas, it confirmed a new nickname: "city of hate."

Dallas: The place where the president was killed.

Yes, Dallas! Dealey Plaza, where it happened, has the same familiar look as it did in 1963. The red-brick building with the sixth-floor window from which the assassin fired fatal shots is still there. A museum commemorating the event now occupies the same sixth floor with the view held by the assassin. The grassy knoll where terrified spectators fell to the ground in fear of being targets themselves is unchanged. On sunshiny, crowded weekends aggressive salespersons sell lurid and sensationalist five- or ten-dollar tabloids describing the crime in graphic detail and conspiracy theories. The extended pergola is an unforgettable reminder of the place where Abraham Zapruder stood with his Bell & Howell camera. We see first-time visitors contemplating the X marks painted at the approximate place on Elm Street where Oswald's rifle shots, especially the final one, found their target. Visitors lift their heads to stare upward at his sixth-floor window.

Little could we have realized at the time that November 22 marked the end of one era and the beginning of another. Evidence of that fact emerged quickly, though. The modern media brought the events closer than ever to the entire nation, even the world. Neither we in Dallas nor millions of others had ever experienced anything like it. It was especially these days—the twenty-second through the twenty-fifth of November—that television networks began their rapid march to replace the daily newspaper as the primary vehicle for informing the American public about the news of the day. Dimly, as a Dallas newspaper reporter who was there trying to cover so many related events,

I could see it happening. Network television gave live reports for four consecutive days while we newspaper journalists prepared stories for our morning or afternoon editions.

These many weeks, months, and years since 1963, I am among thousands who drive routinely through the assassination site on the way to other nearby destinations. For me, the few others who were here in 1963, and the many younger ones who study the details of the events of November 22, Dealey Plaza is to Dallas what Ford's Theater is to Washington, DC. Ford's Theater, however, does not define our capital city in in the way Dealey Plaza does Dallas.

Many months ago, staying at home to avoid the ravages of the coronavirus and seeking to amuse myself, I found in a dark closet corner my collection of JFK materials, many of which were my own notes taken at whatever scene I was assigned to be as a *Dallas Times Herald* reporter. Among the papers was my years-ago unfinished manuscript about those experiences, written while my memories were fresh and aided by my two reporters' notebooks. I decided to return to that nearly forgotten project. Perhaps there would be some value in publishing my memories as a 26-year-old reporter who found himself intensely involved in covering the story of his life and that of his home city, Dallas.

In the first pages of this memoir/history, as I call it, I briefly look backward to previous presidential visits to Dallas and the ways in which those chief executives were welcomed and entertained—the first being that of Theodore Roosevelt in 1905. As further background, in the appendix I revisit the facts about the previous assassinations of presidents.

I introduce myself as a child of Dallas—one who chose journalism as my profession and began as a general assignments reporter for the *Fort Worth Press* before moving on to the *Dallas Times Herald*. I write about events that made most Dallas citizens fearful that previous actions of extremist right-wing activists during President Kennedy's planned visit would bring further harm to the city's reputation.

Later, as a journalism professor and historian at Southern Methodist University, I started my interests with separate biographies of two famous writers—Frederick Lewis Allen, editor of *Harper's* magazine and author of such popular histories as *Only Yesterday,* and Owen Wister, now a nearly forgotten writer whose novel, *The Virginian,* sparked our lasting interest about the West and its cowboys.

Afterward, I turned to my hometown of Dallas as a primary research interest. Without any specific intention, many of my publications inevitably touched on the assassination. My biography of Sarah T. Hughes, the distinguished federal judge, naturally included her role in giving the presidential oath of office to Lyndon B. Johnson aboard Air Force One. My biography of industrialist J. Erik Jonsson, who was presiding at the Trade Mart while awaiting President Kennedy's arrival and who within weeks would launch his position as mayor to restore the city's spirits and its reputation, also covered many aspects of the assassination. In *Big D: Triumphs and Troubles of the American Supercity in the 20th Century*, I sought to tell the twentieth-century history of the city, including the assassination. An examination of the city and state's racist past came in my biography of the city's first Black judge, Louis A. Bedford Jr., entitled *Quest for Justice.* Other books included a history of the Dallas Citizens Council, the city's so-called oligarchy and acknowledged host for President Kennedy's visit to Dallas.

With a few fellow journalists I was a principal organizer of the thirtieth reunion in Dallas of reporters, editors, and photographers who described their actions at major scenes of the Kennedy assassination. I published and coedited with my colleague Laura Hlavach a transcript of our journalists' comments as *Reporting the Kennedy Assassination: Journalists Who Were There Recall Their Experience*s, published by Three Forks Press. Because of my firsthand involvement in the assassination, I became an occasional speaker and guest at the new Sixth Floor Museum in the School Book Depository building, as well as at other venues.

With my interest in such subjects, it was not surprising that I finally returned to the most significant historical event ever to take place in Dallas, where I continue to live. I hope and believe readers of this memoir/history will gain new perspectives about those horrifying and unexpected events of November 22, 1963, and the preceding and following days.

DARWIN PAYNE

Chapter 1

Earlier Presidential Visits

THROUGHOUT OUR HISTORY a presidential visit has been an important event for any American city, certainly for smaller towns. Such was true for Dallas when on April 3, 1905, shortly after his inauguration, President Theodore Roosevelt launched a tour across the heart of the nation aboard his train, the Roosevelt Special. After brief stops and speechmaking at Pittsburgh, Louisville, St. Louis, and a few other cities, on April 5 he reached Dallas, a rapidly growing Texas town with about fifty thousand residents. It was the state's third most populated city (following San Antonio and Houston), and it had never experienced a presidential visit. Dallas determined to make Roosevelt's stop special.

For Roosevelt it must be admitted that his overnight was little more than incidental. He was headed to San Antonio to reunite with his famous Rough Riders, heroes in the brief 1898 boundary war with Mexico. Typically, when passing through smaller towns, the Roosevelt Special merely slowed down as the engineer sounded a high-pitched whistle for spectators waving flags and hoping for a glance at their famous president. Seldom were they disappointed,

The first president who stopped at little-known Dallas came in April 1905. Theodore Roosevelt's arrival merited many ambitious festivities, including a carriage ride through town. *Dallas Morning News.*

for Roosevelt usually would be looking through a train window, shouting and waving with his special exuberance as it passed without a stop. But for Dallas he did better. He stopped, toured the town, spoke, and spent the night.

Dallas's leaders made elaborate plans, including a carriage ride through downtown streets to show him its progress and special features. City leaders wanted to use six beautiful horses to tour Roosevelt around in a fancy carriage (perhaps as eight horses pulled Napoleon's carriage through the streets of Paris). The president insisted that two horses were enough. His wishes were followed.

A crowd estimated from thirty thousand to a surely exaggerated guess of seventy-five thousand saw their president. Townspeople and their children, shopkeepers, laborers, farm families, cowboys, and even a few who would become more numerous in the future—oil speculators—lined the streets. However many, they gleefully cheered the twenty-sixth president as he traveled up and down the crowded streets, choosing to stand in his carriage. He waved heartily to the men, women, and children who hurrahed him. A few found better vantage points from rooftops and open windows. Spectators with nerve climbed and clung precariously to utility poles for even better views. Flags and bunting were everywhere. The president appealed to the town's aging Confederate veterans, declaring that although he was half-Union blue and half-Confederate gray, he was *all*-Lone Star.

Secret Service agents, six local detectives, four patrolmen, and a mounted guard of honor protected him. Outside the Oriental Hotel at Akard and Commerce Streets, the president spoke to a crowd estimated at twenty-five thousand. Some scuffled over the best places to see him. Inside, the president and some three hundred privileged citizens enjoyed dinner, music, and speeches. The menu included "Saddle Rock Oysters" and "Frog Legs, a la Tartar." Frog legs in Dallas? No problem. But oysters? Such a menu! The president awoke without ceremony early next morning and boarded his Roosevelt Special for San Antonio. His brief stay brought only joy to Dallas. There were no problems, only pleasure, in welcoming this president.[1]

Four short years later, in 1909, Roosevelt's successor, William Howard Taft, the nation's twenty-seventh president, honored Dallas with its second presidential visit. Still on a growth spurt, the city by now had almost doubled its population to some ninety-thousand. Instead of the horse-drawn carriage for Roosevelt, Taft toured town in an actual motorcade. The times were a-changin'. Eight gasoline-powered automobiles, following Taft's chauffeured car, passed crowds on the same streets as Roosevelt. President Taft spoke three times that day—at the state fair, from the balcony at the Oriental Hotel where Roosevelt had spoken, and at an evening banquet.

During the day police officers, deputy sheriffs, and Texas National Guardsmen alike were on duty to control any overeager spectators who wanted to get too close to the Ohio-born Republican Taft. So mindful were the officers and guardsmen of their important responsibilities that Mayor S. J. Hay's wife, although holding appropriate credentials, was nearly arrested when she attempted to join her husband in a protected area.

A far more traumatic event dimmed this day, though. An over-hyped National Guardsman named Sgt. J. L. Manley halted Dallas County's 36-year-old deputy clerk, Louis Reichenstein, as he tried to cross a barricade protecting President Taft at Fair Park. The two exchanged angry words. Manley, his rifle affixed with bayonet, ended the argument by plunging his bayonet through Reichenstein's midsection, front to back. The injury was fatal.

Dallas County's district attorney charged Guardsman Manley with murder. A prolonged legal battle ensued for months and years. City and county officials contended that Manley was guilty of murder. The National Guard argued that Manley was innocent because, after all, he was merely following his orders to protect Taft, but a Dallas County jury convicted Manley and sentenced him to life in prison. Later, his sentence was overturned, but jurors in a new trial in adjacent Ellis County again found him guilty. This time Manley's punishment was reduced to forty years.[2]

Twenty-seven years later, June 12, 1936, Franklin Delano Roosevelt arrived as the city's third presidential visitor. (FDR was

Teddy Roosevelt's fourth cousin.) Accompanied by wife Eleanor, he officially opened the Texas Centennial Exposition—six days late. Hosting the one-hundredth anniversary was an especially proud achievement since Dallas hadn't even existed when Texas won independence in 1836. Led by a trio of prominent bankers, the city was chosen in a state-wide competition.

Some fifty thousand excited spectators roared with approval as the president's open-topped car rolled down a ramp into Fair Park's Cotton Bowl for his speech. The entire nation could listen to this live radio address, presided over by famous broadcaster Ted Husing and newcomer Art Linkletter.

Later at Oak Lawn Park, the president spoke at the unveiling of a magnificent equestrian statue of Robert E. Lee astride his horse Traveler. This 1936 event also occasioned a name change—Oak Lawn Park became Robert E. Lee Park. (The equestrian statue would be removed in 2019 and the park's name changed back to Oak Lawn Park, then to its present name, Turtle Creek Park.)

Prominent in supervising police efforts for crowd control and safety that day was Detective Inspector J. W. (Will) Fritz (who would be prominent in 1963 as chief of the Dallas homicide and robbery bureau and interrogator of Lee Harvey Oswald). Dallas police officers, Secret Service agents, Texas State Highway patrolmen, and others guarded all major intersections where President Roosevelt passed. He rode in the fire chief's seven-passenger touring car (customarily red but painted black, befitting the occasion), accompanied by motorcycle police officers and squad cars. A newspaper headline summarized the day: "Surging Crowds Are Easily Handled During Roosevelt's Visit by Army of Officers." After their full day in Dallas, the Roosevelts' son Elliot drove his parents to his home in Fort Worth to spend the night.[3]

Harry S. Truman, having assumed the presidency after Roosevelt's death in 1945, came to Dallas in 1948, campaigning for a four-year term. Even though I was only a third grader at the time, I retain a fair memory of the hoopla surrounding this visit. There was still something special about a presidential visit, although less for a city that had gained national attention with its Texas Centennial Exposition of 1936. Thousands of spectators lined much of the highway from Fort Worth to Dallas, cheering lustily for Truman; his wife, Bess; and their daughter, Margaret, on this thirty-mile journey. The family rode in a Lincoln automobile, which they had chosen over a proffered Packard. After a pause outside the Chance Vought airplane manufacturing plant in Grand Prairie, the motorcade entered the city via Oak Cliff and stopped for the president to speak at Rebel Stadium, home of Dallas's Double-A minor league baseball team. Some twelve thousand spectators, including my older sister, June, attended.

Public school students were permitted to skip school to see the president. June accepted that opportunity. Truman was much the favorite candidate in our home in this battle against the seemingly sophisticated GOP nominee Thomas E. Dewey, governor of New York. Afterward, June told us how surprised she was to see Black attendees sitting wherever they pleased! Truman's advisers, wanting a good crowd, had guaranteed this right to Black Democratic leaders.

June and many others had never experienced integrated seating. My parents, although not active in civil rights efforts or politics at all other than being regular voters, listened to the news and read about such events. They were pleasantly surprised to learn this. It seemed right to them. And to me, too, age 11.

Such a decision to desegregate the rally had been daring, and in her biography of her father, Margaret Truman observed that this was the first integrated political rally in the South.[4] The *Dallas Morning News* story noted this violation of Southern norms, estimating that about 30 percent of the integrated crowd were "Negroes." June's surprise at desegregated seating was understandable, for in Dallas and other Southern cities, Black citizens had separate neighborhoods and schools, separate seating on buses and streetcars, separate bleachers at the baseball games and other sporting events, separate hotels, water fountains, public restrooms, public parks, and movie theaters.

After the president's appearance, the Truman family was escorted to Union Station to take a train to Bonham to visit Sam Rayburn, minority leader of the US House of Representatives. One of the *News* reporters who wrote an excellent sidebar story about the Dallas visit was Harry McCormick (whom I would see years later on November 22, 1963, under unusual circumstances, which I later describe.)

Dwight David Eisenhower, the famous general in charge of plans for our Allied invasion of Europe, born in Texas but reared in Kansas, and successor to Truman as president, made a brief stop in 1956 in his successful reelection bid. On this tour-by-rail he paused in Dallas only to make a thirty-minute speech at downtown Union Station. Both Republicans and Democrats cheered him.[5]

In fact, the Texas Democratic Party already had rejected Democratic presidential candidate Adlai Stevenson in favor of Republican Eisenhower. This was an early indication of future Republican dominance in Texas, for Ike would carry Texas in 1952 and in 1956. His campaigning was marked by heavy reliance on television and public relations, introducing a new age in campaigning.

Dallas voters that year also replaced their heavily favored Democratic congressman Wallace H. Savage with an avidly conservative Republican, Bruce Alger, who would hold that office for ten years. The appeal of the New Deal liberalism was waning. The war was over. It was time for a change. Eisenhower's moderation looked good to voters, and the GOP and its candidates were stressing that they were not just Republicans but conservatives.

Chapter 2

My Journey into Journalism

WHAT BROUGHT ME, child of an East Texas couple who began their married life as sharecroppers, to the predominantly urban and fast-paced world of journalism? Why did it attract me? What brings others to journalism?

As I began my teenage years I wanted to be a baseball player. As reality surfaced, I realized that I could be no more than "good field, no hit." I modified my goal. I could be a sportswriter. But before long, with the passage of a handful more years in the 1950s and my increasing interest in critical affairs that were confronting the nation (McCarthyism, racism, the Cold War, etc.), I decided to be a reporter of current events.

My parents, especially my father, kept up with local and national politics and always voted, but I am quite certain that in their fifty-plus years as voters and tax-paying Dallas citizens, they never met an elected public official. But it was different for me in my first years as a reporter, as it is for all reporters. Early in my journalism career I met prominent officials and important citizens, even President Nixon and his wife, Pat, at a fancy White House reception. I stood a handshake away from John F. Kennedy in Fort Worth during his 1960 presidential campaign; took a car ride in early 1963 with soon-to-be nominated GOP presidential candidate Barry Goldwater; saw Lyndon B. Johnson at close proximity on numerous occasions; saw and sat not far away from two-time presidential nominee Adlai Stevenson; and came to know on a first-name basis many city and county officials in Dallas and Fort Worth.

Later, as a journalism professor and regular panelist on an evening local television news show established by my friend Jim Lehrer, I talked with future president George H. W. Bush several times; had a private lunch with Judge Sarah T. Hughes (yes, the one who swore in LBJ as president aboard Air Force One and later was presiding federal judge in a three-judge panel in the *Roe v. Wade* case); and shouted encouragement to Barack Obama to enter the Democratic primary as he walked alone on Austin's state capitol grounds at a book festival. He waved back.

Others I interviewed who come to mind include such notables as Mickey Mantle, golfer Ben Hogan, futurist Buckminster Fuller, architect I. M. Pei, various movie stars, and on and on. All right, I agree, long-time reporters would be amused at this insignificant listing of names, but I offer it only as a suggestion that reporters have opportunities that most ordinary people, such as my parents, never had.

My mother, born in Virginia, came with her parents and siblings to Texas in 1913 from near Cumberland Gap in search of a more prosperous life. Because of her own minimal country schooling, she wanted her children to have better educations, and in her loving, nonaggressive way she very much encouraged us in reading. Recognizing that success in school required a love of books, she regularly read to us (two girls and me) at our impressionable early ages. She playfully mimicked the imagined voice of lovable characters we encountered through books, such as Dick and Jane and Bambi. I still remember my favorite children's book about a lifelike four-poster bed that briefly ran away from home, soon recognized the error in its ways, and then happily returned to where it was loved—home.

We didn't disappoint my mother in her wishes, especially my older sister June, who graduated as salutatorian at the very competitive Forest Avenue High in Dallas, noted for having so many smart Jewish students (Stanley Marcus and Aaron Spelling being two of them). I didn't do bad myself, although my elementary teachers sometimes reminded me of my sister's outstanding demeanor and fine grades.

For his part, my dad enjoyed reading, too. As I advanced from my mother's books for children, he introduced me to novels that he had saved from his earlier years and now were stored (improperly) in our garage, notably among them Mark Twain's *Huckleberry Finn* and *Tom Sawyer* and Robert Louis Stevenson's *Treasure Island*, all three of which I read and reread in my preteen and teenage summers. I was puzzled that *Tom Sawyer* seemed to be the most familiar and important of Twain's books because Huck was so much more enjoyable and his story about race relations better, too. Later, I was especially pleased to realize that *Huckleberry Finn* was recognized as being more daring and meaningful. Daddy's collection, which he passed on to me, also included two or three of Edgar Rice Burroughs's Tarzan books, a couple of Zane Grey western novels, and Defoe's *Robinson Crusoe*, all of which I enjoyed reading more than once.

It was at the age of 9 or 10 that I became entranced with baseball. So were most of my neighborhood friends. We played on our street at first, then graduated to the nearby schoolyard, and finally, after we moved in 1950 to suburban Pleasant Grove, I played on junior league teams and then the high school team. Besides playing, I attended many of the Dallas Eagles games in the Double-A Texas League. The stadium was only a streetcar ride away. I read daily newspaper reports about the games and players, dipped into biographies of previous star players such as Ty Cobb, Babe Ruth, Tris Speaker, and Rogers Hornsby, and read as much as I could about faraway but current Major League players—Ted Williams, Joe DiMaggio, Willie Mays, Pee Wee Reese, Roy Campanella, Larry Doby, and others. I was the only boy

I knew who subscribed to the weekly "Bible of Baseball," J. G. Taylor Spink's the *Sporting News* (with no awareness of Spink's opposition to baseball desegregation that would sully his reputation).

I was an inveterate reader of both Dallas newspapers, getting out of bed each morning to grab the *Dallas Morning News* from our front yard, and then in the afternoon the *Dallas Times Herald*. I "threw" both of those newspapers at separate times when every household in our lower middle-class neighborhood subscribed to one or sometimes both papers. Our family also enjoyed subscriptions to *Time, Life*, the *Saturday Evening Post, Ladies' Home Journal*, and *Good Housekeeping*.

In these otherwise quiet Eisenhower years, exciting news caught our attention, including Senator Joseph R. McCarthy's claims of Communist infiltration in the army and federal government, supposed Red ties of CBS's commentator Edward R. Murrow, and the US Supreme Court decision outlawing racial segregation in public schools. Also, of course, everyone read about the simultaneous electric chair execution of convicted spies Julius and Ethel Rosenberg; the first men ever to reach the top of Mount Everest—Edmund Hillary and his Tibetan guide, Tenzing Norgay; the launching of the first atomic submarine, *Nautilus*; and Disneyland's opening in California. I knew that I wouldn't be covering such stories as those at first, but maybe in time?

Locally, important news dealt with such individuals as banker Robert L. Thornton, "Mr. Dallas," who after decades of civic leadership became the city's mayor by winning three consecutive two-year terms. His exploits from cotton picker to mayor were even profiled in the *Saturday Evening Post*. That was impressive for us, even though we had never even seen this fellow Dallasite who certainly moved in different social spheres. I think in retrospect that for my parents, following the news seemed for them to be the obligation of any proper citizen such as they modestly assumed themselves to be. I was now reading Ernest Hemingway with great pleasure, and I added Irwin Shaw and J. D. Salinger to my list of favorite authors.

There was long-standing Democratic leadership at the Dallas County courthouse and city hall with individuals whose names we knew but never had met or even seen. This included persons whom I would come to know during my time as a reporter, such as former FBI agent Henry Wade as he began a thirty-six-year reign as Dallas County district attorney; W. L. (Lew) Sterrett, starting a twenty-seven-year run as the presiding administrative officer of county government; and James Eric (Bill) Decker as Dallas County sheriff, who would hold his office for twenty-four years. These and other officials generally had worked their way up from modest county jobs.

Local news dealt with the 1950s drought that brought a serious shortage to our water supply; feuds with Fort Worth over our airports; the annual State Fair of Texas, held every October at Fair Park; protests concerning the movement of the Black population into previously all-white Dallas neighborhoods; and the election in 1954 of Bruce Alger to the US House of Representatives as the first Republican congressman to serve Dallas or the state since Reconstruction.

In 1952, when I was 15, we favored Democrat Adlai Stevenson for president. While my parents avoided talking politics with relatives and neighbors, it became clear that most others "liked Ike" instead of being "gladly with Adlai." It was the same with almost all my fellow students, their parents, and the entire state, including so many former Texas Democrats. But my dad was never tempted to give up on the Democrats. His first time to be eligible to vote was in 1932, and he was strongly for Roosevelt; in fact, he would never vote for a Republican. The Depression was not that far away from him. Mother followed his suit.

I knew as a high school student that to be a reporter would require me to type quickly and accurately, not to mention be a good writer. I took typing with a vengeance since I knew I would be using the typewriter regularly as a reporter. I won first place in typing speed and accuracy in the district-wide high school competition. I figured that knowledge of shorthand would also help me as I interviewed newsmakers or took notes on fast-moving events. Thus, along with one brave male friend, we took two semesters of shorthand in high school as the only boys among twenty-five or so females who evidently were aspiring to become secretaries. (Yes, those were the times!) We withstood the jokes of our friends.

THE STATE'S MOST PROMINENT journalism school was at the University of Texas in Austin. I enrolled there in the fall of 1955, living at first in a rooming house two blocks from the campus with a clear view from my window of the university's famous Tower,[1] eating meals in the campus cafeteria with breakfast at the nearby Toddle House, and studying routinely in the library's large handsome study halls. Tuition each semester that first year, as I recall, was $15.

The university newspaper, the *Daily Texan,* was just what it said it was—a daily paper, produced by student journalists without professors looking over their shoulders. It provided full and sometimes controversial coverage, including regular criticism of the university's board of regents and of state and national politics.

I was astonished my first year at the impact of its editor, Willie Morris from Mississippi, who wrote a daily column and attacked segregation, censorship, the state's oil and gas interests, and other controversial subjects. Shortly after graduation Willie would become the youngest editor ever of the famous *Harper's Monthly,* then continue with his remarkable writing, including especially his prize-winning autobiography, *North Toward Home.*

In that same freshman year, the *Daily Texan* had another outstanding writer and journalist, managing editor Joe Goulden (his byline then was J. C. Goulden), who also impressed me with his astute columns and articles. Joe, born in Marshall, Texas, would become a noted journalist with the *Philadelphia Enquirer,* eventually heading its Washington, DC, bureau, and author of excellent books, including *Truth Is the First Casualty, The Superlawyers,* and *Korea: The Untold Story of the War.* A much earlier editor of the *Daily Texan* had been Walter Cronkite, by now a CBS radio news reporter.

As soon as I could, I became a student reporter for the *Daily Texan,* also serving for a semester as amusements editor. In that job I dished out assignments for others to review plays, movies, and books (saving some for myself) and filled out one or two pages a day with entertainment news and features. I was proud to accept a young woman's plea to write a short daily listing of the evening's best television programs. It was the *Daily Texan*'s first venture into regular television coverage. Neither I nor other students had regular access to television those days, but TV's future power was evident.

Graduating with a journalism degree in 1959, I was eager to get my first newspaper job, but rather than being drafted for two years, I decided to take an approved shortcut by joining the 49th Armored Division of the Texas National Guard, which was headquartered in Dallas. This required only six months of active duty in the US Army followed by five-and-a-half years of part-time obligations with National Guard duties and an annual summer camp.

For those first six months I was sent to Fort Knox, Kentucky, where for the eight weeks of basic infantry training I learned to shoot the M1 rifle at targets from one hundred to five hundred yards, take my rifle apart and put it back in a hurry, march in formation (enjoyable), exercise and run each morning with my fellow recruits under the harsh command of our platoon sergeant, and occasionally serve for the dreaded "kitchen police" or "KP." The latter was rather torturous work, lasting from about 4:30 a.m. until we finished at 8:00 p.m. or so.

I filled my diary each day with my army experiences. Plenty of material there, I figured, for a huge journalistic exposé about army training for recruits. I returned to my parents' house and my National Guard unit as a private, but of course never wrote my military exposé. I still have the diary packed with all my daily army notes, though.

NOW, FINALLY, I COULD begin my journalism career. I was lucky. My first job was waiting for me. I had been among others of the UT graduating class of '59 to be interviewed on campus by Delbert Willis, city editor of the *Fort Worth Press*. Now came his tentative offer through mail to be a general assignments reporter after I finished my six-month military duty. A UT classmate from East Texas, Jack

Moseley, had accepted a job at the *Press* immediately after graduation and was doing excellent and varied work.

I preferred to work at my hometown *Times Herald* if I could. Back home, and before accepting the *Press*'s offer, I walked unannounced into the *Times Herald* newsroom, found the managing editor, and asked him for a reporting job. I admitted that I was pondering an offer from the *Fort Worth Press* but that I preferred the *Times Herald*. He didn't think long about it. Polite but without further ado, he advised me to take that job at the *Press*. After experience there, he said, try again.

Thus, I began my professional journey in March 1960. The *Press*, one of many in the Scripps-Howard newspaper chain, stressed local news and obtained most of its national and international news from United Press International wire service, which had its own correspondents in the nation's capital and elsewhere. The nation and world were filled with news. Senator John F. Kennedy, despite his youth and Catholic faith, was making surprising progress toward winning the 1960 Democratic presidential nomination over veteran Senate Majority Leader Lyndon B. Johnson and Senator Hubert Humphrey. Headlines spoke of sit-in demonstrations at segregated lunch counters, as prompted by the dynamic rhetoric of the young Black minister Martin Luther King Jr.

Even though Fort Worth was only thirty miles from Dallas, it might as well have been three hundred, for my knowledge of what sometimes was called our "twin city" was minimal. It was strange that I was so near to home and yet everything was so different. Fort Worth's happy claim of being "where the west begins" placed its colorful emphasis on cowboys, cowboy boots, wide-brimmed western hats, and cattle. This contrasted sharply with Dallas's pride in its larger population, its bigger banks, and its broader recognition in being the site of the regional Federal Reserve bank (the nation's smallest city to have one). It also boasted of busy Love Field airport, with direct flight connections to major cities, and of the annual Texas state fair each October. One could see Fort Worth's emphasis on cowboys at Exchange

Avenue's enormous stockyards, yards away from the adjacent Armour and Swift meat-packing plants, the cattle's ultimate destination.

Commuting daily from Dallas to Fort Worth was out of the question, so I moved to Fort Worth. To be a good reporter I needed intimate knowledge of the city—its neighborhoods, its city and county public officials, and its newsmakers of all kinds. My housing needs were simple. I found an upstairs room with a private bathroom a few miles from downtown and in walking distance of Texas Christian University. Maybe, I thought, evening courses there would entice me toward a graduate degree. I ate every meal at restaurants, generally cafeterias or fast food. I assured my parents and Dallas friends that I would visit them regularly on free weekends, and I did. I wanted to keep up with Dallas while learning the ins and outs of Cowtown. By the time I departed three years later, I knew Fort Worth on a far more intimate basis than Dallas.

Moseley, my fellow journalism graduate, was thriving. He was a great help and trusted companion as I sought to learn the ropes. Other friends in the Fort Worth journalism scene quickly emerged, including many from the opposition *Star-Telegram* and radio and television staff. We were all journalists with common interests, yet were eager to beat our opposition when possible. We often attended social events in which all of us were guests. As it would happen, even though we were competitors, as reporters covering the same beats and being together at the locations of the city hall, county courthouse, or police station, we naturally became friends. This would be the same in both cities, Fort Worth and Dallas.

The long-time publisher of the *Star-Telegram*, Amon G. Carter, its principal founder in 1909, was a self-taught former sandwich salesman whose overpowering influence extended westward beyond Fort Worth into the vast West Texas area. His domination in newspaper, broadcasting, aviation, and civic leadership was unparalleled. No single individual in Dallas came close to matching him in influence. Will Rogers, Carter claimed, was his best friend. Carter started radio station WBAP in 1922 and WBAP-TV in 1948, both first-class in their operations and offering good content for their audiences, including Dallas.

The most serious rivalry between Fort Worth and Dallas was their competition for commercial aviation leadership. Carter masterminded his city's strategies. Both recognized aviation dominance as key to growth and progress; both had their own city-owned airports. Dallas's Love Field was busier by far than Fort Worth's Meacham, but surrounding residential developments, schools, and industry limited Love Field's ability to meet the need for runway additions and extensions.

Less serious competition existed in sports, especially between the football teams of Fort Worth's Texas Christian University and Southern Methodist University in Dallas. Also, there was baseball rivalry between the Fort Worth Cats and the Dallas Eagles in the minor Texas League consisting of six other teams in cities of similar size—Houston, San Antonio, Beaumont, Oklahoma City, Tulsa, and Shreveport. In all these matters, including aviation, but without special knowledge of its complications, I had always favored my hometown team.

Work at the *Press* was exciting. I learned how to be a reporter—that is, the kind a sensationalist-minded tabloid demanded, an aggressive and creative reporter with a knack for writing short, snappy leads (spelled and pronounced hereafter as "ledes"). Despite this approach to news coverage, I surprisingly found those veteran editors at the *Press* to have conservative lifestyles, especially welcoming to a newcomer.

The *Press*, as part of the fading Scripps-Howard chain, faced competition from separate morning and evening *Star-Telegram* editions, each with separate staffs. Founded in 1921 as a broadsheet, the *Press*, by the time I arrived, had switched from that standard newspaper format to tabloid. The tabloid format was more appropriate for what the *Press* had promised its readers—"Pep! Punch!! Personality!!!" Undermanned in this struggle, we knew we had to work harder to find unique or exclusive angles for our stories. But the *Press* lacked the budget, news space, and manpower to compete in a realistic way with the bigger and more powerful *Star-Telegram*.

Some years earlier a *Press* senior editor described the paper to a beginning reporter: "The poor folks take us because we're the least expensive newspaper in town; the rich folks take us to find out what we're telling the poor folks."[2] What the readers got—rich or poor— was news with strong angles stressing the story behind the story, displayed most days with the familiar snappy front-page headlines customary on tabloids one might see in New York or London.

The *Press*'s two-story brick building at the corner of Commerce and Jones Street was at a dowdy edge of downtown. Reporters had their own desks and typewriters, and the only private office in the newsroom was that of our genial editor, Walter Humphrey. There was not even an elevator for reaching the water-cooled second-floor newsroom, which posed a daily task for our one-legged city editor Delbert Willis, who had started as a copy boy, lost his leg to a Japanese machine-gunner on New Guinea, and returned after the war to the *Press*. (He would be editor when the paper closed its doors in 1975, having failed to make a profit for the past twenty-five years.)

Humphrey, our soft-spoken editor, seemed out of place. He never— as far as I could tell—interfered with our coverage of news. Sometimes he may have offered second thoughts to Willis about how a story was handled. While he seemed to accept the *Press*'s tabloid bent, he was out of the office often because of so many luncheons and meetings with Rotary Club, Chamber of Commerce, or other well-intended organizations.

Willis, the city editor and most impactful by far of senior editors, including managing editor C. L. Douglas and news editor Sam Hunter, insisted that we make our stories true but as interesting as possible. We must beat our competition with exclusives and hustles on breaking news. Douglas, I soon discovered, was the author of *Cattle Kings of Texas*, published in hardback in 1939 but by now largely forgotten. (Recently, I saw that his book is available today in paperback editions, but prices for good first editions approach $1,000.)

I spent two days a week covering police, working all day from the police station's press room. I had assumed full-time duty there while my friend Moseley, who had become our full-time police reporter, left to fulfill his six-month military requirement. (I was crushed when Moseley returned to the *Press* upon completing his military require- ment and resumed his full-time police beat assignment, which sent me back to general assignments.) Other reporters, especially from the dominant *Fort Worth Star-Telegram* with its separate morning and afternoon editions, spent days and nights in the police press room. TV and radio reporters also hung out in the press room so they could rush away in their news wagons as soon as the police or fire dispatcher reported a major crime, accident, or fire. We newspaper reporters, hearing the same reports, went out only if the story seemed big enough—but always if a fatality was involved.

Willis's appreciation for a good story inevitably earned its reporter a byline. A sampling of my own byline stories appeared under such headlines as "Helpful Bandit Is Quickly Captured," "Drunken Teenagers Beat Victim of Polio," "Arlington Man Slain in Property Line Dispute," "You Could Be Jailed for Not Answering the Census Taker," "Scoutmaster Forgives Stepson Who Shot Him," and "Girls' Pet Dog Killed by Hit and Run Driver."

One of the Fort Worth police reporters was Bob Schieffer of the *Star-Telegram*. Bob, future famous correspondent and news host at NBC, started as a night-time radio station reporter who covered break- ing stories from his KXOL news wagon, later becoming the night police reporter for the *Star-Telegram*. He spent much time at the press room. Since our afternoon *Press* required our police reporters to be there beginning early in the mornings, our paths did not cross. Bob loved his work. "I thought it was about the best job anyone could ever have," he wrote in his memoir.[3]

I also met a *Dallas Morning News* reporter in the press room one day. His stories had caught my favorable attention, especially with his carefully honed ledes. He was Jim Lehrer, who for reasons unknown to the rest of us was visiting Fort Worth that day and getting his bearings for a story. Jim was a blond, crew cut, former marine officer destined to be a close friend and colleague in days ahead at the *Times Herald* and for the rest of our lives. We did no more that day than exchange brief pleasantries. He, like Schieffer, would become a famous national television reporter, moderator for presidential debates, and host for Public Broadcasting Service programs.

On most days I stayed in the *Press*'s second-floor newsroom, but I often filled in at city hall, the courthouse, and the police station for other beat reporters on their off days. Most of the newer reporters, generally three or four of us, rotated on writing obituaries, routinely calling each morning every funeral home in town for information on recent deaths for which they would hold funeral services. As we gathered basic information about the newly deceased, we also called their homes to gently talk to family members or friends to get interesting or important details about the deceased, including times and locations for their services. I saw then, and recognize now, the importance of good obits. Unlike today, when families pay for their own obituaries based on the number of words, I believe most daily newspapers at that time charged nothing for obituaries written by a newspaper's own reporters, whatever their length. We considered the death of every citizen to be worthy of coverage. It was up to us to find the basics and uniqueness of each life.

As I have written, after having grown up in a family that only knew important local leaders through newspaper coverage, I now found myself dealing person-to-person with newsmakers—the mayor, city council members, county commissioners, judges, local or visiting politicians, detectives, a visiting movie star, crime victims, and even prisoners in jail. My family and friends were impressed with my role as a reporter.

In personally dealing with public officials or other regular news sources, I understood conflicting needs: first, make friends with those who seemed compatible and could be helpful in tipping off reporters to stories and providing needed details, and second, retain the freedom to report essential or controversial news even if it offended them. All this was good experience for my generally unassuming nature, but I felt strongly about the press's obligation to gather and supply information—good or bad—if citizens were to exercise their important functions under the First Amendment. This conviction gave me special heart.

Assistant City Editor Mary Crutcher, who had taken over the police beat while the men went to war in the '40s, had become a local legend herself as a hard-nosed police reporter. Veteran detectives often asked *Press* reporters about Mary or sent their regards to her. Now, from her city desk, she rode herd over our police reporters, pressing them to dig deeper to determine the most telling feature of their crime stories. "Did the killer have the knife in his left or right hand?" she might ask. If you didn't know, you'd go back and find out.

Kent Biffle was the talented rewrite man for most of our police stories, as well as others. We gave him the facts, and he put them together, often with unique ledes. Behind a corner panel in our second-floor newsroom sat longtime amusements editor Jack Gordon, looking like he was straight out of the '30s with his Clark Gable–style mustache and hiding behind tall stacks of age-old news releases. Our most prominent reporter was Carl Freund, whose beat included both the courthouse and politics, and who had inside connections on both. Photographers came to be special friends, especially Russ Russell but also chief photographer Gene Gordon and Ken Hardin. Any of our photographers might be assigned to go with us on any particular assignment. I never failed to be impressed with their work.

Sports coverage under legendary Blackie Sherrod, who before finishing his career would be named Texas Sportswriter of the Year sixteen times, was beginning to transform sports writing in Texas and elsewhere. By 1958, though, he had been lured away to the *Times Herald* (and later to the *Morning News*). His influence remained at the *Press* and in sports writing everywhere. Articles were now appearing in which final scores of games might not be found until the fourth or tenth paragraph, instead of in the opening sentence. Dan Jenkins, tutored by Blackie, was now sports editor at the *Press*. Jenkins, Gary Cartwright, Bud Shrake, and other *Press* sportswriters were destined for greater creative writing heights. This newspaper game, I could see, was fascinating, and so were those who practiced it.

Using the crisscross directory was a tool I had not learned in journalism school, but it was essential in the newsroom and especially in the police press room, where immediacy was so important. If, for instance, the fire dispatcher sounded an alarm for a certain address, we quickly could look up the address in the directory, find the telephone number for the house directly across the street, and ask if she—inevitably a stay-at-home housewife in those years—could see a fire at the house across the street. Often her first answer would be that she saw nothing, then suddenly she might be shocked to hear the siren of an approaching fire truck and a trace of smoke from the house. "How did you know that?" she would ask. If she saw nothing, the fire perhaps would be a kitchen fire, too small for a reporter to rush to the scene. If large enough, though, a quick visit to the scene might be advisable.

EXCITING POLITICAL NEWS came in 1960. The Democratic presidential nominee, John Fitzgerald Kennedy, was bringing his campaign to Texas, Fort Worth and Dallas included, in September. Young Kennedy had won the presidential nomination in the first ballot over veteran Senate Majority Leader Lyndon B. Johnson.

Kennedy, faced with the difficulty of selecting a strong vice presidential candidate and despite opposition from some key backers, thought Johnson could bring electoral support from Texas and the South. Some thought that Johnson surely would not yield his strong position as Senate majority leader. But to the surprise of political analysts, as well as some of Kennedy's closest advisors, Johnson accepted the offer.

Despite being relatively unknown outside of the Northeast, Kennedy was no political newcomer. He had represented Massachusetts for six years in the House of Representatives (1947–1953) and he had been one of the state's two US senators since 1953.

The freshness of Kennedy, his wife, Jacqueline, and his entire family captivated much of the nation. His personality contrasted sharply with dour Republican opponent Richard M. Nixon, who as vice president had stood in Eisenhower's shadow. September polls showed a virtual tie between the Kennedy-Johnson team and the Republican pair, Nixon and Henry Cabot Lodge.

Kennedy's large entourage for Fort Worth included Lyndon Johnson, Speaker of the House Sam Rayburn, Fort Worth Democratic congressman Jim Wright, and others. Their noon September 13 rally was to be at downtown Burk Burnett Park. The previous night in Houston Kennedy faced a group of conservative Protestant preachers in a thirty-minute, nationally televised appearance, the subject being the nominee's Catholic faith. Dallas's First Baptist Church pastor, W. A. Criswell, had warned that "the election of a Catholic as president would mean the end of religious liberty in America."[4] If elected, would the president's Catholicism be a dominant factor in the White House? Would pronouncements from the pope in Rome impact any of his policies? Kennedy's responses to such questions on television seemed comforting, and the question of his faith in fundamentalist Texas now lost much significance (although all four Baptist ministers on the program still opposed Kennedy). The task for Kennedy and his Texan partner, campaigning together for the first time, was critical. They must bring the state's twenty-four electoral votes back to the Democratic Party, having lost them to Eisenhower in 1952 and 1956.[5]

I held hopes of helping cover the rally in some way, possibly in a brief sidebar, but nothing was said about that until I arrived in the newsroom early the morning of the event. Delbert Willis summoned me to his desk and handed me a paper press credential to hang around my neck. It guaranteed me a seat on the Kennedy press bus as it left Fort Worth and headed to Dallas. My assignment was simple, he said. I would ride on the press bus behind Kennedy's open-topped limousine through two brief campaign highway stops. There would be nothing for me to write about since our noon deadline would be far over.

With a confident twinkle in his eyes, Delbert said I would be "insurance in case somebody takes a shot at him." That, he added, would be about the only way we could get anything at all into the

In 1960 John F. Kennedy, campaigning at a downtown Fort Worth park, gave
me the opportunity to see him and vice presidential candidate Lyndon B.
Johnson for the first time. *Dallas Morning News* Collection, the Sixth Floor
Museum at Dealey Plaza, donated by the *Dallas Morning News* in the interest
of preserving history.

paper at that hour. We both knew nothing of such magnitude would
happen. It wasn't much of an assignment, but I was pleased. I would
see Kennedy and his entourage at close range, and I would ride briefly
in the bus with the nation's elite news corps.

Before the noon event, I walked to the pleasant midtown
park. A joyous crowd of lunch-hour office workers, composed

predominantly of women, it seemed, were already there. A few flimsy pickets favoring Nixon were evident, but they were hardly visible in the pro-Kennedy crowd. Before Kennedy appeared on the speaker's platform, the pro-Nixon signs seemed to have melted away. After all, a debonair contender for the presidency was visiting. "Jack Be Nimble, Jack Be Quick, Jack Jump Over Tricky Dick," was one of the wittiest signs. Near to it was this one: "Baptist for Kennedy." A *Star-Telegram* headline the next morning accurately described Kennedy's appearance as that of a "matinee-idol."[6]

Working to get closer, and using my newfound reporter's sense of privilege, I maneuvered through the crowd where the candidate and his large entourage, including vice presidential candidate Johnson, milled about. Close up, I was impressed to see that Kennedy lived up to advance publicity. I had assumed I might be disappointed, skeptically sensing that he would be something less than his media image. His trim figure, however, suggested natural-born athleticism. He smiled broadly and constantly, displaying confidence without appearing to be jaunty or cocky. Maybe he seemed so striking because he was such a contrast after Eisenhower's two terms and a long military career and the nearly four terms under wheelchair-bound Franklin Delano Roosevelt. Here, in the person of Kennedy, was a young man calling for a new frontier, which so many believed we needed in this new age.

Before Kennedy spoke, Lyndon Johnson, obviously confident in his own state and seeming to know everyone, stood on the platform, waving and gesticulating as he spotted specific individuals in the audience. He was Texan through and through. I would have felt no hesitancy at all in walking up to him as if I had known him all my life—"Hey, buddy, how's it goin'?" Kennedy, although friendly and presidential, exhibited New England reserve.

Nearby, seemingly little more than a spectator, sat another Texan, Sam Rayburn, already holding history's longevity record as Speaker of the House. Both Johnson and Rayburn wore white Stetsons in a town where Stetsons were common, even for the richest businessmen.

More Stetson hats certainly were visible here than in any other large Texas city.

Texas's US senator Ralph Yarborough, a liberal Democrat but no special friend of the more moderate Johnson, was there. So was Fort Worth congressman Jim Wright (whom I later would come to know quite well), a future successor to Rayburn as Speaker of the House. Yarborough especially, and Wright to a lesser extent were well-known in Dallas. Lyndon's wife, Lady Bird, sat demurely on the platform, alone as her husband glad-handed so many. Finally, an actual touch of Hollywood screenland was noted through the presence of Kennedy's sister, Pat, married to movie star Peter Lawford. Maybe this stylish Englishman friend to Sinatra was in Hollywood that very day. If Jacqueline Kennedy had been present, she would have overshadowed everyone, but pregnant with her second child (John Kennedy Jr.), she was home in Georgetown with daughter Caroline.

Kennedy spoke with the New England accent that still sounded odd to Texan ears. He had done his homework, though. He praised Fort Worth's World War II role through its military "bummer" plant (as Fort Worthians fondly pronounced it), where bombers such as the B-24 Liberator had been built.

Noting that Texas and Massachusetts were two thousand miles apart, Kennedy contended they were really "sisters under the skin." His late brother, Joseph P. Kennedy II, was flying a Fort Worth–built B-24 Liberator when he lost his life during the war in a crash over the English Channel. Dying with him was a Fort Worth man, Wilford Wiley, whose widow sat on the speakers' stand. Kennedy's older brother had been believed to be their father, Joe's, anointed choice to become president, but that wish had descended upon his next oldest son, John, now standing before us.

As Kennedy's speech ended, the tide of departing spectators (estimated at fifteen thousand), began pushing me away from my press bus assignment. Panicking that it might leave without me, I struggled against the flow and reached it just in time. The "elite" Washington press corps, in which I hoped one day to be included, looked like nothing more than an exhausted bunch of Rotarians after a hot summer softball game against Kiwanians. For these journalists, representing such papers as the *New York Times, Washington Post, Boston Globe,* and *Chicago Tribune,* the magic of traveling in a strenuous presidential campaign already had faded. It now seemed routine to them, not just because of the irksome job of getting in and out of the bus at every stop, but also because they needed every day to find a new angle from a speech or spontaneous comment.

On the bus a familiar face surprised me. It belonged to Seth Kantor, who had left the *Press* only a month or so earlier for the *Times Herald.* Seth, a veteran reporter in his mid-30s with a trim mustache, motioned for me to sit across the aisle from him. It was comforting to see an actual friend. Not long afterward he became Scripps-Howard's Washington correspondent, a fine career step.

As our bus moved out, I could see Kennedy's open-top limousine ahead, led by motorcycle escorts going slow enough so spectators on both sides of US Highway 80 could see the president. In suburban Arlington the motorcade stopped as scheduled. Police halted highway traffic briefly so Kennedy could say a few words. Reporters on the bus pondered whether it was worth their effort to get off. For me this was no decision. I wanted to see everything, so I got off. Only a few reporters joined me. Kennedy stood on the limousine hood, gesticulating as he spoke through his bullhorn. LBJ stood behind him, waiting to make a few words of his own. As JFK finished, Johnson grabbed the bullhorn. "Come on over with us to Dallas. Let's show how we can give a real Texas welcome," he shouted, waving his big hands and displaying the take-charge manner that had done him so well for many years. He was, after all, still the Senate majority leader.

A few miles farther down the road at Grand Prairie, the motorcade made a longer stop adjacent to two side-by-side aircraft plants, Chance Vought and Temco. An estimated six thousand workers poured from their workplaces and gleefully surrounded the limousine. Here, Kennedy, though obviously happy with the Fort Worth crowd, ramped up his energy. He could count on these workers for their support.

My assignment for the visit was simple—ride in the press bus to see that the president made it safely from Fort Worth to Dallas. In this crowd I stood anonymously. Andy Hanson Collection, the Sixth Floor Museum at Dealey Plaza.

Once again, I left the bus to be as near him as possible. Kennedy again spoke from the back of the limousine with Johnson just behind him. In the same limousine sat Kennedy's Dallas County campaign manager, Congressman Barefoot Sanders and Sanders's co–campaign manager, Texas criminal district judge Sarah T. Hughes. Meeting Kennedy for the first time, Judge Hughes was squeezed partway between him and Johnson in the limousine's back seat. (She later recalled that ride, which soon would extend into downtown Dallas before enormous crowds of admirers, as "one of the most exciting experiences I ever had and one which I will never forget."[7])

With Dallas just ahead, my assignment ended. I needed to find the Greyhound bus station and return to Fort Worth, but as I left I noticed a short, bald-headed man standing alone, lighting a cigarette. I recognized him as the famous Sam Rayburn. I snapped his picture without a word, not wanting to bother him. (The speaker had little more than a year to live before dying of pancreatic cancer. Kennedy, as president, would make a quiet and unannounced trip to Dallas to visit him in the hospital just before his death. Four former or future presidents attended his funeral in Bonham, Texas—Truman, Eisenhower, Kennedy, and Johnson.)

Down US Highway 80 in the distance, the presidential motorcade would reach Dallas, the Texas city acknowledged to have the highest conservative rating and home of the state's only Republican congressman, Bruce Alger. However, the next day's morning *Star-Telegram* described Kennedy's visits to Fort Worth and Dallas as the "greatest welcome any candidate ever received in Texas."[8] Minutes away in Dallas he would be seen, according to Police Chief Jesse Curry, by 175,000 persons in a short motorcade of several blocks—compared to the 50,000 to 75,000 who had seen Nixon a few days earlier on his longer motorcade route through the city. A crowd of some 9,500 supporters cheered Kennedy as he spoke afterward at Memorial Auditorium.

As enjoyable as it would have been to be in Dallas to see Kennedy's reception, my few hours with him were over. I returned to the *Press* on a nearly empty bus. There was no story for me to write; no one had "taken a shot" at him. But for me, 23 years of age, the day was a memorable, not-to-be forgotten occasion.

I would see Kennedy again before the month ended—but this time on our television set from my chair at home in Dallas with my parents and sisters. So did millions of other Americans. The Kennedy-Nixon debates we watched were the first nationally televised debate between presidential candidates.

A few days later as I walked into the newsroom I saw a young face working intently at a typewriter. It was Martin Frost, a promising Paschall High School student beginning the first of three summer internships at the *Press*. Some two-and-a-half decades later, Martin would be elected to Congress, serving from 1979 to 2005. He rose to leadership positions, and in the 2002 race to be House minority leader, he lost to Nancy Pelosi, his more liberal challenger.[9]

It was time now for some local reporting on the race between Kennedy and Nixon, and high school student Frost helped us. Delbert, as I understood was his usual practice, assigned reporters to visit particular county precincts, interview as many potential voters as possible, and report which candidate the residents seemed to favor. Each report was accompanied by the writer's byline and a half-column photo of ourselves taken by one of our photographers. The four-column headline for my story was "Religious Issue Predominant in Another Fort Worth Precinct," accompanied by a sidebar, "Typical Pct. 101 Leans GOP Again."

REPUBLICAN PARTY MEMBERS were finding much to admire about an Arizona conservative named Barry Goldwater. In fact, after Kennedy's election in November 1960, they were looking toward the former department-store mogul as a possible future presidential candidate. Goldwater's short but well-respected *Conscience of a Conservative* was published that year (ghostwritten by William F. Buckley's brother-in-law, Brent Bozell Jr.). I didn't know much about Goldwater, but I recognized that moderate Republicans such as Nelson

Rockefeller on the East Coast were of a different ilk. Goldwater, in his second term as a US senator, was gaining attention as a more aggressive, new-style conservative Republican.

I had the pleasure of meeting Goldwater soon afterward when Delbert gave me another easy assignment. Goldwater was coming to town in late September to speak at a fundraiser for Nixon. One of his Fort Worth supporters was picking up Goldwater at the airport and giving him a ride to town. This supporter—I don't remember his name—had agreed that one of our reporters could accompany him and ride back to town with him and Goldwater, just the three of us in the car. Even though I had no choice in accepting or declining any assignment, I certainly would not have rejected this one.

With no ado and no other greeters present—not even from the *Star-Telegram*—we picked up the senator at Meacham Field. I understood he had flown solo in his own airplane. I sat in the car's back seat and mostly listened as the two men chatted on the way to downtown. "My, this town has grown so much," Goldwater said in perhaps the only comment I now can remember.

Goldwater was quiet and well-mannered, not eager for political small talk. It would be presumptuous, I thought, to press him on his viewpoints on what might be considered a social automobile ride. It was good to take measure of the man who one day might be a presidential candidate or even president. My story was nothing but a brief advance about his arrival and fundraising speech. In essence, it would give the *Press* an entrée to the future, just in case. (And, indeed, Goldwater became the GOP's 1964 presidential candidate.)

I knew enough about Goldwater's conservative brand of politics to know that I wouldn't favor him in an election. And, in fact, despite the growing ultraconservative mood he represented, I was pleased to be with him for these minutes on the cusp of his growing popularity. I didn't attend his speech, but I read how he, a brigadier general in the Air Force Reserves, advocated that evening for the United States to resort to whatever means possible to remove Castro from power.

Chapter 3

"The Prettiest Bunch of Women I Ever Saw"

B Y READING AND SEEING regular news accounts on my frequent visits to Dallas, I continued to follow events there. The same voters who had supported Eisenhower found much to like about his potential successor, Richard Milhous Nixon from California. With Texas's outcome a toss-up in the few days remaining of the Kennedy-Nixon battle, voters needed a strong reminder that Johnson was one of their own. Did they forget that Lyndon Baines Johnson was a Franklin D. Roosevelt favorite who had served the state in the House from 1937 to 1949 and the Senate for twelve years? Or forget the unusual fact that he was simultaneously running for vice president and his present office as senator from Texas in the 1960 election? The Democratic ticket needed Texas's twenty-four electoral votes, but Johnson was deeply disturbed. What if he and Kennedy won the national election but his native Texans supported Nixon? "We just must not win the nation and lose Texas," he wrote to fellow Texan and Secretary of the Navy John B. Connally."[1]

Eisenhower had carried Texas in the last two presidential elections. Nixon very well could do the same. Dallas and Fort Worth voters were important for the Kennedy-Johnson ticket. Four days before the election, Kennedy sent Johnson, accompanied by Lady Bird, to a Democratic reception at Dallas's finest hotel, the Adolphus. I followed reports of extraordinary events occurring when Lyndon and Lady Bird arrived there for a noon luncheon in their honor. So, although not a firsthand account, my following description is based on many reports, film accounts, and research.

The raucous reception that confronted this native Texan couple on their November 4 arrival brought national and worldwide attention. It marked for certain the city's pronounced turn not just to conservatism but also to a strong element of extremist Republican conservatism.

On this same morning, Dallas's Republican congressman Bruce Alger called upon his "Alger Girls" to meet him downtown, ostensibly to pin Nixon buttons on shoppers. Alger, recognized often as the most conservative member of Congress, described his female supporters as "the prettiest bunch of women I ever saw."[2] Besides Alger's own movie-star looks, conservative Republicans were attracted to his three-step approach when considering proposed congressional legislation: (1) Is it needed? (2) Is it a proper function of the federal government? and (3) Can we afford it?

A tall former realtor and neighborhood leader in Dallas's Casa Linda area, Alger was born and reared in Webster Groves, Missouri. He was a 1940 graduate of Princeton and varsity football player who earned a unique degree in philosophy of art. As an undergraduate he had become acquainted with Albert Einstein, a resident Princeton scholar. Alger was said to have shared ideas with him. After graduation and the United States' entry into World War II, Alger became an Air Force pilot who flew low-altitude bombing raids over Tokyo.

Upon marrying a Dallas woman, the couple moved to her city. Alger began working as a real estate salesman in the new Casa Linda residential area and quickly involved himself in civic activities, inevitably being elected president of such organizations as the area's chamber of commerce, its Kiwanis Club, and chairman of the downtown YMCA. This polished, ambitious, and conservative man, blessed with

These politically conservative but peaceful-looking Alger supporters await the arrival of Vice President Lyndon B. Johnson and Lady Bird outside the Adolphus Hotel in the 1960 campaign. The atmosphere got far more spirited when the couple arrived. Bill Winfrey Collection, *Dallas Morning News*, the Sixth Floor Museum at Dealy Plaza.

a mellifluous voice, had won his first race for Congress as a staunch supporter of Eisenhower, defeating his overconfident and better-known Democratic opponent, Wallace Savage, who had been state chairman of the party's executive committee and had been a shoo-in to handle Alger with ease. Alger's campaign pitch was "You Elected Ike—Now Support Him."

Just how many buttons Alger Girls attached to lapels and dresses that morning is uncertain—perhaps only a few—for their obvious purpose was to demonstrate against Lyndon and Lady Bird. Dressed colorfully in red, white, and blue outfits, the "Girls" congregated outside the Adolphus Hotel to await their arrival. All but a few Democrats, some two thousand of them, were already inside at luncheon tables or milling about while waiting. Republican partisans were outside on the sidewalk, yielding professionally designed protest signs. There were some GOP men, too, but it was the women's ferocity that turned the day and captured the nation's attention.

A youthful John Tower, a political science professor at Midwestern University in Wichita Falls who hoped to replace Johnson in the Senate, was there. He announced his eagerness to engage Johnson that very day in a face-to-face debate. This, grim-faced Tower certainly knew, had no chance of happening. But Tower, short of stature, was showing his supporters that he had no fear of facing the towering "Landslide Lyndon."

If the crowd intended merely to demonstrate, the day immediately turned into something else as soon as the Johnsons stepped out of their chauffeured automobile and encountered pugnacity such as they had never experienced. A Maginot Line of anti-Kennedy and anti-Johnson protestors screamed and waved their pickets. Even Lady Bird, who emerged from the car just before her husband, was targeted. One Alger Girl snatched Lady Bird's dainty dress gloves and tossed them into the gutter. Another taunted her with a sign, "Down With Lady Bird." Most pickets were aimed at her husband, though. "Smiling Judas Johnson" and "LBJ, Traitor" were among countless placards. "Texas Tombstones for LBJ" was another. Alger, dressed in a dark suit, white shirt, and tie, waved a large sign, "LBJ sold out to Yankee Socialists."

Where were the Democrats? There seemed to be no Democratic presence in this crowd. All but a few were inside the grand ballroom, waiting for the Johnsons.

Lyndon and Lady Bird had to struggle with demonstrators, face-to-face, elbow-to-elbow, to reach the ballroom. Earlier, having recognized that a gathering storm awaited the couple outside the hotel, police offered to slip the couple inside through a side door. Johnson shooed them away. "If the time has come when I can't walk through the lobby of a hotel in Dallas with my lady without a police escort, I want to know it," he said.[3] Later it would be observed that Johnson envisioned a mob scene that would shame the GOP and win votes for the Democratic ticket.

Lady Bird said she was never so frightened in her life. It was, she said, the worst hour in politics she had ever experienced. Spittle and insults flew as the crowd shouted, "We Want Nixon." *Dallas Morning News* political editor Allen Duckworth described them as howling, chanting, and jeering. A reporter called it the "nearest thing to an uncontrollable mob" he had seen since the wildest days of Dallas's Texas-Oklahoma Friday evening football rallies.[4]

The incident was described across the nation by reporters. The images of angry protestors captured by television cameras and newspaper photographers were shocking. The way Texans treated their own vice presidential candidate and majority leader of the US Senate, and his East Texas–born wife, was unimaginable. The impact on Johnson's prominent Senate pal from Georgia, the veteran and much-admired Richard Russell, was immediate. Russell, who for years had not campaigned for the national Democratic ticket, called Johnson afterward and offered his support. Johnson accepted, and for the few days remaining, Russell campaigned through Texas with Johnson.[5]

In a rare front-page editorial, the *Times Herald* observed that the scene was "completely foreign to usual Dallas manners and hospitality—even in the heat of dying campaign days."[6] It declared this wild scene an embarrassing setback to Dallas's presumed reputation for cordiality and its image as a progressive and friendly city. Other Texas newspapers had similar reactions. An editorial in the *Abilene Reporter-News*, from the deeply conservative town in West Texas, commented that "a mob in Dallas yesterday wrote a new chapter that stands to the shame of our state and people."[7] When the Johnsons arrived at their next stop in Houston, they were greeted at the airport with a crowd in which individuals were holding signs that said, "We Apologize. We Love You."[8]

Despite the negative publicity and its own criticism of the event, our politically moderate *Times Herald* endorsed Nixon as president; those were the orders from upstairs. The conservative *Morning News* did what was expected, also urging its readers to choose the Nixon-Lodge ticket.

How about Dallas voters? Despite the Adolphus being fresh on their minds and despite the overwhelmingly hearty welcome they had offered Kennedy two months earlier, they gave an outstanding majority to Nixon-Lodge—149,000 votes to 89,000. Texas voters, though, supported Kennedy-Johnson, 976,000 to 917,000. Many ascribed this to their disgust with the GOP's storm trooper actions at the Adolphus.

Perhaps Alger's own description of the Adolphus event, appearing in a full-page advertisement in the *Dallas Morning News* one day before the election, made a difference. No violence and very little jostling had occurred, he argued, other than what one normally would experience in a tight crowd. The alleged female "goon squad," he said, was simply three hundred young ladies who had volunteered to come to town for his "Nixon Tag Day."[9]

At twenty-five, now old enough for my first presidential vote, I cast it for Kennedy. (Although recognizing my professional obligation to be strictly nonpartisan in writing news articles, I never refrained from voting.) My parents and sister June also voted for Kennedy, with conviction. My sister Sally, 15, was too young to vote.

John F. Kennedy, at age 43, became the youngest elected president in American history. However, with Johnson's Senate seat becoming vacant, the little-known Tower won the May 1961 election to replace him, then would be reelected for three additional full terms, serving until 1985 when he resigned. Just as Alger was the first Republican congressman from Texas since Reconstruction, Tower was Texas's first Republican senator sent to the nation's capital since Reconstruction.[10]

The demonstration was an early warning signal for what was to come in November 1963.

AT ABOUT THIS TIME I was promoted at the *Press*—with some trepidation, since I enjoyed reporting—to assistant news editor and wire editor. This desk job included choosing stories from the UPI wire service machine, writing headlines, designing pages, and selecting a new page-one story and headline for the financial edition. Our publisher, Walter Humphrey, seemed to share my trepidation. In his Home Towner column he announced that he was "giving a shot" at the job to this young reporter Darwin Payne. Such a comment didn't display much confidence in me. It perhaps was recognition that my approach to news stories failed to exhibit our tabloid's required flamboyance. Truth is, the position was no challenge. I felt confident in my abilities and soon proved myself.

Before too many months of this work (which I thoroughly enjoyed) had passed, in August 1961 the world situation and my own changed. The Soviet Union unexpectedly closed its section of the divided four parts of Berlin with an ugly and impenetrable solid concrete wall, known simply as the Berlin Wall. This violated postwar agreements sectioning Berlin into one each for the United States, Great Britain, France, and the USSR, allowing free passage from one to the other. The Soviets' action prompted a stern response from Kennedy: activation of National Guard units and the recall of Army Reservists.

I watched the news on my UPI wire machine with special interest. The activation included my Texas National Guard unit, 49th Armored Division, and Army Reservists as a warning. The 49th's small information office, of which I was a part, was in Dallas, where our regular weekly and occasional Sunday meetings were held. With more than a hundred thousand other guardsmen and reservists from across the country, we were ordered to the previously closed army base at Fort Polk, Louisiana, for a year's additional training for possible action against the Soviets.

During my time away from the *Press*, one of my pleasant duties included writing a folksy column for our new Fort Polk weekly newspaper, *The Peacemaker*. We filled it with the usual assortment of military news, principally about training activities, internal sports teams, profiles of enlisted men and officers, and other typical items. It was a triumph for our small staff. We wrote stories and headlines, designed pages, took photographs, and hired a weekly newspaper in DeRidder to publish the paper. After ten months passed and the international crisis ended, we were released from active duty in the summer of 1962. I returned to the *Press*, where my position as wire editor and assistant newspaper awaited. I was deeply appreciative.

Not long after returning, my personal life changed. The girlfriend I had met and dated in Fort Worth, Patsy (Pat) Patterson, and I were married in her home city of Houston. We found an apartment on Blaylock Drive on the east side of Lake Cliff, the small lake in the Oak Cliff section of Dallas. (Only after the assassination would we learn that Lee Harvey Oswald and his Russian wife, Marina, lived on the other side of the lake. Marina told her interrogators that she and Oswald enjoyed occasional picnicking there.[11] Could we have seen them there with their first young daughter? Possibly, we supposed.)

As an exception to our normally sedate social life, Pat and I and a few friends occasionally saw interesting characters at a beatnik joint known as The Cellar, located in a seedy, unfurnished basement in downtown Fort Worth. The Cellar was a harbinger of the new cultural, antiestablishment beatnik phenomenon emerging in the early '60s. Its uniqueness brought much attention, even nationwide. The Cellar's owner, Pat Kirkwood, the bearded, black-garbed son of an infamous Fort Worth–area gambler, had leased this space, thrown some large pillows atop cement floors, got some wild musicians to perform on occasion, hired young and sometimes scantily clad females as waitresses, and intrigued journalists, police officers, and lawyers to come and enjoy free (under-the-table) mixed drinks. The place did not have a liquor license. Other customers paid for nonalcoholic setups or brought their own booze. A couple of my young reporter friends, their dates, and Pat and I were there on occasion. Also, we enjoyed my journalistic standing, which brought us free alcoholic drinks. (On the late evening of November 21, 1963, Secret Service agents charged with protecting President Kennedy were curious enough to visit The Cellar under the guidance of *Star-Telegram* reporter Bob Schieffer. A considerable amount of public criticism followed this late-hour visitation by Secret Service agents on the evening before the assassination.)

AS MUCH AS I HAD come to know and appreciate Fort Worth, I continued to harbor wishes to return to my home city. So, with three years' experience at the *Press*, including my ten months of active duty after the Berlin Wall crisis, I decided in the spring of 1963 that I might be sufficiently toughened up for the *Times Herald*.

On my impromptu visit there to check it out, new managing editor Hal S. Lewis Jr. heard me and listened carefully to my *Press* experiences and my unsolicited comment about once being a *Times Herald* paperboy. After only a few minutes he directed me to city editor Kenneth Smart. Before the day ended, I was hired. I would be a general assignments reporter. My duties were about the same as when I had first joined the *Press*—covering police two days a week, substituting for the city hall and courthouse reporters on their days off, writing features, and taking turns with other reporters on obituaries. Eventually I became full-time courthouse reporter and then city hall.

The greater space available for stories in the *Times Herald* and its much bigger staff permitted more in-depth reporting with less emphasis on sensationalism. Its circulation of more than two hundred thousand was quadruple that of the *Press*. Its location in a handsome building at Griffin and Pacific streets was convenient, and there would be no more walking up stairs to the newsroom; instead, elevators carried us to our fourth floor. The newspaper had a long history, dating to 1888 when the existing *Dallas Times* and *Dallas Herald* merged. The *Times Herald* was the city's only afternoon paper. Later I would observe that compared to the *Press*, the *Times Herald* was more like being in a country club than waging daily war with the *Star-Telegram*'s morning and afternoon editions.

Although the *Dallas Morning News*, founded in 1885, had a far better national reputation and larger circulation extending over a broader area, the *Times Herald* had more circulation within the city and Dallas County. Consequently, its reporting emphasis was on local news. Our news staff came almost exclusively from graduates of Texas colleges who had sharpened their skills on smaller papers before moving to the *Times Herald*.

While Delbert Willis at the *Press* had control of the city staff, the *Times Herald* had a large hierarchy of administrators largely removed from the reporting staff. Their principal offices were upstairs. At top was John W. Runyon, publisher, who had started his career at the *Times Herald* in 1911 in advertising sales. He was rarely seen in the newsroom. Next in line was James F. Chambers Jr., president since 1960. Chambers had started newspaper work as a copy boy at the old *Dallas Dispatch*, which had an aggressive approach to the news resembling that of the *Press*. As a reporter Chambers had witnessed the lawmen's fatal 1934 ambush of Clyde Barrow and Bonnie Parker in Louisiana. Afterward, he rode back to Dallas in the hearse that carried Barrow's body. Now, as president, he had removed himself from daily news coverage and, like Runyon, was rarely seen in the newsroom.

Felix R. McKnight, a former sportswriter and Associated Press staff member who after sixteen years at *Morning News* had risen to the position of editor, had been lured away by the *Times Herald* in 1957 to be its vice president and executive editor. McKnight sat in his own newsroom office.

Managing Editor Lewis, at one time the paper's police reporter, had an office at the front edge of the newsroom. News editor Charles F. Dameron Jr., a native of West Texas and a World War II and Korean war veteran, sat between city editor Kenneth Smart and the entrance to the composing room, where linotype operators set stories in type and printers put together the pages.

But it was city editor Smart, a quiet-mannered Dallas native who had taken the position at the age of 29 and now was 31, who really ran the newsroom, sending reporters on various assignments, taking a first look at their copy, and selecting beats for the best reporters. Smart was another graduate from North Texas State, where the well-known professor C. E. "Pop" Shuford was busy supplying many of the state's newspapers with journalism graduates.

One of Smart's assignments reminded me of something the *Press* might have done. My time at the *Press* possibly inspired him. Smart had obtained a wig typical of the outlandish hairstyles of the new and sensational Beatles. Would I be willing, he politely asked, to put on this crazy wig and walk downtown? One of our photographers would be on the other side of the street with a long camera lens, quietly taking photos of individuals' shocked expressions as they saw me and my fake hair. It might be fun. Well, yes, I said, I would do that. So I did, my story earning jovial comments from fellow reporters who enjoyed the unlikely stunt.

The editorial department was under the leadership of the witty and literary A. C. Greene, now approaching his prime as an author and commentator. His assistant was the equally witty and intellectual John Weeks, book lover and former assistant city editor.

My new position gave me my own desk (as I had at the *Press*), but I was surrounded by a much larger group of reporters, including veteran copyeditors who, from a large table, took final looks at our stories, wrote headlines, and seemed to have stimulating conversations among themselves as they worked. Among them was Bill Sloan, who had gone to my high school and now became an even better friend.[12]

Political writer Keith Shelton had come to the *Times Herald* in 1959 after a stint as wire editor at the *Wichita Falls Record-News*. Other than going to political events, much of his work was done through telephone contacts with his major sources. City hall reporter Al Hester had a different routine. Each day, after politely greeting the city manager's secretary, he walked past her into City Manager Elgin Crull's office for a daily chat. At 10:00 a.m. or so he joined Park Superintendent L. B. Houston, City Secretary Harold Shank, and a couple of other city officials for coffee at the White Plaza Hotel across the street. When I or others substituted for him, Al insisted that we do the same. He didn't want his privileges lost—and the officials had no problem with that. The reporter for the *Morning News* was not part of this group; its city hall reporter arrived later in the day because of later deadlines.

James C. (Jim) Lehrer, the writer whom I had met briefly in the police press room in Fort Worth when he was with the *Dallas Morning News*, became a special friend. Jim had resigned instantly from the *News* when its editors declined to print a story of his that revealed irregular and perhaps illegal activities by certain local public officials. He went immediately to the *Times Herald*, which hired him to be one of its top reporters and eventual city editor. Jim was especially dedicated to the role of journalism in American culture and government, but he also had the long-range goal of becoming a novelist. A graduate of the University of Missouri's top-notch journalism school, he was especially popular in the newsroom.

As a boy, Jim's father—and mother—spent years working in the bus business, with the dream of starting their own commercial bus line. It was Jim's dream, too, and he did everything he could to help. As a teenager his first job was working at a bus station as a "caller." As an adult Jim and his wife, Kate, sometimes held lively but respectable parties in their home. The highlight of every one of those parties, and those to follow for the rest of his life (even when receiving an honorary doctorate from Southern Methodist University), was his famous "bus call." He would imitate a bus caller in a familiar tone heard at bus stations everywhere, announcing departure times followed by a long list of small towns where it would be stopping.[13]

It was Jim and Kate who introduced my wife and me to their liberal-inclined First Community Church, Congregational denomination. It was a popular church that had as its pastor the much-admired Rev. W. B. J. Martin. Members included District Attorney Henry Wade and his wife, Yvonne; the *Times Herald*'s progressive women's editor, Vivian Castleberry; Blackie Sherrod's wife, Marilyn; and musicians from the Dallas Symphony Orchestra. Vivian was not content to have her women's pages devoted strictly to weddings, engagements, society, fashion, and foods, as was the custom. She was becoming a leader in transforming her women's section to include the need for women to escape the limited versions of women's "proper" roles in life.

Among the other city-side reporters was the colorful Jim Featherston, a Tennessean who had come to the *Times Herald* in 1962 from Vicksburg, Mississippi, where he was one of five reporters jointly winning a Pulitzer Prize in covering a devastating tornado. "Feather," as he was called, spoke with a heavy Southern drawl. He was a favorite colleague in the newsroom.

Of course, our photographers were critical assets for their work on news coverage and features. One who would gain the greatest fame for his skills was Robert (Bob) Hill Jackson, a sports car enthusiast and son of a cofounder of a Dallas savings and loan association. Jackson and his wife lived in our neighborhood. Other special photographers were my friend Russ Russell, who like me came to the *Times Herald* from the *Fort Worth Press*, and the outstanding Andy Hanson. It would be customary for a photographer to accompany me or any of our writers when we were given special assignments. Almost inevitably it was the photographer who drove us to our designation in his car (there were no female photographers on the staff). Of these mentioned persons, all serious professionals, only Hanson made a lifelong career at the *Times Herald*, remaining there until the newspaper closed in 1991. Not only did the photographers take numerous pictures for a single story, exploring every angle and presenting their best ones to the editor, who made the final decision on which to use, but each photographer also did his or her own darkroom work. I suppose I was like other reporters who particularly enjoyed going out on an assignment with a photographer.

On the police beat, which I covered twice a week before moving to the courthouse beat, reporters shared a press room adjacent to detectives' offices at the north end of the third floor. Copies of daily offense reports, usually describing overnight activities, were regularly delivered there for the reporters to sift over as they sought basic information on newsworthy events. If already assigned to specific detectives, usually a pair of detectives for major incidents, we could interview them for more details.

Often detectives would ask a nearby police reporter to their office to confirm with our signature, in the presence of an accused person, that his (or her, although I don't recall such for a female) written confession had been given voluntarily without coercion. This had been a typical practice in Fort Worth, too.

Over the press room intercom, reporters could hear transmissions from the police dispatcher to uniformed officers as they patrolled their designated areas. Another speaker in the press room carried the fire department's dispatcher with instant alerts about fires, their locations, and their needs (two or three or four alarm, for instance).

None of the other beats (such as education, medicine, education, politics, and science) provided a press room exclusively for reporters. Their less occasional newsworthy events were not tied to a central location, and their interaction with journalists was not so frequent as to require all-day facilities for reporters.

Chapter 4

"What the Hell's the United Nations for, Anyway?"

ULTRA-REPUBLICAN CONSERVATISM was becoming dominant in Dallas. Surely no large city in the nation was more recognized for its right-wing politics. Encouraged especially by the political influence of the *Dallas Morning News*, far-right activities included paying for billboards that urged the impeachment of Chief Justice Earl Warren; making ultraconservative statements from organizations with members such as propagandist oilman H. L. Hunt; choosing Dallas as the site for the ultraright John Birch Society regional headquarters; admiring the state's sole Republican congressman Bruce Alger, generally considered to be Congress's most radical conservative; and controversial former Army general Edwin A. Walker selecting Dallas as his home and headquarters. Walker's exaggerated claims about the spread of Communist influences throughout the federal government and the United Nations, by teachers and professors, the art world, and intellectual endeavors reflected the influence of Joseph McCarthy, the late senator from Wisconsin whose tirades created the so-called Red Scare of the 1950s.

All this found a ready audience, even as the national Democratic Party was becoming more and more favorable to the working class and minorities. Local oilmen, rich since the 1930s from huge new East Texas oilfields, were supported in their push for the federal government to fatten their wallets by recognizing their claims for the oil-rich tidelands off Texas's lengthy Gulf Coast.

Even Protestant ministers in Dallas were combining conservative politics with their fundamentalist religious beliefs. Any mention of Dallas's prominent archconservatives should include the First Baptist Church's pastor, W. A. Criswell, who had opposed Kennedy's election and preached against the evils of school desegregation as contrary to biblical command. He said Kennedy was "either a poor Catholic or he's stringing the people along." From his pulpit he endorsed Richard Nixon as president.[1]

Among the popular and influential ultraconservatives was Dan Smoot, a 61-year-old former FBI agent who since the late 1950s had been publishing a weekly newsletter entitled *Dan Smoot Report* and broadcasting a political television show from Dallas under the same name. Handsome and smooth-talking, Smoot's past work as an FBI agent gave supposed credence to his allegations about Communist infiltration into the federal government.[2]

Another ultraconservative boasting of proper credentials but soon discrediting himself with his new and outlandish beliefs was Robert J. Morris, president of a small and struggling Catholic university bearing the name the University of Dallas. Morris moved to Dallas in 1960 from his native New Jersey after losing his bid in 1958 for a US Senate seat. This one-time moderate conservative converted almost overnight to incessant political anti-Communism rants, such as his claims that President Kennedy was planning a merger with the Soviet Union to establish a world government controlled by the United Nations. Government leaders in Washington, he had concluded, were working toward this goal. He indoctrinated many of his students with such propaganda, but his shocked colleagues at the university forced him to resign in 1962. By then many of his students had become familiar figures in ultraright crusades and joined Edwin A. Walker in his efforts.[3]

Walker's decision in 1961 to make Dallas his home and center for his beliefs won enthusiastic approval. He earlier had won praise as the heroic general who commanded federal troops protecting Black students as they entered previously all-white public schools in Little Rock. Now, revealed as a conservative who under growing pressure resigned his military commission for indoctrinating troops with a "pro-blue" John Birch Society program, Walker, although Texas-born, had never lived in the city.

In his first highly anticipated local speech before an adoring crowd of 5,500, he proclaimed that he "could no longer be a collaborator" in turning over American sovereignty to the United Nations. Dallas's appreciative but naïve mayor, conservative Democrat Earle Cabell, publicly welcomed him that evening as he presented him with a new Stetson hat. That wasn't all. Former Texas governor Coke Stevenson chaired a Texas Welcome Home committee to coordinate Walker's speeches throughout the state and nation. *Newsweek* put the former general's picture on its cover with the words, "Thunder on the Right" (Dec. 4, 1961).

The rugged-looking former major general moved into a large two-story house on Turtle Creek Boulevard near exclusive Highland Park. He posted an upside-down American flag in his front yard, explaining that it was a sign of distress because a determined and pro-Communist movement was endangering the nation. A confirmed bachelor, he attracted to his home a regular group of especially aggressive young right-wing zealots, many of them college students.

But overconfident of his popularity with such a small but vocal group, Walker made a fatal error in 1962 by running for governor in the Democratic primary. He finished last in a field of six. Besides going too far in his extremism, he failed as a speechmaker. Worse, he became even more pathetic when federal marshals arrested him in September for promoting riots on the University of Mississippi campus to prevent Black student James Meredith from entering the all-white university.[4]

The turmoil over Meredith's effort in Mississippi captured the nation's attention. The riots prompted my wife and me to buy our first television set—black-and-white—to watch the dramatic events in which two individuals were killed. Federal marshals arrested Walker for inciting a riot. Held in custody so government psychiatrists could examine him, he was deemed sane. In the eyes of his young zealots, he was a patriotic former major officer whose superiors had attempted to muzzle his warnings about a Communist takeover.

The John Birch Society was especially strong in Dallas. Its regional headquarters oversaw an estimated thirty-five chapters. The Birchers opened in the city their own American Opinion Book Store, specializing in right-wing propaganda. The Birch founder, retired candymaker Robert Welch of Massachusetts, made frequent visits to speak and recruit new members. Meetings started with the Pledge of Allegiance, followed by individual presentations, film viewings, discussions, and progress reports. When chapter memberships reached thirty, they were directed to divide and form an additional chapter, intending on further growth for the organization.[5]

One day in 1962, seeing only a small newspaper notice that Welch would speak at a downtown hotel (surely his October 6 appearance at the Statler Hilton Hotel), Pat and I, disgusted with the Birchers' politics and curious to see this increasingly famous founder, decided to attend. I had no intention of writing a news story about it. Wanting to avoid conversations with Birchers who would likely see us as compatriots instead of critics, we arrived only a couple of minutes before Welch's talk. Only a few, perhaps no more than thirty to forty, were there. Attendees were well-dressed and mature. We sat—inconspicuously, we hoped—in the back of the small meeting room. Despite Welch's supposed skills as an organizer and propogandist, this ultraconservative leader in his early 60s was one of the most boring speakers we had ever heard. As expected, he emphasized his anti-Communist and anti-UN viewpoints, but unlike so many of his followers, he displayed no passion or fervor.

Near the end of the meeting, Birch Society members were asked to stand, possibly so prospects could be singled out. As far as we could tell, everyone except us stood. Those who turned to survey the room and saw us seemed to display curiosity and perhaps a grain of hostility, but no more. At the conclusion we hustled out before anyone could engage us in conversation. Later, we were pleased to boast that we had dared see and hear the famous propagandist at a Birch Society meeting.

One notable member of the Birch Society possibly present that evening was H. L. Hunt's son, Nelson Bunker Hunt, who, like his father, was a wealthy oilman. But his father, sometimes described incorrectly as the richest man in the world, was a far more prominent ultraconservative. In a single-minded way he wrote and published tracts such as *We Must Abolish the United Nations* and *Hitler Was a Liberal*. He sponsored "LIFELINE" radio programs, bombarded newspapers and magazines with letters to the editor, and led a tax-exempt organization called Facts Forum.[6]

One of the most aggressive critics of the federal government's alleged association with Communism was a new organization, the National Indignation Convention, which erupted spontaneously in September 1961 when news reports revealed that four pilots and four mechanics from Communist Yugoslavia were being trained at Perrin Air Force Base in Texas. Knowledge of this federally authorized assistance came when a Texas Air National Guard officer asked innocently to borrow from Perrin some equipment for ground training his unit. That would be fine, he was told, but the equipment was being used by the class with the Yugoslavs in it. The officer, angered, wrote to US senator John Tower to complain, and the story of this "treasonous" action was widely reported in the media, especially in Dallas.[7]

Secretary of State Dean Rusk explained that although Yugoslavia was a Communist nation, its ruler, Josip Broz Tito (commonly known simply as Tito), was doing his best to maintain independence from the Soviet Union. To encourage him the Truman, Eisenhower, and now

Kennedy administrations were selling to Yugoslavia certain aircraft and training their technicians to maintain them.[8]

This news alerted 32-year-old Dallasite Frank McGehee to initiate vigorous reactions to this alleged government act of treason. The startling news aroused so many protestors that McGehee rented Dallas Memorial Coliseum for a rally. Relatively few attended that first evening, but the meetings continued every night, with media coverage, from October 13 through October 21. Attendance reached as high as five thousand. McGehee and his stalwarts organized committees to advance their cause. Protest sessions emerged in Chicago, Los Angeles, Milwaukee, and smaller towns as thousands of like-minded individuals launched their own protest chapters known as the National Indignation Convention. Members demanded that Congress cease military aid to any Communist regime and to dismiss all responsible government officials. McGehee became the organization's vociferous leader.[9]

The Dallas Morning News, a crusader in the early 1920s against Dallas's large Ku Klux Klan chapter (especially because the KKK insisted that the *News* was under Catholic control), had grown adamant in editorial tirades against what it perceived to be Kennedy's socialist tendencies and support of the Civil Rights Movement. The editorial page nodded approvingly as the city's extremist elements gained strength. Its ultraconservative editorials gained wide attention and praise.

Few if any of Dallas's mainstream but conservative city leaders openly endorsed the extremists. The exclusive business-oriented and private Dallas Citizens Council was very protective of the city's image. Its leaders viewed extremists as a problem because they damaged Dallas's reputation, but the organization did not fund or align with far-right extremists such as Walker. Nor did they disown or discourage such individuals or groups whose aggressive conduct and statements were becoming more and more obnoxious.

There were, of course, liberal-minded citizens and organizations in Dallas. They could be found in elements of the Democratic Party identified as liberals such as US senator Ralph Yarborough, churches such as First Unitarian and Northaven Methodist, faculty members at Southern Methodist University, and organizations such as the Dallas Council on World Affairs, the League of Women Voters, and the American Civil Liberties Union.

Occasionally, these contrarian individuals or organizations challenged Dallas with enlightened projects. A notable example was when the Dallas Council on World Affairs, joined by the League of Women Voters, announced a local celebration of United Nations Day to be held on October 24, 1963. Its special feature would be a visit and speech by UN ambassador Adlai Stevenson, who as such was detested by the isolationist right-wingers.

I remembered that when I was 15 our family made a short pilgrimage in October 1952 to see Stevenson at an outdoor rally at Fair Park as he campaigned for the presidency. Our admiration of the former governor of Illinois was strong. Despite our parents' family roots as Southern sharecroppers, we felt close to this politician who identified as an intellectual.

An intriguing factor that endeared him to us and many others was a famous photograph taken on Labor Day in Flint, Michigan, that appeared in a September 1952 issue of *Life* magazine. As Stevenson sat on the speakers' platform, he momentarily crossed his legs, revealing a hole in the sole of his well-worn shoe. *Flint Journal* photographer William G. Gallagher promptly snapped the shot for his newspaper, and it was reprinted in *Life*. For this crowd-pleasing photo the Pulitzer committee awarded its 1953 journalism photography prize to Gallagher.[10] Erudite, intellectual, and well-bred though Stevenson was—and we believed that—we saw the photo as evidence that he was really a man of the people.

Most of our nonpolitical relatives and friends favored Republican candidate Dwight Eisenhower. And why not? As commander of the D-Day invasion leading to the end of World War II, he was a bona fide hero. And now he pledged that if elected he would go to Korea, where that dismal war needed an end. He offered a special treat for Texas oilmen. As a proponent of states' rights, he believed that tax revenue derived from underwater oil sources such as the coastal tidelands belonged to states rather than the federal government. Texas had an abundance of coastal tidelands.

As I recall, our father (Daddy to us) came home late that afternoon from work and suggested that our family attend Stevenson's rally that evening at Fair Park. That location was just down Second Avenue from our small frame duplex in South Dallas. So, of course, we eagerly agreed. Fair Park we knew very well. Often on Sunday afternoons we would go there to see exhibits or free events or just walk around the grounds where the State Fair of Texas reigned every October and the 1936 Texas Centennial Exposition had been held.

The crowd was larger than we had expected. Attending political rallies was something our parents had never done. After finding a parking spot for our trusty green '39 Ford, we walked to a grassy spot in front of the iconic Hall of State, perhaps a hundred yards away from the speaker's platform.

Having heard earlier that "organized disorder" might occur, the 50-year-old governor doubted it. "If fascism ever starts in this country, I don't believe it will start or even live in the fiercely free heart of Texas," he said. Minor disturbances between Democrats and Republicans did break out before the governor spoke, but without too much difficulty Democrats outshouted the few anti-Stevenson supporters. Throughout the evening, though, occasional shouts could be heard: "What about Hiss?" "What about Acheson?" "What about Korea?"[11]

Of course, Eisenhower was elected by a wide majority, prevailing over Stevenson in Texas as well as the nation. In 1956 he won a second term, again defeating Stevenson. Dallas, the state of Texas, and the entire Southland were giving up their historic Democratic ties to be conservative Republicans.

But that family outing to see Stevenson was exhilarating.

NOW, ELEVEN YEARS LATER, with news of UN ambassador Stevenson's forthcoming event in Dallas, Walker and his allies began planning their own pro-US and anti-UN day. It would be held at the same Memorial Auditorium where Ambassador Stevenson would speak the next evening. Stevenson had not visited Dallas since 1952; he had avoided Texas in his 1956 presidential campaign. Texas governor John B. Connally, who had served for a year as Kennedy's first secretary of the navy, unwittingly sanctioned this "patriotic" event as Mayor Cabell had done when he honored Walker with a cowboy hat. Connally surely did not know that harsh right-wing strategies to spoil Stevenson's appearance on the following evening would be planned in this auditorium.

Approximately 1,400 individuals attended the US Day rally to hear Walker claim that the Communists, Alger Hiss, and "that crowd" had founded the UN. "The main battle in the world today," Walker stressed, "is right here in America, and it involves the United States versus the United Nations." Texan conservative activist and author J. Evetts Haley won loud applause when he bragged that he didn't want to impeach Supreme Court chief justice Earl Warren. No, he wanted to hang him. "Tomorrow night," Walker told the cheering crowd, "there will stand here a symbol to the Communist conspiracy and its United Nations." It would be waged, he claimed, from the podium at which Stevenson would appear. The question "boiled down to which side you are for—the United States or the United Nations?"[12]

John F. Kennedy and former presidents Eisenhower, Roosevelt, Truman, and Vice President Nixon were targets of the venomous Walker. Messages from Dallas's congressman Bruce Alger, Senator Strom Thurmond of South Carolina, propagandist Dan Smoot, and Robert Morris were read aloud. Twelve area mayors, invited pro forma to attend that night, were asked to stand. Seeing no one standing, the crowd booed lustily. And when Walker read the list of organizations sponsoring the next night's UN Day, the crowd again shouted its disapproval.[13]

The first evidence of work done by Walker and cohorts to spoil Stevenson's UN Day event came the next morning. Leaflets bearing simulated police mug shots of President Kennedy under the headline "WANTED FOR TREASON" had been spread throughout the city.

When I arrived that morning at the newsroom, reporters and editors were studying these leaflets with contempt. No source for the handbills appeared. The listed "charges" included Kennedy's supposed sympathy with Communist objectives, such as turning the sovereignty of the U.S. over to Communist controlled United Nations and his encouragement of Communist inspired racial riots. We could imagine several sponsors, certainly including Walker and his supporters, but as far as we were concerned, such ridiculous propaganda did not warrant news coverage, so we disregarded them. However, the handbills were alarming. (Walker's responsibility for these handbills would become known later.)

To me, and I suppose to others, the outlandish leaflets suggested a strong probability that demonstrators would be present this night. I suggested to Pat that we simply must attend to see what would happen. She agreed.

It would take no more than ten or fifteen minutes to get there from our apartment. After all, out of curiosity and total disdain, we earlier had attended that John Birch Society meeting to see the candymaker himself. Stevenson's speech would be covered by our political writer, Keith Shelton. It would also be televised live by local CBS-TV affiliate KRLD-TV. We would be there as UN supporters, though, not as part of the media. As it soon turned out, my expectations of trouble were far less than what happened.

On Stevenson's morning arrival at Love Field for his evening speech, Jack Goren, Neiman Marcus executive vice president and new president of the Dallas United Nations Association, warmly welcomed him. One of the newsmen, aware of the previous night's US Day rally and the expectation of intense anti-UN picketing, asked Stevenson if he expected a friendly reception. Stevenson had been alerted, but he innocently replied, "I don't know why not."[14] The ambassador might not have seen a small airplane flying overhead tugging a banner with the words, "GET THE US OUT OF THE UN."[15]

A limousine carried Stevenson to the Sheraton Hotel for a noon luncheon where he was guest of honor. Stanley Marcus had arranged it. When the usual western hat was presented to Stevenson, he said that having been through Texas on his campaigns, he already had about sixty-five such hats. Then, as he more thoughtfully examined it, he managed to recover—"but of all of them, this is the best one." A news conference followed at the Press Club, adjacent to the Baker Hotel.

Wes Wise, Press Club president, future mayor of Dallas, and a familiar newsman known especially for his television sports reporting on KRLD-TV's ten o'clock evening news, shook hands with the ambassador. Wise later would note his surprise at Stevenson's "small stature and red face."[16] But he described his handshake as firm and friendly. Wise would see Stevenson again that night, for he had been assigned to cover the speech for KRLD-TV.

The brief press conference went well. Afterward, the elevator carrying Stevenson and Wise downstairs was crowded with individuals who seemed friendly enough. But as the two stepped out at ground floor, one of the passengers, a 30-something man, muttered loud enough for the ambassador to hear: "What the hell's the United Nations for, anyway?"[17]

Stevenson likely retreated to his presidential suite at the Sheraton for an afternoon nap and perhaps a final review of his evening comments. He surely read with interest a page-one story in that day's *News* describing the previous evening's US Day event, noting that he would speak at the same place. Neither would he have missed Walker's unqualified declaration that a "war" existed between the United States and the United Nations.

Marcus, who had invited Stevenson to come to Dallas, and Jack Goren, chairman of the local United Nations Day committee, had been assured that ample security would be present. Former FBI agent William de Gan, at Goren's request, had visited Police Chief Jesse Curry to stress the need for enhanced protection. Curry assured him that adequate protection would be provided. A few days later, confidential reports had made it evident that picketing would be heavier than expected. De Gan made yet another plea for additional security.

Curry assured him that he would arrange additional protection. Maybe
he did, but if so, it made little difference.[18]

As evening came and the dark of night replaced the disappearing
sun, Dallas Memorial Auditorium on downtown Canton Street, with
a seating capacity of 1,770, began to fill. As Pat and I approached, we
could see protestors around the entrance waving signs and shouting.
Most noteworthy was the notorious segregationist Bobby Joiner,
candidate for the Texas Legislature representing the Indignant White
Citizens Council. Costumed flamboyantly in an Uncle Sam suit,
he carried an American flag and shouted to one and all that the UN
was for Communist race mixers. Some protestors were well-dressed,
having been advised beforehand by their organizers to look especially
respectable. But they carried picket signs, one of them stating "Adlai,
Who Elected You?"

Inside, as seats were being taken, heated exchanges between far–
right wing elements and UN supporters broke out. The protestors

Further emergence of far-right groups, evidenced by attacks on UN ambassador
Adlai Stevenson a month before the president's approaching visit, caused
urgent concerns about his safety. *Dallas Morning News* Collection,
the Sixth Floor Museum at Dealey Plaza, donated by the *Dallas Morning
News* in the interest of preserving history.

represented not just Walker's supporters but also the John Birch Society, McGehee's National Indignation Convention, Young Americans for Freedom, college students from Robert Morris's University of Dallas, and at least a few from North Texas State College (now University of North Texas). A separate category seemed evident, too—independent old-timers, both men and women, who must have been disgusted for years with the federal "guv'ment" and the United Nations.

The auditorium, already electric, was filling up, but we found a good place to sit on aisle steps leading to the balcony. Harangues grew louder and louder. Looking around, I did my best to calculate the separate numbers of protesters and supporters. It didn't seem difficult to distinguish between them. By my rough approximation, as many as half of the audience were right-wing extremists, easily identified by their actions, looks of disgust, and miniature American flags held upside down. Sedate UN supporters looked about in shocked disbelief. A few earnestly requested the protestors to be quiet. Inevitably, this only prompted louder and louder exchanges. The first two rows in the auditorium were designated for the press, but we didn't try to sit there. We were just spectators.

PROCEEDINGS STARTED WHEN US district judge Sarah T. Hughes, the well-known Dallas liberal recently appointed to the federal bench by Kennedy, read the president's proclamation declaring UN Day. Stanley Marcus next stepped to the podium to give Stevenson a proper introduction, but this venerable and respected Neiman Marcus legend was obviously shocked by boos and catcalls such as I'm sure he had never experienced. As Stevenson moved to the podium, Frank McGehee, strategically seated at front and neatly attired in suit and tie, quickly arose with bullhorn in hand. His amplified voice rang out throughout the auditorium: "Before you speak, Mr. Ambassador, we demand that you first answer these questions."

UN supporters angrily shouted at McGehee to shut up. I found myself joining in the shouts. The situation was disgraceful. Stevenson at first sought to ignore McGehee, evidently thinking his challenger could be ignored, but McGehee's outlandish demands, enhanced for all to hear, were impossible to ignore.

There were thirty policemen on duty at the auditorium. But where were they? Finally, Stevenson responded lamely, "I'll be pleased to give you equal time after I have finished." Finally, an older, white-haired man near the front had had enough. He stood up, rushed to McGehee, and tried to grab the bullhorn from him. A brief standing wrestling match ensued, accompanied by the shouts of the highly agitated crowd. A handful of Dallas police officers reached McGehee, grabbed him, and escorted him outside to the cheers of the UN supporters.

Stevenson, now regaining composure, said, "Surely, my friends, I don't have to come here from Illinois to teach Texans manners, do I?" But the interruptions were not over; they had just begun. Throughout the ambassador's speech, extremists sought to disrupt him, waving their signs, booing, shouting interjections, laughing derisively, coughing incessantly, and walking up and down the aisles while clicking small tin cricket noisemakers. "How about Cuber?" was a common shout, ridiculing Kennedy's tendency to add that invisible *r* to its ending, and "How about Hungry [*sic*]?" and "How about Katanga?" The evening continued as a struggle of wills between the two opposing groups, with the demonstrators holding the advantage because of their dogged determination to be spoilers.

At one point, rather incredibly, the large and handsome banner high above the speaker bearing the words "Welcome Adlai" was flipped over to reveal an opposite message. In equally large letters it now had these words: "UN Red Front." An approving roar greeted the turnover. The trick banner had been planted the night before.

Still, the worst was yet to come. Instead of leaving when the oft-interrupted speech ended, a hundred or more hardline demonstrators congregated outside the auditorium, intent on confronting Stevenson when he left. Seeing their ill intentions, Pat and I waited, too, concerned about what further might happen. It was certain that the troubles were not over unless Stevenson somehow managed to slip away unseen. His departure was delayed by a short reception inside, limited to the UN Day sponsors. The demonstrators waited patiently, keeping watch.

Finally, accompanied by a few police officers, Stevenson, Marcus, and a handful of supporters, which included our own reporter and supporter Val Imm, exited from a side door, walking calmly toward the adjacent parking lot.

"There he is!" a demonstrator sounded, and with that the crowd raced toward their prey with animallike roars and cries of "Communist," "traitor," and more. We went along, too, but silently. Near us, we saw police officers handcuff a resisting college student who was furiously shouting and spitting at Stevenson and the arresting officers.

Our political writer, Keith Shelton, was off to the side, taking notes as fast as he could. I rushed to him to offer help. Keith, nonplussed, said he could manage it, which he did. I was disappointed. It appeared to me that plenty of help was needed.

Stevenson, still the gentleman, rather foolishly thought that he could reason with the mob. He turned toward their first arriving wave to engage in conversation. Immediately, though, more and more protestors arrived, shouting and waving their signs. One irate demonstrator, a matronly woman later identified as Cora Frederickson, held a cardboard sign with the words, "Down With the UN." She slammed it on Stevenson's head, afterward claiming that someone had pushed it. We could see the two exchanging a few words, but in the clamor we couldn't hear what they said. A few police officers arrived to grab her. Stevenson, still the gentleman, asked them to release her so he could reason with her.

"What's the matter with you?" he asked her. "What's the trouble?"

"Don't you know?" she responded.

"Know what?"

"I know, everybody knows. Why don't you know?"

"It's all right to have your own views . . . but don't hit anyone," Stevenson said, ending the tortured dialogue.[19]

Wiping spittle from his face, Stevenson had had enough. He was quoted next day as having said, "Are these human beings or animals?"[20]

Finally, Stanley Marcus pushed Stevenson into the waiting car for departure. But the crowd, surrounding the car, began rocking it from one side to the other, clearly intending to turn it over. At long last, at Marcus's urging, the driver sped away.

Wise, in the midst of the angry crowd and filming everything he could, saw Val Imm next to Stevenson. Knowing that the regular 10:00 p.m. local newscast was approaching, Wise asked her to rush him to the KRLD-TV newsroom so his film could be processed and shown. She agreed. They got there just in time for the film to be on the news. The next day Walter Cronkite showed the film on his late afternoon CBS-TV news program, congratulating Wise as "our alert young cameraman Wes Wise."[21]

The fierceness of the attack, widely seen on network television's recently expanded news programs and extensively reported by wire services from East Coast to West Coast, went far beyond what had happened to LBJ and Lady Bird at the Adolphus. ABC radio commentator Edward P. Morgan said that "Big D now stands for disgrace." *Time* echoed his words: Dallas now was "A City Disgraced" (Nov. 1, 1963). *Christian Century* dug deeper a few weeks later in a thoughtful piece entitled "The Dallas Image Unveiled" (Nov. 20, 1963). Was Dallas the progressive, forward-thinking place its leaders, notably the Dallas Citizens Council, claimed? The article blamed the fiasco on the failure of civic leaders to respond to previous extremists' behavior. Only slightly less critical was *Time*, calling the threatening crowd "Dallas' adult delinquents" (Nov. 1, 1963) and the *Washington Post*'s description of them as "creatures from a jungle swamp" (Oct. 26, 1963).

A HUGE PROBLEM AWAITED. The president and his wife, Jackie, were scheduled to come to Dallas a month later with a group including, among others, Vice President Johnson and his wife, Lady Bird, and Texas governor John B. Connally and his wife, Nellie. That similar riots would greet the president was a terrifying thought, especially for city leaders who were seeing Dallas's former reputation for civility fading.

The ultraright's major target was Kennedy, not Adlai Stevenson. Nothing less than the attack on Stevenson and the aggressive demonstration against the Johnsons at the Adolphus could be expected. Would Dallas be able to handle whatever arose?

Chief Curry, facing broad criticism for having failed to protect Stevenson despite advance warnings, was defensive. He falsely blamed Stevenson for breaking away from his police escort to talk to the approaching, screaming crowd. "There is no way to protect a person who does this if he insists in going into a crowd of unfriendly people," the chief said.[22]

Chagrined and embarrassed by the significant UN event, which they had not bothered to attend, Mayor Cabell, whose father and grandfather years before had been mayors of the city; Erik Jonsson, chairman of the Dallas Citizens Council and a founder of Texas Instruments, Inc.; and Robert B. Cullum, incoming president of the chamber of commerce whose family had been prominent in the city since the nineteenth century, were joined by a hundred other citizens who sent a telegram of apology to Ambassador Stevenson. Dallas, they wrote, was "outraged and abjectly ashamed of the disgraceful and discourtesies you suffered at the hands of a small group of extremists."[23]

Small group? Already the city's sensitive leaders were minimizing the actual number of demonstrators. The term "small group" was not at all descriptive of their number or their outrageous antics. Mayor Cabell, though, urged Dallas citizens to reject the radical right just as it finally had rejected the Ku Klux Klan in the 1920s when the city was home to the largest Klan chapter in the nation. (This I had not previously known, but it inspired me later to research and write about Dallas's Klan chapter and its dominance in official bodies at the highest levels.)[24]

The *Times Herald* deplored "storm troopers" who had ruined Stevenson's visit. "What has happened to Dallas?" The display of malevolence brought a sickening realization. "We must quit preaching hate," the editorial continued. The right-wing *Morning News* was less concerned in its conditional apology, although it editorialized that "if the time had come when a distinguished gentleman in his position cannot express his beliefs without abuse, then this city should examine itself."[25]

Despite his usual reluctance to address Dallas's tolerance of extremist political opinion, Stanley Marcus had had enough. Normally circumspect as a member of the conservative Dallas Citizens Council, he wrote a highly critical letter to the *Morning News*'s Joe Dealey. "Your paper has been one of the contributing factors to the development of a hard core of unreasonable people intolerant of any views opposed to their own . . . preaching a doctrine of criticism of the Government and of the United Nations while at the same time giving solace to the extreme rightists like General Walker and his ilk."[26]

Serious questions arose. Should the president cancel his visit to Dallas? At first Stevenson thought so. Kennedy aide Arthur Schlesinger Jr. congratulated Adlai for his coolness at the scene, to which Stevenson responded, "But, you know, there was something ugly and frightening about the atmosphere."[27] Some of the city's leading people, Stevenson acknowledged, wondered if the president should go to Dallas. With President Kennedy now emphasizing that he indeed would go to Dallas, the somewhat chastened ambassador changed his tune. He also downsized the mob's hostility and numbers, reducing the crowd to "a minute handful" and "a few zealots," forgetting that the auditorium's seating capacity was 1,770 and that there had been standing room only.[28] In an obvious misstatement, Stevenson contrasted five thousand cheering supporters inside with fifty outside protestors.

Bob Walker, news director for Dallas's WFAA-TV, wrote to Stevenson that idiot fringe elements were "winning their fight in Dallas." US attorney Barefoot Sanders, Kennedy's Dallas County campaign manager for 1960, wanted the president to cancel his Dallas visit. So did US district judge Sarah T. Hughes. When Stanley Marcus told Vice President Johnson that it would be "a grave mistake" for the president to come to Dallas, Johnson responded, "I don't care what you think, nor does it make any difference. . . . He is coming to Dallas, so go out and raise the money."[29]

The president would not be intimidated. He was, after all, a "profile of courage" and representative of a "new generation." Besides raising money, the Texas feud between its conservative Democrats, led by Governor Connally, and its liberal Democrats, represented by US senator Ralph Yarborough, needed attention. Although brief, the schedule included stops in Houston, San Antonio, Austin, Fort Worth, and Dallas.

President Kennedy told Connally that as Texas's governor and chief executive, he should assume authority over decisions concerning his visits. Prompted by the upcoming crisis sure to catch the nation's attention, Connally came to Dallas to meet with leaders of the Dallas Citizens Council—Mayor Cabell, Robert Cullum, Erik Jonsson, and the aging banker Robert L. Thornton. At Connally's urging it was decided to describe the Texas visits as either "political" or "nonpolitical." Dallas and Fort Worth visits would be dubbed as nonpolitical—that is, the hosts would be civic and business leaders instead of the Democratic Party. Thus, the Dallas visit would be hosted by the supposedly nonpolitical Dallas Citizens Council, whose exclusive membership, dominated by conservative businessmen, had been the city's most important force since its founding in 1937.[30]

This business-leadership sponsorship was an especially devastating blow to the local Democratic Party. Finally, in defense, the Dallas Citizens Council added the little-known Dallas Assembly and the Science Research Center as cohosts, which provided hardly any diversification. The Dallas Assembly was a "junior" citizens council composed of no more than one hundred invitation-only members between the ages of 25 and 50 who were destined to become members of the Dallas Citizens Council. The Science Research Center was a collection of scientists organized by Jonsson and his fellow Texas Instruments executives (who formed the nucleus of leadership in what would become the University of Texas at Dallas). The county's Democratic Party, which had worked so hard for Kennedy's election, still had no role in the visit. At most they would be allotted a certain number of tickets for the noon luncheon.

AS POWERFUL AS THE Dallas Citizens Council had been for nearly three decades, it was hardly known by the public, even though it was a major behind-the-scenes force in influencing major events. Its founding came after the city's most prominent bankers surprisingly led the drive to secure Dallas as the site of the 1936 Texas Centennial, which would honor the state's one-hundred-year anniversary of independence from Mexico. State officials decided that no less than a world's fair should be held during the Depression as an attention getter for Texas. The site selection committee stressed that the state's romantic history should be a major theme in its location. San Antonio, with its inspiring and world-famous Alamo, was a logical place. Equally likely was the state's most populous city, Houston, conveniently located near the victorious San Jacinto battlefield. As for Dallas, it had no romantic or historical justification. It didn't even exist in 1836. Yet a trio of its influential bankers—led by Robert L. Thornton, with the special aid of Nathan Adams and Fred Florence—together masterminded an energizing campaign that won the prize.

So successful was the Texas Centennial that this team of leaders decided to continue the next year with another world's fair for Dallas, this one the Pan-American Exposition of 1937. Since the centennial had celebrated our freedom from Mexico, the Pan-American boasted of our friendships with Mexico and Latin America.

The city that for years had been ignored by the national press now was praised because of its sponsorship during the Depression of not just one but two world expositions. The national media—largely print, of course—concluded that Dallas was an unusual city of enterprise, culture, and imagination. The *Readers' Guide to Periodical Literature*, which annually indexes articles appearing in the nation's periodicals, reveals that between 1933 and mid-1935, Dallas merited only one lonely article. In the following two years, twenty-five articles related to Dallas and its expositions appeared, and eighteen more in the next two years. So if the centennial was "the year America discovered Texas," its historian Kenneth B. Ragsdale believed especially that it was the year it had discovered Dallas.[31]

After the 1937 exposition ended, the self-made Thornton proposed that his banker friends Adams and Florence join him in establishing an exclusive leadership group consisting only of what he called "boss" businessmen, who—unlike the elected Dallas City Council or Dallas County Commissioners—could act quickly with muscle to achieve significant things for the good of Dallas. Membership would be limited to those at the very top of their businesses who could make important decisions without having to run back to their offices for permission.

Finally, when bylaws for this Dallas Citizens Council were established, excluded from membership were practicing attorneys, doctors, educators, journalists, government officials, and labor leaders. Membership was limited to presidents or general managers of businesses located in Dallas. Meetings were closed to the public and the press. The charter did not prohibit women, Blacks, or Latinos from membership, although none were among the original members. Jews and Catholics were prominent among these first board members, as they would continue to be.

With so many normal residents, they had reveled at every minor mention of Dallas in a national publication, movie, or television. In fact, up to this time if a character in a movie happened to utter the word "Dallas" in the least significant way, spontaneous cheers and clapping would erupt. And what a sensation to hear "I'm From Big D" in Frank Loesser's popular Broadway musical, *The Most Happy Fella*. (Later, this would not be the case. In other cities, cheers and jeers would follow its mention. In Dallas, there would be only a thoughtful silence.)

FEAR THAT RIOTOUS RIGHT-WING extremists would spoil President Kennedy's visit created the most angst-filled weeks in the city's history. Big D's once-proud image could be irreparably, possibly everlastingly, damaged if hard-core zealots spoiled what in the past had brought good publicity. In preparation, the Secret Service began examining photographs of the principal antagonists at the Stevenson affair. Wise's film was especially useful for Secret Service agents, who met with him in five or six sessions lasting two to three hours each. The agents arranged for Wise and his wife, Sally, to sit with them at the Kennedy luncheon, too. Wise would be able to point out those protestors who had been so active or who "looked suspicious."[32]

With utmost sincerity Mayor Cabell stressed the necessity for Dallas to redeem itself by giving the president and party a warm and generous welcome. Four days before the president's arrival, Cabell and elected members of the Dallas City Council (not to be confused with the Dallas Citizens Council) passed a new ordinance prohibiting individuals from interfering with public assemblies. Harsh in toto, it prohibited "any person, singly or in concert with others from interfering with a public or private assembly by use of insulting, threatening, or obscene language or intimidation."[33]

Curry himself held a conference in which he told the press that police would take immediate action against anyone who would attempt to disturb the president's visit. "We will take immediate action if any suspicious conduct is observed, and we also urge all good citizens to be alert for such conduct. . . . Citizens themselves may take preventative action if it becomes obvious that someone is planning to commit an act harmful or degrading to the President."[34] Free speech under the First Amendment was one thing, but disrupting a public meeting, hitting a dignified UN ambassador on the head with a protest sign, and spitting on him were beyond free speech. Even former president Nixon, visiting the city briefly, publicly urged Dallas "to give President and Mrs. Kennedy a courteous reception."[35]

Could Dallas possibly provide Kennedy the proper and dignified greeting usually afforded a president of the United States? There was no assurance, only fears.

Chapter 5

"Welcome Mr. Kennedy to Dallas"

D ALLAS HAD A NEW nickname: "city of hate." Such a stinging moniker for a growing, prosperous, and business-minded place where image meant everything. As the November days grew fewer and fewer, the Kennedy visit closer and closer, tension heightened. Soon he would arrive. What then? A saturation of newspaper articles and radio and television messages from leading citizens, public officials, civic organizations, and others emphasized the absolute necessity to offer an overwhelmingly graceful reception for President John F. Kennedy, Jacqueline, and the entire presidential party, including Vice President Johnson and Lady Bird and Texas governor John M. Connally and his wife, Nellie.

The city's now ultraconservative presence could not easily be erased. A mere four days before this big November 22 event, the demagogic segregationist governor of Alabama, George Wallace, showed up. Wherever he went, controversy followed. I was pleased to be assigned to cover his speech before an increasingly conservative group of well-heeled Dallas women known as the Public Affairs

Luncheon Club. I wanted to see this conservative and dynamic troublemaker at close hand.

Wallace was almost certain to be a conservative Democratic candidate opposing Kennedy in the 1964 Democratic primary. He soon would confirm that intention. As an avowed opponent of desegregation, this one-time Golden Gloves boxing champion, judge, and legislator had stood at the University of Alabama's school doors as the state's governor to stop two Black students from enrolling, living up to his inaugural speech in which his concluding words had been, "Segregation now, segregation tomorrow, segregation forever."

Wallace's Dallas speech was scheduled for a noon luncheon on Monday, November 17, at the Baker Hotel, cater-cornered from the Adolphus and considered to be the city's second most prominent hotel. That day, as requested by the club's female president, I arrived two hours early so the governor could hold a press conference. I was among some eight or ten newsmen representing print, television, and radio. A press aide passed out news releases with the familiar list of racist resolutions.

Promptly at 10:00 a.m. the slick-haired, dark-eyed governor, who before capitalizing on his success as a strict segregationist had been defined as a populist, walked briskly into the room. He was of short stature, which we all knew, and right away he displayed the confidence so often associated with his younger pugilistic days. His bearing suggested that he expected no trouble in handling challenging questions from a handful of newsmen who would ask questions about his well-publicized prejudices. Before opening with a statement as to why he was in Dallas, he moved down our orderly line of standing reporters, shaking hands with each of us one at a time, always offering a few pleasantries. This bit of cordiality and formality, whatever its motivation, was rarely exhibited by newsmakers at such press conferences.

When my turn came, he looked straight into my eyes with right hand proffered and said simply, "I'm George Wallace." He seemed to study me as if determined to remember my name.

"The *Times Herald*," he repeated knowingly after I identified myself. His amiable nods suggested that he was well familiar with my paper. As much as I disagreed with the governor's distasteful segregationist beliefs and actions, I couldn't help being impressed with his show of sincerity. Possibly, I thought, this was a secret for many demagogues. Giving him the benefit of the doubt, though, I acknowledged to myself that there might be more to the man than I had realized.

He paid the same close attention to each reporter. Finished finally with such introductions, he fielded the ensuing questions with a practiced air. The "Negroes," he contended, had a better life in Alabama than those living above the Mason-Dixon line. The East Coast press, he said, distorted the situation in the South by concentrating solely on the area's problems, without bothering to cover its own racial disturbances, of which, he said, there were many. As for the 1964 presidential election, without mentioning himself as a possible Democratic primary candidate, he thought Barry Goldwater would be a fine choice for the Republicans. He believed that Kennedy would fail to be elected to a second term.

The press conference ended after a nervous, aging, Mexican American reporter from a Spanish-language San Antonio newspaper asked a long question in halting English. Mexican Americans, the newsman said, were afraid that if he—Wallace—became president, he would discriminate against them just as he discriminated against Black people. Wallace answered carefully, insisting that he held no grudge against "Negroes" or Mexican Americans, that he was in fact their friend and had done much to help them.

Afterward, as the hotel's adjacent Crystal Ballroom began to fill up for the luncheon, the well-coifed women looked as affluent as their reputations held them to be. Among a handful of men scattered about, one could see H. L. Hunt and Edwin A. Walker at nearby but separate tables, both easily recognizable. I had anticipated that this crowd of some 450 well-educated and handsome women would behave with decorum in greeting Wallace. But I was wrong. As soon as he entered the room, those immaculately attired women jumped to their feet, vigorously cheering and applauding. I had expected a favorable welcome, but not a standing ovation. We newsmen, very appropriately, stayed seated at the long table designated for us.

As the luncheon began, television filmmakers with their hand-held cameras focused their attention on ex-General Walker, sitting quietly and chatting with female tablemates. When Wallace began his speech, lambasting Attorney General Robert Kennedy and the "sex perverts, narcotics addicts and common criminals" who had invaded Alabama disguised as "civil rights workers," most of the cameramen backed away.

The last, though, George Phenix, representing Dallas's KRLD-TV (part of the *Times Herald* broadcast family), edged between tightly packed tables and chairs for even more close-ups of Walker. Not a good idea, I thought, for plenty of close-ups already had been taken and the program had begun. But Phenix, a newcomer who had been on the job for only five weeks, was persistent.

Finally, the former major general, tired of Phenix's annoying attention, stood up angrily, and shouted, "I've had enough. Get out of here." Phenix responded, "One more picture." That was too much. Walker shoved Phenix backward onto the next table, pounding him on the back with both fists, knocking over a chair or two, spilling their occupants, as well as glasses of iced tea and plates of food, and finally landing Phenix awkwardly onto a woman's lap—all this very noisily.[1]

The shocked audience applauded. Walker, appearing as cool as a cucumber, as a former high-ranking military officer should, turned to the now-silent Wallace at the podium and apologized: "Excuse me, please." His fisticuffs completed, Walker sat down as waiters quietly but hurriedly rushed to repair the damages. Wallace resumed his talk.

This unexpected episode occurred minutes before our last edition deadline with the financial market's closings. I briefly considered pushing through the tables to get Walker's comments, but it would have been another awkward interruption. Besides, there was hardly time for more than a paragraph or two. I hurried to a hotel telephone to tell the city desk what had happened. Sufficient time remained to get seven paragraphs on the front page under the headline "Walker Shoves Lensman." My brief story began with this sentence: "Former Maj. Gen. Edwin A. Walker turned camera-shy in the midst of Alabama Gov. George Wallace's speech and shoved a television cameraman, interrupting the governor's talk before the Public Affairs Luncheon Club." Associated Press and United Press International picked up our brief paragraphs for their national wire services.

The luncheon was ending when I returned to the ballroom. The club's president approached me, but to my surprise, not in anger and not blaming Phenix. Instead, she said she was embarrassed and regretted that Walker was there. She had feared what his controversial presence might bring. He was not even a member of the club, she told me, and certain members had brought him as their guest. On the previous evening the same members wanted to bring him to a small dinner party, but she had declined that request. Yet she could not prevent them from bringing him today.

My friend Phenix was still around, and we left the hotel together to walk to the nearby *Times Herald* and KRLD-TV complex. I was eager to see how members still there would treat him as we departed. Unlike their president, these women blamed Phenix, not Walker, for the disturbance.

"I wish you newsmen would leave the general alone," one said, referring to me as well as Phenix.

"Poor General Walker can't get a minute's rest without somebody pestering him," said another.

One lady went on and on in mock sympathy. "Did it hurt much?" she asked Phenix. "Such a pity. We're just so-o-o-o sorry." Phenix took the criticisms good-naturedly with quiet smiles, but he told me he felt so much anger inside he could burst.

The Dallas Morning News had a well-displayed story about Wallace's speech the next day and a sidebar on the disruption.

I REMEMBER THIS WAS the same day our editors were making plans for covering the president's first public visit to Dallas since his campaign appearance in 1960. As anticipated, he and Jacqueline would be accompanied by a large and prestigious presidential party, including Vice President Johnson and Lady Bird, Governor Connally and Nellie, and lesser but well-known congressmen and political figures. They would arrive at Dallas's Love Field airport after a short flight from Fort Worth, where they would spend the night and have a public breakfast.

Coverage would present a particular challenge for us. The 11:30 a.m. arrival time would be our usual deadline for our important home edition. But for this newsworthy arrival, we would extend our deadline by an hour so we could at least provide material about their reception at the airport, their motorcade through the city streets, and the opening minutes of the Trade Mart luncheon for some 2,400 guests.

Kennedy's short Texas campaign had begun in San Antonio on November 21, continued that same day to Houston, and then moved to Fort Worth before reaching Dallas. The final climactic stop would be in Austin, the state's capital city. The goal was to raise money and ameliorate liberal-conservative friction among Texas Democrats, especially between conservative Connally and liberal Yarborough.

In those days the public relied almost exclusively on newspapers for news of their community, state, nation, and world. We were acutely aware of that (although those days were destined to end). This, I was certain, might be the most important story I had ever helped cover. And as far as I could see from our preparations, the same was true for others. Our plans involved every reporter, rewrite person, editor, and photographer, not to mention Linotype operators, printers, pressmen, and others.

Would there be jeers along the motorcade mixed in with cheers? Scads of anti-JFK pickets? Scuffles? Blockades?

Each stationed reporter would call by telephone to relay his or her information to an assigned rewrite person who would compose a separate story or an insertion for the overall story. As usual, we would type with triple-spaced lines (providing space for editing by pencil before Linotype operators set the story in type). Additionally, a specific editor was assigned to oversee each news items for editing, including writing headlines for stand-alone stories.

Political reporter Keith Shelton and our Washington correspondent, Bob Hollingsworth, would be on the arriving press airplane. Keith and Hollingsworth would then transfer to one of the two campaign press buses for the motorcade and onto the Trade Mart for the luncheon. There we would have six other reporters and two photographers, plus as many as two others outside.[2]

Reporters' earlier stories for the first edition would be updated as the day moved along. Only then could our printing back shop and others complete necessary and elaborate processes prior to loading the trucks with organized bundles for delivery to designated locations throughout the city. Finally, the irreplaceable paperboys would fold their papers, place rubber bands around each of them, hop on their bicycles with their heavy cloth bags stretched across the handlebars, and distribute them to some two hundred thousand *Times Herald* home subscribers. And, of course, there were newsstands throughout the city also waiting for newspapers.

So what was my assignment? Would I be able to see Jack and Jackie, Lyndon and Lady Bird, Connally and Nellie, and the other important individuals? All of them would pass through town in open convertibles.

No! I would not. I was designated rewriteman for our Jackie Kennedy sidebar story. I would sit at my newsroom desk, press my telephone to my ear in a holder to free both hands for typing as information came from reporter Val Imm at Love Field, begin writing from those notes, and finish the sidebar when our reporter at the Trade Mart, Constance (Connie) Watson, could tell me about the arrival there. I would blend her report with Val's information into a single Jackie story. One thing we knew: readers would be keenly interested in the beautiful and fashionable Jackie, who with the possible but unlikely exceptions of Eleanor Roosevelt or Mary Todd Lincoln was the most intriguing and highly publicized presidential wife in our history.

Maybe I shouldn't have been disappointed at my assignment. In describing the plan, news editor Charles Dameron said those of us chosen for rewrite would be "very experienced, fast writers, experienced people who could turn copy out by the ton." Did I fit that description? I wasn't so sure, especially concerning the time restrictions. But it was a fine compliment.

Live television coverage, aside from its technical aspects, seemed simpler. By now, television news had come a long way. Only two months earlier, with much hoopla, the major networks' late afternoon news programs had expanded their usual fifteen-minute evening newscasts to thirty minutes. Virtually every American home viewed network news at dinnertime with anchors such as Walter Cronkite on CBS-TV and Chet Huntley and David Brinkley on NBC-TV. Local television news was growing in popularity too, for besides regular evening newscasts, broadcast reporters in mobile units regularly scoured the city day and night covering crime, fires, sports, and other spot news for radio and television.

On Thursday morning, one day before arrival, the city's hopes for a warm welcome suffered a crushing blow. Leaflets with two fake mug shots of the president, similar or identical to the ones distributed anonymously before Adlai Stevenson's speech, had been scattered throughout town. They displayed the same huge headline, "WANTED FOR TREASON." Among the spurious claims was that Kennedy had turned over the nation's sovereignty to the United Nations. Another was the false statement that he had lied to the American people about not having had a previous marriage before Jacqueline. (It was learned later that Robert A. Surrey, an associate of General Walker's, arranged the printing for five thousand of these leaflets.)[3]

But that was just the beginning. On the morning of the arrival, an even more shocking protest appeared as a full-page advertisement in the *Dallas Morning News*. A funereal black border surrounded the entire page. In huge capital letters its mocking title was "**WELCOME MR. KENNEDY TO DALLAS.**"

WELCOME MR. KENNEDY

TO DALLAS...

...A CITY so disgraced by a recent Liberal smear attempt that its citizens have just elected two more Conservative Americans to public office.

...A CITY that is an economic "boom town," not because of Federal handouts, but through conservative economic and business practices.

...A CITY that will continue to grow and prosper despite efforts by you and your administration to penalize it for its non-conformity to "New Frontierism."

...A CITY that rejected your philosophy and policies in 1960 and will do so again in 1964—even more emphatically than before.

MR. KENNEDY, despite contentions on the part of your administration, the State Department, the Mayor of Dallas, the Dallas City Council, and members of your party, we free-thinking and America-thinking citizens of Dallas still have, through a Constitution largely ignored by you, the right to address our grievances, to question you, to disagree with you, and to criticize you.

In asserting this constitutional right, we wish to ask you publicly the following questions—indeed, questions of paramount importance and interest to all free peoples everywhere—which we trust you will answer...in public, without sophistry. These questions are:

WHY is Latin America turning either anti-American or Communistic, or both, despite increased U. S. foreign aid, State Department policy, and your own Ivy-Tower pronouncements?

WHY do you say we have built a "wall of freedom" around Cuba when there is no freedom in Cuba today? Because of your policy, thousands of Cubans have been imprisoned, are starving and being persecuted—with thousands already murdered and thousands more awaiting execution and, in addition, the entire population of almost 7,000,000 Cubans are living in slavery.

WHY have you approved the sale of wheat and corn to our enemies when you know the Communist soldiers "travel on their stomachs" just as ours do? Communist soldiers are daily wounding and/or killing American soldiers in South Viet Nam.

WHY did you host, salute and entertain Tito — Moscow's Trojan Horse — just a short time after our sworn enemy, Khrushchev, embraced the Yugoslav dictator as a great hero and leader of Communism?

WHY have you urged greater aid, comfort, recognition, and understanding for Yugoslavia, Poland, Hungary, and other Communist countries, while turning your back on the pleas of Hungarian, East German, Cuban and other anti-Communist freedom fighters?

WHY did Cambodia kick the U.S. out of its country after we poured nearly 400 Million Dollars of aid into its ultra-leftist government?

WHY has Gus Hall, head of the U.S. Communist Party praised almost every one of your policies and announced that the party will endorse and support your re-election in 1964?

WHY have you banned the showing at U.S. military bases of the film "Operation Abolition"—the movie by the House Committee on Un-American Activities exposing Communism in America?

WHY have you ordered or permitted your brother Bobby, the Attorney General, to go soft on Communists, fellow-travelers, and ultra-leftists in America, while permitting him to persecute loyal Americans who criticize you, your administration, and your leadership?

WHY are you in favor of the U.S. continuing to give economic aid to Argentina, in spite of that fact that Argentina has just seized almost 400 Million Dollars of American private property?

WHY has the Foreign Policy of the United States degenerated to the point that the C.I.A. is arranging coups and having staunch Anti-Communist Allies of the U.S. bloodily exterminated?

WHY have you scrapped the Monroe Doctrine in favor of the "Spirit of Moscow"?

MR. KENNEDY, as citizens of these United States of America, we DEMAND answers to these questions, and we want them NOW.

THE AMERICAN FACT-FINDING COMMITTEE

"An unaffiliated and non-partisan group of citizens who wish truth"

BERNARD WEISSMAN,
Chairman

P.O. Box 1792 — Dallas 21, Texas

Despite determined local efforts to make the president's visit a happy event with no signs of hostility, this angry full-page newspaper ad appeared on the morning of his arrival. The Sixth Floor Museum at Dealey Plaza.

There were no photographs, but twelve accusatory questions followed, such as:

"**WHY** have you ordered or permitted your brother Bobby, the Attorney General, to go soft on Communists, fellow-travelers, and ultra-leftists in America, while permitting him to persecute loyal Americans who criticize you, your administration, and your leadership?

"**WHY** has Gus Hall, head of the U.S. Communist Party praised almost every one of your policies and announced that the party will endorse and support your re-election in 1964?

"**WHY** have you scrapped the Monroe Doctrine in favor of the 'Spirit of Moscow'?"

Finally, it said: ". . . we **DEMAND** answers, and we want them **NOW**."

The ad was attributed to The American Fact-Finding Committee, described as "an unaffiliated and non-partisan group of citizens who wish truth." The ad was signed by an individual none of us knew—Bernard Weissman, chairman.

Copies of this shocking advertisement were being passed around in horror in the newsroom when I arrived that morning. Only five days earlier the *News*, despite its ardent political opposition to Kennedy, had published a front-page article headlined "Incident-Free Day Urged for JFK Visit" (Nov. 17, 1963). What impact would this advertisement have on his arrival? Granted that the *Dallas Morning News* had become ultraright in its editorials, why would this respected newspaper accept such an advertisement, especially at a time when the city's decency was under question throughout the nation?

Besides, who was this "Fact-Finding Committee"? Who was Bernard Weissman, the self-identified chairman of the committee? None of us, even the most senior reporters and veteran executives, had the slightest idea. The *News* easily had legitimate grounds to decline such an advertisement because of its obvious falsehoods. Would the famous *New York Times v. Sullivan* decision of 1954 on free speech protect falsehoods such as these? An important exception to this US Supreme Court ruling was whether the libel was published with actual malice—that is, knowingly false or with a reckless disregard of the truth. It appeared here that actual malice applied; it was a knowingly false publication and it almost certainly exhibited a reckless disregard of the truth.

Later it would be learned that the Fact-Finding Committee was nothing more than a group of three wealthy oilmen who solicited funds and used some of their own money to pay for the advertisement. Its leader was Joseph P. Grinnan, coordinator for the local John Birch Society. Others were H. L. Hunt's son, Nelson Bunker Hunt, and H. R. "Bum" Bright (later briefly owner of the Dallas Cowboys football team). Weissman, a right-wing extremist and newcomer to Dallas eager for recognition, agreed to place the advertisement under his name.[4]

ARRIVING IN FORT WORTH on Thursday, the presidential party spent the night at the Hotel Texas and enjoyed an early breakfast sponsored by the Fort Worth Chamber of Commerce before a sold-out crowd with hundreds in attendance. The enthusiastic crowd was seated and applauding as the president and special guests were announced and took their seats at their table.

But where was Jackie? The large crowd was impatient for her. She was still in the couple's hotel room, preparing herself to look her absolute best for the event and the following day in Dallas. The president, recognizing the crowd's eagerness, explained from the podium that this was understandable: "It takes her a bit longer, but then she looks a lot better than Lyndon and me." The crowd roared with appreciation, and just a few moments later, as if by magic, she entered the room to loud applause, looking even lovelier than anticipated, wearing the same raspberry—usually described as pink—outfit that within a handful of hours would be stained with her husband's blood.

Only a few may have known that her arrival had been plotted for dramatic effect. Julian Read, public relations advisor to Governor Connally, later revealed that Jackie's delayed arrival had been planned and executed on cue.[5] Julian and others, including Texas's senator Ralph Yarborough, staff members, Secret Service agents, and others from the nation's capital were with the president.

Air Force One was due to reach Dallas's Love Field Airport at about 11:30 a.m. after its unusually short hop from Fort Worth, thirty miles away. As our political writer, Keith Shelton, later described it, the fifteen-minute trip was like no other. Before the takeoff was complete, preparations for landing had already commenced.

Sixty-eight traveling reporters would arrive simultaneously at Love Field in a separate airplane, fifty-eight from Washington, DC, and ten others who joined the tour in Texas. These reporters would ride in two motorcades and to the luncheon. A few other vehicles, aside from the numerous local police motorcyclists, would ride in two convertible press photo cars, a local press photo car, and a car for the AP and UPI.

As arrival drew near, the handbill and full-page *News* advertisement brought even more fear. This day might be anything but cordial. I believe few if any of us—normal citizens, city officials, police officers, and journalists alike—thought otherwise. We did not know that the president already had seen the scurrilous advertisement in Fort Worth, where the *News* had circulation. As Air Force One approached Dallas, President Kennedy showed the advertisement to his wife, who was horrified. "We're heading into 'nut country' today," the president warned.[6] In other words, Fort Worth's enthusiastic cheers had been expected, but Dallas, just thirty miles away, was "nut country." The message was clear: be prepared for anything.

The city's law enforcement contingent certainly appeared ready. Chief Curry said that a third of the entire police force, 350 officers, were assigned to keep trouble away. Added to this were 40 state police officers and 15 deputy sheriffs. (Later, the figures were calculated to show that 447 Dallas police officers were assigned for various aspects of the visit. Of this number, 178 were on the motorcade route; 63 at the Trade Mart parking area; and 150 inside the Trade Mart. In all, it was the largest security detail ever assembled in the city.)[7]

Every one of us was on alert to look for troublemakers. If observed, they would be a key part of our stories. If treatment of Adlai Stevenson had been rough, would any of the extremists be bold enough to do something worse? Uninvited individuals certainly would not be inside the Trade Mart.

The weather was also uncertain. There had been early showers that morning, with the possibility of more. If rain continued, the portable bubbletop of the presidential limousine would keep the Kennedys and Connallys dry. But if used, the bubbletop would spoil spectator views of the president and his lady as they passed by street-side admirers. Kennedy himself preferred to ride without the bubbletop, being especially conscious of the positive image his bearing and looks conveyed to his supporters—not to mention those of Jacqueline on the fewer times she joined him in public appearances.

Our federal beat reporter, Jim Lehrer, was writing an advance story for the early edition. With showers possibly continuing, he wanted to know if the bubbletop would be taken off or left on. He made a quick call, possibly to Forrest V. Sorrels, the special Secret Service agent in Dallas whom he knew. Sorrels's source didn't know, but at Jim's request he agreed to call the official who presumably would know (possibly Winston G. Lawson, the advance Secret Service agent for the Dallas visit). The quick answer, with Lehrer overhearing, was that a decision hadn't yet been made. But then the decision-maker, evidently looking up at a clearing sky, said something like this: "What the heck. We'll take it off." So the Kennedys and Connallys rode through the streets of Dallas without the bubbletop.[8]

At Love Field the official greetings committee stood patiently as Air Force One, having landed, drew near enough for their passengers to descend. Committee members included J. Erik Jonsson, outgoing president of the Dallas Citizens Council, and his wife, Margaret; Robert B. Cullum, incoming president of the Dallas Citizens Council, and his wife, Dorothy; Mayor Cabell and his wife, Dearie; and a few other dignitaries. Notably mind relieving was the unexpected and unofficial presence of a huge throng of cheering, extraordinarily

Kennedy had alerted his wife, Jackie, that they were landing in "nut country," but a large and enthusiastic crowd at the airport erased fears of angry demonstrators. *Dallas Times Herald* Collection, the Sixth Floor Museum at Dealey Plaza.

exuberant Dallas residents—men, women, and children—separated from the welcoming committee and the anticipated presidential party by a temporary chest-high, chain-link fence, presumably erected to keep away hostile demonstrators.

MRS. KENNEDY STEPPED OUT via Air Force One's stairway just ahead of her husband. The starstruck crowd greeted her instantly with screams of delight and cries of "Jackie, Jackie." Normally reluctant to be politically involved, the president's wife was clearly overjoyed at this unexpected reception. Having heard her husband's warning a few minutes earlier about entering "nut country," she surely had expected something different, perhaps opposite to the jubilant scenes in Fort Worth. Governor Connally and Nellie, exiting Air Force One a few steps behind the Kennedys, seemed unnoticed.[9]

Val, my on-the-scene reporter, was excited herself at such jubilant sights and sounds. Above the background squeals she described for me handwritten signs: "Welcome Jack and Jackie to Dallas"; "We Welcome You With Vigah, J.F.K."; "Onward, JFK"; "All the Way with Jack"; and many, many others. A few anti-JFK and pro–Barry Goldwater signs could be seen, but they were so vastly outnumbered that they virtually disappeared among the others. A careful observer could spot a small picket that favored Republican senator Barry Goldwater in 1964: "AuH2O for President." The most visible sign of opposition was a huge Confederate flag, bigger and flying higher than Texas's Lone Star flag.

Above the background noise, Val told me of the huge bouquet of red roses that Mayor Cabell's wife, Dearie, had presented Jackie. Val did her best to describe, rather breathlessly above the noise, the first lady's beautiful double-breasted raspberry suit with dark navy trim, topped off with a matching pillbox hat. The president and his wife, so encouraged, ignored the protective chain-link fence and moved directly against it so they could exchange personal greetings with the excited, enamored supporters. Veteran White House correspondent Robert Pierpoint said it was one of the few times he ever saw Jackie engaged in "any kind of crowd-pleasing politics."[10] Also surprised by her obvious joy, Charles Roberts, White House correspondent for *Newsweek*, asked her if she now liked campaigning. "It's wonderful, it's wonderful," she exclaimed.[11]

Val had done her homework. She earlier had gathered quotes from awaiting spectators, asking why they were there. All were positive. These and her other notes of what she was seeing constituted my working material. I sat at my typewriter, doing my best to recapture the festive scene she had described, hoping that I was one of those "experienced people who could turn copy out by the ton." I was very aware that the story needed a good lede followed by a few opening descriptive paragraphs. Then I must finish with additional information from Connie, waiting at the Trade Mart for the president's arrival.

First, though, the motorcade would pass through the streets of Dallas, including downtown Main Street, in a ten-mile stretch led by

A temporary fence intended to protect the presidential couple from crowds
was disregarded as the Kennedys and their excited supporters happily came
together. Eamon Kennedy, photographer, *Dallas Times Herald* Collection,
the Sixth Floor Museum at Dealey Plaza.

Chief Curry driving his own car with passengers Sheriff Bill Decker
and Secret Service agents Forrest Sorrels, in charge of the Dallas
office, and Winston G. Lawson from the Washington, DC, office.
They were followed by three advance police motorcycles and then five
more accompanied the presidential limousine (an extended Lincoln
Continental) carrying the Kennedys and the Connallys, with Secret
Service agents William R. Greer and Roy Kellerman on front bench
seats. Behind the limousine was a black Cadillac convertible loaded
with eight Secret Service agents and presidential aides Dave Powers
and Ken O'Donnell.[12]

Other vehicles bearing Secret Service agents followed Lyndon and
Mrs. Johnson, Senator Yarborough, a White House pool car for its
reporters, convertibles for photographers, two press buses, and still
others. Except for Mayor Cabell and his wife, Dearie, who stayed with
the motorcade, those on the greeting committee hustled directly to

the Trade Mart so that once again they could greet the Kennedys and Connallys. One was Jonsson, who as president of the Dallas Citizens Council would preside at the luncheon.

Our reporters stationed along the motorcade route and at the Trade Mart were calling their rewriters, who, like me, listened on their telephone headsets as they typed copy "by the ton." There were no "hunt and peck" typists in this newsroom.

Somehow, though, I couldn't compose the attention-getting lede that I knew my story required. The minutes were passing away. Finally, I put my opening paragraphs in city editor Ken Smart's basket. Amid his hectic work, he perused it briefly, then looked at me from a dozen feet away with a perplexed look.

"This isn't your lede, is it?" he shouted above the ongoing hubbub.

"Well, yes, I intended it to be," I answered hesitantly. I could see what was coming. "You don't like it?" I asked, already knowing the answer.

Ken, quiet-spoken, competent, and always amiable, didn't. "I thought maybe it was your second take and you were going to put your lede on top of it. We need something that gives more of a total picture of what was going on out there," he said.

He tossed back my copy. I realized what he meant. It should be grander, more encompassing, illuminating the scene in greater depth. Still, my own emphasis was on Jackie, not the president. I forget just how my unacceptable opening sentence went, but I had written it in desperation. The rejection didn't surprise me. So, back to the typewriter.

Hunter Schmidt, working that day as the copyeditor assigned to my story, was listening and watching. Seeing my frustration, Hunter, a fine friend, laughingly suggested, "How about Jackie came, Jackie saw, and Jackie conquered." He was halfway serious, probably simply trying to loosen my imagination. But no, that was just a joke. I kept trying.

The motorcade route, which our paper had displayed exclusively on a map the previous day, was being strictly followed with no protestors interrupting the cheering crowds. Our stationed reporters were calling to their rewriters as the motorcade departed the airport down Lemmon Street, then went along Cedar Springs to Harwood Street, where a right turn at the police station brought it to Main Street. Thousands cheered and waved welcome signs from both sides of the street. The motorcade now headed to the green lawns of Dealey Plaza, which marked the end to downtown's commercial district and the beginning of a fast route to the Trade Mart.

Certainly among the onlookers were those who might be critical of the president, but there was no evidence of that. All along the route our reporters described the unusually favorable actions of adoring crowds who cheered loudly for this young president and his attractive wife. Our Washington correspondent, Hollingsworth, riding in one of the press buses, was surprised at seeing such unanimously positive reactions with no protestors in sight.[13]

Finally, after what I hoped had not been too many wasted minutes, I ripped off a proper lede, something like "Jackie Kennedy conquered the eyes and hearts of thousands of cheering Dallasites Friday, waving cheerfully as she stepped off Air Force One to be greeted with enthusiastic exclamations from hundreds of greeters." It was not the best, I supposed, but there was no time to polish it. At least Ken didn't complain. And I had already turned in descriptions of the crowd and of Jackie and her fine attire. They were being processed. Minute-by-minute telephone reports were coming from veteran police reporter George Carter, who was at the police station's press room listening to the police dispatcher. Smart was repeating these reports. We all were listening with one ear as we worked.

Suddenly Ken stood up with a horrified look that I'll never forget.

"They're sending an ambulance and homicide unit to the Triple Underpass, code three," he shouted.

At first I didn't connect this to the president, thinking that something else had happened in the large crowds, probably related to the passing of the motorcade and the excitement it was generating. Perhaps a heart attack. We knew, though, that "code three" meant a need for officers to speed urgently to the destination with sirens and flashing lights. Carter was hearing more information from the police dispatcher while he talked to Smart.

Looking paler than ever, Smart shouted to the rest of us. "He's been hit! The president has been hit."[14]

"Hit? What with?" I shouted, joining a cacophony of questions. My first thought was that the president might have been struck with a protestor's placard, the same as Adlai Stevenson. My question was lost in the tumult. A dozen or so of us who had been hearing Smart as we worked were on our feet, surrounding him, desperate to know what that meant. The sound of clattering typewriters had stopped. Whatever stories we had been typing for the minutes before deadline had to be forgotten. Was this a terrible mistake with an easy explanation?

Smart was pumping Carter for more, and it came quickly. "He's been shot; they're taking him to Parkland," Smart said, clearly distressed.

The president's condition? They don't know, Smart said, still repeating what he heard from Carter. But early word was that it was bad.

Dameron, sitting behind Smart, had heard enough. He picked up his telephone to the adjacent composing room where typesetters and make-up men were waiting. Dameron's apparent calmness surprised me. He quietly told a printer to pull out "that huge blockbuster type" used only for a rare advertisement. Give me two headlines, he said: "PRESIDENT SHOT" and "PRESIDENT DEAD." Both would fit across the top of page one.

This, we all knew, was the biggest story we would ever cover.

Chapter 6

"Can You Get Me Some Macanudo Cigars?"

S MART SHOUTED AT ME, "Forget Jackie, get to the Triple Underpass fast as you can."

I jumped up, my unfinished story in my typewriter. I grabbed pen and notebook as Smart looked around. One reporter wasn't enough. He spotted Paul Rosenfield, now our Sunday magazine assistant editor. "Paul," he yelled, "go with Darwin."

Paul and I rushed to the elevator but realized we simply should hustle down the stairs to the street four floors below and run. Driving would take too long. The Triple Underpass was only five or six short blocks away at the downhill edge of a landscaped area known as Dealey Plaza.[1]

I knew the location well. It was the city's birthplace. A wandering frontiersman from Tennessee named John Neely Bryan had camped there in 1841 with the unlikely notion of founding a town named for his anonymous friend Dallas. Now, downtown's three principal streets, Main, Commerce, and Elm, converged through the landscaped and park-like Dealey Plaza to pass beneath overhead railroad tracks, thus the name Triple Underpass.

We ran, trotted, and occasionally walked so we could catch our breath. Huffing and puffing, we hardly talked except to express our astonishment in a few words.[2] Surely ultrarightists had been the shooters, there was little question about that. Dallas's newly aroused extremists had taken their hatred of President Kennedy to an unbelievable level. Was the president wounded? Dead? Could the report that Kennedy had been shot or even killed be true? How about Jackie? Governor Connally? Others in the motorcade? Would the assailant or assailants already be caught? Was a shootout with police impending? We had no idea, but we feared the worst. Would one of Dameron's huge headlines actually be needed?

We saw only a few individuals walking rapidly on the other side of Elm Street in our same direction. Grim faced, they seemed concerned.

A few blocks away we arrived at Dealey Plaza, the more specific site, where we confronted an agitated, tormented crowd of spectators milling about in front of the adjacent Texas School Book Depository building. The Triple Underpass itself, some one hundred yards downhill, was forgotten. Individuals in anguished tears, wrought with pain, paced about aimlessly, some comparing stories with one another of the still incomprehensible sights they had witnessed. They knew that shots had been fired, that the president had been at least seriously wounded, as well as another individual, possibly a Secret Service agent, but few had been near enough to know for sure. Friends and strangers alike were comparing stories as best they could to make sense of it. No one was in charge to help them.

Paul and I knew what we must do: locate police officers or witnesses who could tell us as precisely as possible what had happened. We separated and went to work.

Increasing numbers of police officers, some with rifles and shotguns, were looking upward to the top windows of the depository's seven-story building. I had never seen a police officer armed with a shotgun. Someone high inside the building surely had fired rifle shots. Hook-and-ladder fire trucks were parked beside it, poised, I assumed, to lift officers to high places where the sniper or snipers might yet be hiding.

The motorcade ended horrendously at Dealey Plaza as rifle shots rang out.
The city editor, urging utmost speed, sent me and another reporter there.
We saw armed officers and tearful spectators, confused as to what they had
seen. William Allen, photographer, *Dallas Times Herald* Collection,
the Sixth Floor Museum at Dealey Plaza.

I hurried to the building's entrance where a stone-faced police sergeant stood guard. The officer, E. B. Howard, absolutely refused to let me inside, assuring me that no one had been allowed to enter or leave the building since he had stood at the entrance four or five minutes after the shots had been fired. "I let no one out," he said. Only officers and detectives were inside, he said.

Most witnesses who weren't immediately adjacent to the street didn't feel confident in describing what they thought they had seen. Whatever had happened before their very own eyes seemed too unreal to comprehend.

Some thought the first loud noise they had heard was backfire from a motorcycle or truck, perhaps a firecracker, but the following shots eliminated that possibility. Those closest had seen the president's head explode in an awful burst of blood, brain, and flesh. Then they had seen Jackie crawling perilously toward the back of the open-topped limousine as if trying to escape.

Captain Will Fritz, chief of Dallas's police homicide bureau, and Dallas County sheriff Bill Decker, along with detectives Richard Sims and Elmer Boyd, all arrived shortly after Rosenfield and me. The officer guarding the depository front door told them that the shooter possibly was hiding in the building. Fritz, Decker, and the others began a floor-by-floor search, seeing nothing but police officers already posted on each floor.[3]

I envisioned a handful of armed extremists, perhaps two or three of them, likely involved also in the Stevenson affair, blockaded high in the building. For a killer or group of killers to have escaped from the top floor of a building, alive with employees and surrounded by spectators and officers, seemed impossible. A shootout between police and the assassins, once they were located, seemed certain. I wanted to be as near that as possible. Yet nothing was found.

Two innocent bystanders were pointed out to officers as possible suspects. Police took each to the sheriff's office across Houston Street for questioning. Many, presuming their guilt, vehemently cursed them as officers walked each one to the sheriff's office. Their innocence was quickly established, and they were released with sincere apologies.

Unknown to me, my uncle, Gene Payne, was an onlooker standing near the sheriff's office when police took in one of the innocent suspects. Gene recalled to me how shockingly white-faced the man was as he plaintively insisted that he had nothing to do with the shooting. With his innocence quickly confirmed, he departed.

No one seemed to acknowledge or realize that Governor Connally had been seriously wounded. In those early moments, the wounded Connally in his civilian clothing might have been mistaken for an agent. How badly off Connally was, no one knew.

AS WOULD BE LEARNED later, before passing out Connally had exclaimed in sudden pain, "My God, they're going to kill us all." In fact, one of the Secret Service agents assigned to sit in the presidential limousine, Roy H. Kellerman, testified to the Warren Commission that when a bullet hit the president in his upper shoulder, he heard him exclaim, "My God, I am hit." Having been with the president for three years, Kellerman said he was "very familiar" with the president's Boston accent and was certain of what he heard. No one else in the limousine heard such an exclamation, and it is highly improbable that Kellerman did either according to medical experts' opinions.[4]

Doctors later testified that this second shot, which entered Kennedy's lower neck, although very serious, would not have been fatal. But four or so seconds later, the third and final shot ripped off the back of the president's head. This was the fatal injury.

Dealey Plaza must have seemed a convenient meeting place that day for many spectators who came together. One group was there to wave to accompanying police motorcyclists with whom they were friends. Mary Ann Moorman, 31, and Jean Hollis Hill, 32, were among them. Hill was wearing a full-length red coat to make certain that motorcyclist Billy Joe Martin, with whom she was personally involved, would see her. Stavis (Pete) Ellis, commanding rider of the motorcyclists, was related to Bill and Gayle Newman and their two children, who were also waiting at Dealey Plaza to wave to him. Moorman, Hill, and the Newman family were among several who fell to the ground for safety when shots were fired.

I didn't know then but learned later that three newsmen, two of whom I knew quite well, went immediately inside the depository and accompanied officers and detectives as they searched every floor. The two friends were Pierce Allman, program director of WFAA radio, and Kent Biffle, my colleague at the *Fort Worth Press* who recently had joined the *Dallas Morning News*. The third one, Tom Alyea, was a cameraman and reporter for WFAA-TV, whom I later came to know.

When Biffle joined officers rushing inside the depository with pistols drawn, he removed his press badge so that he might be assumed to be a detective. Allman, who saw the impact of the shots on the president, dashed into the building and asked a young man who appeared to be leaving where the nearest telephone was. The man pointed toward a telephone. Later Allman realized from pictures that the departing man must have been Lee Harvey Oswald, leaving as discreetly as possible.

Robert MacNeil of NBC-TV heard the first shot from his seat on one of the press buses. "Was that a shot?" he asked. Some said yes, others no. When MacNeil very distinctly heard the second and third shots, he jumped from his seat and shouted, "They were shots! Stop the bus! Stop the bus!"

The driver stopped for a moment to open the door. MacNeil jumped out and saw people screaming in terror and others throwing themselves down on the grass. A few reporters got off with MacNeil. Others stayed on the two press buses, one going to Parkland Hospital and the other to the Trade Mart, carrying most of the reporters with them.

MacNeil, rushing into the depository, also saw a young man leaving. Desperate to call his office, MacNeil asked him to point to a telephone. Afterward, like Allman, he thought the man was Oswald. After calling his NBC-TV newsroom, MacNeil went back outside and paid a passing driver five dollars to take him to Parkland Hospital.

One wonders how Oswald, having fired three shots from the sixth floor amid a crowd of spectators and lawmen, escaped. He surely had thought it would be almost impossible to flee from the building with a frenzied crowd below and officers who most assuredly would have run into the building from which the shots had been fired. As it turned out, he was stopped, then let go. On his way out Oswald caught the attention of police motorcyclist Marrion L. Baker, who had immediately raced inside with his pistol drawn. Baker, accompanied by building superintendent Roy Truly, spotted Oswald moving away and was suspicious. "Come here," he summoned Oswald, as Officer Baker pointed his revolver directly toward him. "Do you know this man?" Baker asked Truly.

"Yes," Truly responded, "he works here."[5]

Baker, satisfied, turned away, and resumed his race toward the top of the building from where he believed the shots had been fired. Later, from photographs, Baker identified the suspect he had stopped as Oswald. To Baker and Truly, Oswald was simply an employee, beyond suspicion. He was free to escape because the officer and everyone in Dallas had expected that any trouble associated with the presidential visit would come from ultraright-wingers, not from an employee at the Texas School Book Depository.

HAVING BEEN TOO LATE myself to get inside the depository, I continued to question especially those whose demeanors suggested that they personally had witnessed something beyond belief. My best information came from a distressed group of three or four young women. Their tears suggested the horror of what they had seen so vividly from their proximity. More than others I had interviewed, they were especially specific. My newfound but excellent sources said they had gone outside to find the best location. When the motorcade appeared, Kennedy was smiling and waving to cheering onlookers. President Kennedy definitely had been hit in the head, they agreed. They saw much blood and were confident that he had suffered severe, probably fatal injuries. I had found no others who had been so conclusive. Now they were returning to work in the Dal-Tex Building across the street from the depository. Their employer, they said, was Abraham Zapruder, co-owner of the Jennifer Juniors dressmaking firm, who had been taking film of the passing president with his Bell & Howell camera when the shots were fired.[6]

One of the women, Marilyn Sitzman, Zapruder's receptionist, was bracing his legs as he stood on an elevated concrete structure (the Bryan Pergola, named for the city's founder) for the best view. Her fellow office workers were a few feet away. Their mention of the camera especially caught my attention. Obviously, a closeup film depicting the shooting would be of critical importance. I asked if they would take me to see Mr. Zapruder. They readily agreed. One of the young women, a payroll clerk at Zapruder's office, identified herself to me as Mrs. Charles Hester. I instantly recognized Charles Hester as the name of a former schoolmate of mine. Mrs. Hester's first name, I learned, was Beatrice. She and Charles, she said, had been standing on the grassy knoll near Zapruder when shots were fired.

As I walked with them toward the seven-floor Dal-Tex Building, Mrs. Hester gave me a brief description of what she and the others had seen. With my notes recorded in longhand, I omitted obvious words to save time.

"I was waving at Mrs. Kennedy," she said. "I heard three [shots]. One [other person] heard two shots. My boss [Zapruder] was on [the floor] [a reference to his departure from the Bryan Pergola]. Seemed like [it] hit him [Kennedy]. Could see blood. Jackie grabbed him."

Now, some thirty minutes afterward, they were weeping, agreeing that the president couldn't have survived such a shot accompanied by so much blood and matter. Still, they couldn't be certain as they grasped flimsy straws for the unlikely possibility that doctors might save him. Our conversations continued as we rode the elevator to their fourth-floor offices, adjacent to a large open area where other women were back at work on the popular Jennifer Juniors apparel.

Zapruder was not yet there, but the black-and-white television set in the large office was tuned to CBS-TV. We watched anchorman

Walter Cronkite acknowledge that the president had been wounded, but he carefully avoided definitive statements about his condition. I had never met Cronkite, but I felt closer to him as a fellow University of Texas graduate than I had any right to.[7]

I rang city desk to give notes from my interviews, describing what I had seen and continued to see from the company window overlooking Dealey Plaza as I waited for Zapruder. News from Parkland Hospital, where the president had been taken and where Governor Connally was also being treated, offered almost no hope for Kennedy. No hints mentioned possible suspects.

My *Times Herald* telephone companion, Bill Bates, agreed that Zapruder's film, if any good at all, could be an outstanding addition to our coverage. I could hear background chaos in the newsroom as we talked. The film, however startling, could not be processed in time for this day's paper. Moreover, we couldn't even know if any of it was usable. Because of the critical time factor, I continued to talk to Sitzman and Beatrice Hester so I could give additional comments to Bates. I could overhear a few reporters, evidently standing just behind Bates, listening to our conversation and watching as he typed the words.[8]

From my window vantage to Dealey Plaza, I could see more armed officers arriving. The building was barricaded; certainly no one besides officers now was coming in or out. Spectators continued to come too. I kept my eye on the office door, waiting for Zapruder.

MINUTES LATER A DISTRAUGHT, balding man in his late 50s wearing dark-rimmed glasses rushed into the room with his camera. Obviously Zapruder. I told Bates to hang on while I followed Zapruder into his adjacent office, introducing myself as he held tightly to his camera. (Later, Zapruder's granddaughter, Alexandra Zapruder, wrote that he was "in a state of shock" when he returned to the office, "kicking and banging" his desk. If he did, I didn't see it.[9]

"I got him," he said right away when I asked him what he had seen. "I can't talk," he then exclaimed. "I'm too upset." But he couldn't resist talking, and once again I took notes in longhand. "I saw it [hit] him in [the] head. They were going so fast. [The president] slumped over with [the] first shot—he bent over and grabbed [his throat]. Second [of] two shots hit him in [the] head. It opened up. [He] couldn't be alive. She [Mrs. Kennedy] was beside him. After [the] last shot she crawled over [the] back of the car . . . He's dead. I know the president couldn't live."

But as we watched on television, Cronkite continued to be cautious about the president's condition. Knowing that the media and our newspaper would hold the same caution, I felt certain that the president's chances were far less hopeful than what Cronkite was saying.

Yet the emotional Zapruder continued to talk about what he had seen. We moved to the outer office to keep up with CBS-TV's breaking news. Reports left open the possibility that the president could be alive but seriously wounded. Zapruder knew better. "Yes, I got it all," he told me. "It was awful, just terrible. I was standing right there looking through my camera. The president's head just exploded, like a firecracker. You see it. Blood went everywhere." I wrote down every word. I knew it was a much-needed descriptive quote.

Cronkite's tentative reports, Zapruder insisted, were entirely wrong. Zapruder, Russian-born but a Dallas resident since 1941 and a fervent Kennedy admirer, was convinced that he alone knew the truth, no matter how much Cronkite or anybody might have a smidgen of hope for recovery. As he talked, Zapruder continued occasionally to shake his head grievously, sometimes slapping his forehead with his hand as if to remove the horrible and unforgettable image.[10]

The sight of Jackie's dangerous crawl toward the rear of an open-topped moving car with a sniper shooting from above was as puzzling to Zapruder as it was to others. Marilyn Sitzman and Beatrice Hester told me that they believed the only explanation was an effort to escape the shooter's aim. (Only several days later came information that Jackie had been trying to grab a piece of her husband's shattered skull or brain, a fact she confirmed.) The seriously wounded Connally, still conscious with his wife, Nellie, beside him, had heard Jackie exclaim, "They've killed my husband. I have his brains in my hand."[11]

With Zapruder's precise description, I reminded him of his film. He was keenly aware of its probable significance. I stressed that the *Times Herald* would be extremely anxious to develop his film, and that we would do it under any conditions he wished to impose, including payment.

He would have none of it. Of course, I was mindful that the film might not portray what he seemed so certain about. But I didn't want to display doubt. Zapruder's consistent response was that he wanted "to turn it over to the Secret Service and no one else. It's too important."

I persisted, although trying hard not to irritate him. I said he could turn it over to the Secret Service after he watched us develop the film. We worked regularly with the FBI and Secret Service, I said, and we easily could arrange this. The procedure should take no more than a few hours.

The film, he continued to insist, should be turned over only to the Secret Service or FBI. As he emphasized this determination, I offered new possibilities. A *Times Herald* employee could drive here—to this very office—pick him up with his camera, take him to the newspaper, and from there call the Secret Service to come after the film. We could make that connection for him.

But he would not be swayed. "I've got to be sure," he said. "I've got to make sure the Secret Service gets it."

Zapruder's camera rested atop a filing cabinet not far from me. For a fleeting moment I had a vision of simply grabbing and running with it. But I knew I wouldn't do that.

Cronkite continued to report that the president had been seriously wounded. By now I had been with Zapruder for about thirty minutes, both of us hearing increasingly pessimistic reports. With Zapruder's absolute certainty as to what he saw through his viewfinder, I understood that the president surely was dead.

Bates and I continued to keep an open line. I reinforced to him Zapruder's determination to turn over his camera and film to the Secret Service or FBI, not to me nor accompanying me to the paper. I urged Bates to find a high-level negotiator who could speak with greater authority, preferably James F. Chambers Jr., our newspaper's president, although I had never even met him.

Bates relayed my request to city desk. I could hear him say excitedly that I was with a man who had filmed the shooting from a close vantage point. Others had been there with cameras too. We all knew that was certain; I had seen them among the spectators.

Around me the women had hardly dried their tears. They stood around their desks, not sure what to do. One sat down at a huge typewriter and began pecking away at the keys on what appeared to be a payroll sheet. I apologized for holding the telephone line so long. I had been on it for almost an hour.

Cronkite, continuing with updates from his CBS-TV news desk, acknowledged only that the president had been gravely wounded. Zapruder continued to criticize his announcements.

"No, I know he's dead," he continued to exclaim. "I was looking through the viewfinder. I saw his head explode like a firecracker. He has to be dead." His tears flowed the more he talked.

At 1:11 p.m. early reports from Parkland Hospital indicated finally that the president was dead. A physician had told Eddie Barker, a familiar face in Dallas because of his nightly news reports on KRLD-TV (CBS-TV's affiliate) that the president was dead. Barker gave his scoop to Cronkite, who then turned live to Barker at the hospital.

Another local newsman, Bert Shipp of WFAA-TV (ABC-TV's Dallas affiliate) saw Dallas County sheriff Bill Decker leaving Parkland. The sheriff told Shipp that no man could live with the severity of the president's head wound. Tom Wicker of the *New York Times*, Hugh Sidey of *Time*, and Sid Davis of Westinghouse Broadcasting all saw two priests leaving the hospital after giving last rites to the president. On that basis they indirectly confirmed his death.

I was with Zapruder and a few of his office workers, anxiously watching the television together, when at 1:38 p.m. Cronkite, removing his glasses and lowering his sad eyes, confirmed that all hope was gone. The president was dead. The news brought a new eruption of moans, sobs, and tears from Zapruder and the office workers.

(I did not know that one of the other Jennifer Juniors employees, Peggy Burney, a cousin of *Times Herald* women's editor Vivian Castleberry, had called her to say that she had witnessed history on this day. She, presumably with Castleberry's help and encouragement, wrote her own first-person story about what she had seen. Her story appeared in our last edition that day.)

Afterward, with Zapruder away on one of his occasional interludes to his private inner office, I sat ruminating at the fourth-floor window, watching the depository and Dealey Plaza. A dramatic thought of jumping to death to the concrete sidewalk four floors below flashed through my own mind. How melodramatic and foolish, I knew, and the thought instantly vanished, just as had my image of grabbing the camera and running with it. Remembering nothing about it other than as a dry history fact, I thought of President McKinley's assassination at the turn of the century. I wondered if my wife, parents, sisters, and friends already knew what had happened today and how they were reacting.

From the window I could still see throngs gathered against a roped-off area around the front of the depository. Inside that perimeter, policemen, plainclothes officers, firemen, sheriff's deputies, newsmen, and other officials still wandered about.

I still felt I couldn't leave Zapruder. There remained the matter of the camera and the film. Finally, Bates had corralled Jim Chambers to the telephone. Even if I had never met our *Times Herald* president, this was no time to be deferential.

Doing my best to describe what Zapruder had told me, I suggested what I thought might be good strategy. Above all, I said, Mr. Zapruder needed to be certain that we would take him and his film to the Secret Service or FBI. If the film was good at all, I told him, it should be sensational. I further suggested that Chambers could send a car here to pick up Zapruder with his camera and film, preferably a car bearing the words *"Dallas Times Herald."* Speed was imperative because I had no idea how long Zapruder would remain here.

Chambers asked if Zapruder wanted money. That did not appear to have entered his mind, I said, but I thought the film might be unbelievably valuable. An offer of a fair payment surely would be helpful. Suddenly I realized that in my first conversation with the *Times Herald*'s president I was being emphatic in telling him how to conduct this transaction. It seemed an unusual way to start an acquaintance with my newspaper's president. "Mr. Zapruder is in his office. Hang on and I'll get him for you," I told him. Laying the telephone aside, I dashed into Zapruder's office.

"James Chambers, the president of the *Times Herald*, is on the telephone," I said. "He's the man who runs the entire paper."

Zapruder picked up his telephone. I returned to my own telephone and listened as a third and silent party. I heard Chambers assuring Zapruder that the film would be well taken care of. "We'll pay you for it," he said without special emphasis.

I was disappointed. The *Times Herald* president sounded half-hearted, unwilling to make a commitment. I thought that we should be offering him a thousand dollars or as much as the newspaper could afford. Why didn't he assure Zapruder of a personal escort instead of letting him think he might be asked to walk or drive to the newspaper with his camera? Zapruder appeared to be waiting for anything to grasp, but nothing was offered. The conversation ended.

Later I was surprised to learn that at about 8:15 that very morning Chambers and Kennedy had talked on the telephone. The president had requested a personal favor. "Can you get me some Macanudo cigars?" he asked Chambers. "They don't have any over here in Fort Worth."

"Sure," said Chambers, presumably pleased that the president knew him well enough to make such a request.

"Well, get me about a half dozen," Kennedy told him. Chambers did. He bought six of these expensive, hand-rolled cigars at Dallas's United Cigar store, intending to give them to the president at the luncheon.[12]

Kennedy certainly would not have called E. M. (Ted) Dealey, publisher of the *Morning News*, for the same favor. Dealey famously had insulted the president in October 1961 at his White House luncheon for Texas newspaper moguls. Dealey chided him by saying the nation needed "a man on horseback" to deal with the Soviet Union instead of one "riding Caroline's tricycle."[13] Chambers was among those present at that famous White House luncheon. It may have been the first time he had met President Kennedy.

Bates and I continued talking. I told him of the crowd gathering around the depository. As far as I could tell no one had been arrested, although I had known of the innocent suspects being taken to the sheriff's office and adjacent jail. Possibly, I thought, not knowing how carefully the depository had been searched, the assassin was still hiding somewhere inside. At any rate, I would not give up my key vantage point from Jennifer Juniors. If anything broke out, such as an exchange of shots from an upper depository building floor to the ground below, I might see it all.

Tears continued to flow. I felt like crying myself. Zapruder was in his own office, his head on his desk. The office girls wandered aimlessly about, their eyes usually on the television as Cronkite elaborated on the dark news. Outside, crowds of people were straining against additional rope barriers while officers continued their watch. There was no doubt in my mind that the attacker or attackers had been part of Dallas's extremist right-wing crowd. Rather than a single assassin acting alone, I envisioned a group of maddened plotters who had lain in wait for the president to appear beneath their depository window.

WITH SUCH THOUGHTS a great light suddenly dawned. I realized—or speculated—that I very possibly possessed an important clue that might help identify the assassins. That list of vicious anti-Kennedy resolutions given to me and other reporters at George Wallace's speech had come in envelopes bearing the return address of a schoolbook depository, not the Public Affairs Luncheon

Club. The resolutions followed the same disturbing tone as the *News*'s full-page advertisement and the "Wanted for Treason" handbills distributed anonymously the day before.

How many schoolbook depositories could there be in Dallas? I knew of none. It was likely, I felt, that the envelope's return address was that of the Texas School Book Depository itself. While the luncheon club itself no doubt consisted primarily of more respectable ultraconservatives, whoever prepared those resolutions also may have provided the envelopes. The envelope and resolutions were on my desk in the newsroom. As I contemplated the matter, it dawned on me that someone in that group or someone with a connection to it could have plotted the assassination. As one local minister was to say a few days later, he had heard a member of his congregation say at a party that he likely would have taken a shot at the president himself.

I told Bates what I was thinking. He, too, saw the possibility of connections and agreed to get the envelope and resolutions from my desk to confirm the name of the book depository. If they matched, the Secret Service or FBI could be alerted. Bates gave my information to Executive Editor Felix McKnight, who relayed the information to the Secret Service.

Afterward, there was little for me to do but sit at the window with the telephone and continue to tell Bates what I could see outside the depository. How much more, if anything, could be produced for the paper at this late hour was doubtful. As far as I could tell, nothing new had developed. I was beginning to feel restless. Almost an hour had passed since I had been with Zapruder.

Police reporters often think they can recognize detectives or FBI agents by their clothing or manner. I had this feeling when the office door opened and three men in dark suits appeared, displaying an air of confidence. When the last man in the group entered, I felt that my suspicions were right, for although he wasn't a detective or FBI agent, he was someone I recognized as Harry McCormick, a veteran and renowned police reporter for the *Dallas Morning News*.

I had seen him on one of his rare stops at the police press room. I don't believe we had exchanged a word on such occasions, and I doubt that he recognized me. How McCormick had weaseled his way into this situation I didn't know. But I didn't doubt that he had. The leader of the three was Forrest V. Sorrels, the Secret Service agent in charge of the Dallas office.

Later I would learn that the third well-dressed man was none other than Zapruder's business partner, Erwin Schwartz, who had shown them the way to Zapruder's office.[14] Sorrels had helped plan the JFK motorcade route through Dallas. McCormick knew him well from his years as a Dallas reporter. When shots were fired at Dealey Plaza, Sorrels was riding in a lead car with Police Chief Curry. McCormick was already at the Trade Mart luncheon when he learned that shots had been fired, and he raced in his car to Dealey Plaza. He saw among the frenzied crowd the visibly distraught Zapruder with his camera. McCormick asked him if he had pictures. Zapruder said he did but refused McCormick's importunities to go with him to the *News* to develop the film. McCormick, however, wrote down Zapruder's office address.

Anxious to tell Sorrels, McCormick found him in the sheriff's office. He had a man "over here" who had pictures "of this whole thing." Sorrels, intrigued, said, "Let's go see him." It was shortly before 2:00 p.m. that Sorrels and McCormick came to Jennifer Juniors, where they first encountered Schwartz, Zapruder's business partner, who accompanied them to Zapruder's office, where I remained. I watched as Sorrels told Zapruder that they needed to talk to him privately in a small adjacent room. Concerned because McCormick worked for the opposition, I followed them into the room. "Who are you?" Sorrels asked me.

I introduced myself as a *Times Herald* reporter, only to be brusquely informed that they were there on confidential business and that I could not come in. I stood for a second, looking at McCormick, pondering my situation.

"You'll have to leave," Sorrels told me again, curtly.

McCormick was eyeing me too.

I had been with Zapruder and his camera for so long, doing my best to get his film for the *Times Herald*. To allow Sorrels and McCormick to take it away was an appalling thought. No doubt I would see at least a frame from Zapruder's film next morning in the *News*. I decided that if I had to leave, so did McCormick. "How about Mr. McCormick, then? If he's in here," I said to Sorrels, "then I have to be."

"He'll have to leave too," Sorrels said.

So McCormick, without protest, stepped out of the room and waited outside the door with me. We didn't exchange a word. I returned to the telephone, where Bates was still waiting, and explained the situation.

When the office door opened, Sorrels, accompanied by Zapruder, holding tightly to his camera and followed by Schwartz and McCormick, walked toward an elevator at the rear of the building. I raced after them to ask where they were going. But they would not respond.

I ran to the telephone and told Bates I would follow them. But first I had to catch them.

"Stay with them. Don't let that film out of your sight," Bates, also excited, shouted. So for the first time I hung up the telephone and raced through an adjacent area to see the four men disappear on a freight elevator.

A stairway wasn't near, and I waited helplessly for the elevator to return. By the time I reached the first floor, the four were nowhere in sight. I was disappointed. But it seemed senseless to try to find and follow them on these busy streets. After telling the city desk of my situation, we agreed it simply was best to cross the street and return to Dealey Plaza, still alive with police officers and a rapidly growing group of spectators. It was now a few minutes after 2:00 p.m.

I learned later what happened. McCormick led the group to the *News* to have the film developed there. Lucky for me and the *Times Herald*, I suppose, it couldn't be done there because of special needs for 8 mm film. While waiting at the *News* with the film, Zapruder was interviewed briefly at the next-door WFAA-TV studio by program director Jay Watson, who was on the air and unable to concentrate on his interview with Zapruder. The quick interview, now available on the internet, lasted just six minutes. When finally it was learned that Eastman Kodak's Dallas lab could process the film, it was taken there. Later, Zapruder accepted *Life* magazine's offer of $50,000 for print rights, then a few days later $150,000 for all rights.

A further word about McCormick as a police reporter. He resembled and took on the air of one of the hard-boiled, aggressive, old-time newsmen portrayed in movies of the 1930s and 1940s. The story was often told how he had obtained an exclusive interview with notorious outlaw Raymond Hamilton, an associate of Clyde Barrow and Bonnie Parker. Thinking that neither his editors nor anybody else would believe he had such an interview, the crafty McCormick persuaded Hamilton to press his handprints on his auto windshield as proof. The incident, occurring in 1935, is related by Cronkite, at the time a *Houston Press* reporter.[15]

During these hours the *Times Herald* presses stopped as many as eight times to insert new information. As shown in a photograph by Andy Hanson, an eager group of businessmen wearing coats and ties surrounded a newsstand cashier at Love Field with coins extended to buy our papers bearing that huge headline, "PRESIDENT DEAD" (see p. 129). Our reporter Keith Shelton noted seeing people lined up outside the *Times Herald* to buy papers as they rolled off the presses. Never before had he, or any of us, seen such a sight.[16]

Chapter 7

At the Assassin's Lair

M Y THOUGHTS DURING THESE hours often turned to Lincoln's assassination, in which John Wilkes Booth recruited a handful of like-minded individuals to help him. The possibility of a solo rifleman with no Dallas accomplices at all never entered my mind.

Leaving Zapruder's office, I returned to the School Book Depository. A far bigger group of journalists, including additional *Times Herald* reporters and photographers, now were there. Police officers still swarmed the grounds. Could the assassin or assassins even now be hiding in the building? Officers continued to scour the interior. I waited outside with other reporters for whatever new information they might bring us. Through the glass front doors, I could see a crowd. Since no one was allowed to leave, I assumed that all were undergoing interrogation, or perhaps the roll was being called to see if all employees were still there.

John Schoellkopf, Joe Sherman, Paul Rosenfield, photographer William G. (Willie) Allen, and I were there from our paper. John, just arrived, had important news. A police officer had been shot and killed

After a long interview across the street with eyewitness Abraham Zapruder,
I returned to Dealey Plaza. Detectives emerged from the School Book
Depository with evidence found on the sixth floor. I'm there, asking questions
and taking notes. William Allen, photographer, *Dallas Times Herald* Collection,
the Sixth Floor Museum at Dealey Plaza.

in Oak Cliff. At least one of us, he thought, should go there because of its possible connection with the assassination. I didn't volunteer because I didn't envision a connection. My immediate thought was how strange that a police officer could be killed more than a mile away in Oak Cliff within two hours of the assassination. There were no more details at the time.

The action for me was at the depository. I preferred to stay because I still had not given up the possibility that the assassin or assassins might yet be hiding inside the building. I continued to expect a shootout in a police encounter. Neither Sherman nor Rosenfield volunteered

Schoellkopf, however, had a different thought that turned out to be correct. He did envision a relationship. He caught a ride with a police officer headed for Oak Cliff, where a suspect roughly matching the description of a missing employee at the Texas School Book Depository had been seen shooting the officer at a residential corner. The shooter was seen by nearby residents, who called the police and described him. He also had attracted the attention of others as he darted in and out of store entrances on Jefferson Boulevard, where he had fled. Finally he had been seen entering the nearly empty Texas Theatre. Schoellkopf got there in time to see the handcuffed suspect, his face bruised after a brief struggle with the arresting officers, placed in a police car taking him to the downtown station. Hugh Aynesworth, a *Dallas Morning News* reporter who had not had a specific assignment for the day, had been moving even faster. He alone of the reporters managed to witness the suspect's arrest inside the theater.

As this news became clearer, I gave up my idea of witnessing a shootout. By now, about 2:15 p.m., the largest contingent of reporters had left the depository and Parkland Hospital. With the arrest of the young suspect, Lee Harvey Oswald, most of them found their way to the police station where he would be interrogated. Other arriving reporters from distant cities were going there too.

Most of the reporters remaining at Dealey Plaza—about a half dozen, including me—were there when Inspector J. H. Sawyer, a Dallas detective, emerged from the depository with news. He had details of the assassin's hiding place on the sixth floor. The shooter, he said, had fired the shots from the depository's corner window facing Elm Street just below a decorative ledge. Officers had found on the floor three empty shell hulls and a rifle.

What kind of rifle? "It might have been a Japanese rifle," Sawyer said. "It wasn't as large as a 30.06 and looked like a .25 or .30."

As for additional suspects at the depository, Sawyer didn't know. "We have taken lots of witnesses down for interrogation. Most of them saw something," he said.

How many? "Maybe thirty," he responded.

A few minutes later two other Dallas detectives, L. D. Montgomery and Lt. Marvin Johnson, emerged from the building. Our *Times Herald* photographer Willie Allen took photographs as they displayed what was believed to be important evidence tying the assassin to the crime. The most important, shown by Montgomery, was a long brown paper sack in which the assassin was said to have concealed his rifle. Johnson held a shorter sack holding pieces of fried chicken and a Dr Pepper bottle, mistakenly believed to have been the killer's lunch. I stood next to both detectives, taking notes as they displayed their finds before sending them to the crime laboratory for analysis.

As it turned out, I unknowingly happened to be in three of Allen's photographs. They later would be shown in numerous publications, some identifying me. In one of them I was standing with my notebook interviewing Montgomery with his long paper sack. In another I was interviewing his partner, Detective Johnson.

IN THE NEXT FEW MINUTES, at approximately 2:45 p.m., something unexpected happened. Detectives invited a small group of us—reporters and photographers—to accompany them into the building to see where the evidence had been found on the sixth floor. Among us were fellow *Times Herald* journalists Joe Sherman and photographer Willie Allen, reporter Kent Biffle and photographer Jack Beers of the *Dallas Morning News*, Dan Owens of WBAP-TV in Fort Worth, and *Fort Worth Star-Telegram* photographer George Smith. Why so few? That was about all of us who were still at the depository.

Detective L. D. Montgomery holds the long paper sack in which the
supposed assassin earlier had hidden his rifle. That's me at the right.
William Allen, photographer, *Dallas Times Herald* Collection,
the Sixth Floor Museum at Dealey Plaza.

Aside from Biffle and three others—Allman, Alyea, and MacNeil, now elsewhere—we were the first admitted into the building. Deputy Police Chief George L. Lumpkin had instructed that our group be shown the shooter's site, probably as a sign of police cooperation with the press.[1] Detective Charles Dellinger led us upward on the open-door freight elevator, moving so slow that we could see each floor on the way up. On the second floor we saw an officer armed with a rifle, then another officer with a rifle on the fifth floor. We stopped at the sixth floor, where five other officers were posted. The large room, otherwise unoccupied, seemed to be just waiting for us. It was eerily quiet, and so were we.

It was odd that the assassin who had fired shots from this relatively remote corner would be able to escape unnoticed from the sixth to the first floor. Why hadn't some of the other workers seen him racing downstairs? Wouldn't they have suspected something right away? There were no other employees on the floor at the time of the shooting, we were told. As it was a storage area, the only reasons for an employee to go there would be to retrieve books ordered by customers.

From the elevator we crossed the sixth floor through stacks of unopened boxes containing textbooks. At the southeast corner window, Dellinger showed us the assassin's hiding place. Hidden by a neat row of four or five stacked boxes, he would not have been visible to a worker who entered the floor unless, by chance, he or she needed to go to that very corner to respond to a book order. Two or three boxes were placed closer to the window.[2]

Detective Dellinger told us that three rifle hulls had been found in no pattern beneath this corner window. Dellinger, a pleasant, easygoing man whom I knew slightly from the police beat, told these few things to us with no signs of emotion.

Someone pointed out the approximate locations on Elm Street where the president and Connally had been hit. Not too difficult a shot, we agreed. Dellinger said that the rifle, which he believed to be Japanese made, was equipped with a telescopic sight. (Later it was

I'm standing behind fellow *Times Herald* reporter Joe Sherman as we wait our turn
to see the assassin's hiding place on the dark warehouse floor on the depository's
sixth floor. The photographer is either Ira (Jack) Beers of the *Dallas Morning News*
or Willie Allen of the *Dallas Times Herald*, Darwin Payne Collection.

found to be an Italian-made Mannlicher-Carcano rifle, purchased
under the pseudonym of A. Hidell, in March 1963 from a Chicago
sporting goods company at a cost of $19.95 plus $1.50 for shipping
and handling.)

Our accompanying photographers took pictures as one at a time
we looked from the window to Dealey Plaza below. From this point
we could easily see the Houston and Elm intersection where the
motorcade had turned to Elm Street. We had a clear view of the street
curving gently toward what Jackie Kennedy had said she thought
would be a cool place out of the sunshine. That "cool place" was the
shaded Triple Underpass. (A photograph, later displayed regularly at
the Sixth Floor Museum without our identifications, showed Sherman
and me waiting our turns to look out the sixth-floor window.)

Photographer Allen and two other photographers in our group recorded the
same view the assassin had seen from the window. William Allen, photographer,
Dallas Times Herald Collection, the Sixth Floor Museum at Dealey Plaza.

As my former *Press* colleague Kent Biffle and I together looked
through the window to the street below, we estimated that the distance
of the fatal shots must have been about 150 feet. By propping the rifle
with a telescopic sight on the window ledge, Kent and I—each army
veterans with plenty of rifle-range experience—declared to one another
that the gunman didn't have to be an expert to hit his target at this
distance. (Authoritative studies later indicated that the first shot from
an uncertain distance missed, the second hit the president's shoulder
and neck area from 190 feet away, and the third and fatal shot struck the
back of his head at a distance of 265 feet.[3])

From the window we also could see Stemmons Freeway stretch-
ing in the distance to our right. Visible was the Trade Mart, a new,
expansive building where the president was to have spoken. On the
other side of the freeway and opposite the floodplain of the Trinity
River was the area of Oak Cliff. The photographers in our group, of
course, also spent time at the window to capture the assassin's view

and the arrangement of boxes that concealed the shooter's presence from employees who might have entered the room. We all breathed in the scene deeply. Finally, Dellinger led us back toward the elevator. We were awed, but less than I would have thought to be so close in space and time to the president's assassin.

On our way to the elevator, a distance of about seventy-five feet, Dellinger showed us where the assassin, on leaving, had shoved his rifle underneath a flat of boxes containing books entitled *Builders of Educational Programs*, published by Scott, Foresman and Co., Chicago. (I wanted every detail!)

BACK ON THE FIRST FLOOR Sherman and I saw reporters interviewing a man who evidently had news, so we joined them. The man was Roy S. Truly, superintendent of the depository. He was puzzled and deeply concerned at what had happened. Here, I thought, was a supervisor in a tough spot. He no doubt felt a sense of responsibility. When Truly earlier had taken an inventory of employees, he said that only one employee was missing—a fairly new worker named Lee Harvey Oswald. Oswald instantly had become a primary suspect.

Truly said there were eighteen to twenty workers in his shipping department, and they sometimes went to the sixth floor to fill book orders. The depository, he explained, stored textbooks for publishers and distributed them as orders arrived. Overall, from forty to fifty employees were involved in that operation. Some publishers also maintained their own offices in the building.

I asked Mr. Truly if any police officers had checked his building before the motorcade.

"They never did that I know of," he answered.

"Would you definitely have known about it if they had?" I pressed.

"I would think so," he said, giving an inflection that seemed to mean that someone most certainly *should* have. Looking back on it, I was quite naïve to think that the Secret Service somehow could examine all tall buildings in a large city along the path of a presidential motorcade.

"What did you do, Mr. Truly, when you heard the shots?" another reporter asked.

He said he had been just outside the building to see the president pass by when he heard three shots. "I didn't know the shots came from here, but then I saw the police running toward my building after ten to fifteen seconds and so I went back in. I rushed back to go upstairs, saw a policeman running up, and I went with him. About ten or fifteen seconds after the shots were fired I was with police in the building and we went straight to the seventh floor and roof. By the time we came down, policemen were already on the other floors."

Still, nothing had been found except the rifle and hulls. Truly was puzzled about this. He did not believe any of his employees had been working on the sixth floor that morning or noon hour. Fifteen to twenty minutes after the assassination, Truly conducted his roll call and found that Oswald was the only one not there. "I've got a boy missing over here," he already had told detectives.

"His job [Oswald's] was filling orders," Truly elaborated. Oswald had worked at the depository for about two months, and he was "very quiet, with very nice manners and a nice appearance." Truly didn't know much more about him, but he did know that he was married with at least two children. He had never talked to him about his political views, nor had he seen any need to.

Until these moments my own theory had been that someone had slipped into the building, making his way to the rarely visited sixth floor. That it could have been an employee really didn't seem likely to me. But, of course, there was that envelope given to me containing the anti-Kennedy resolutions, perhaps linked to this building. I had already forgotten about that.

This incredible, developing story of the assassination of a president obviously had moved elsewhere. No assassin had been found in the building. It appeared that the officers and detectives were clearing out the employees now and allowing them to leave the building.

Joe and I called the city desk and gave more of our notes for rewriting. I was asked to return to the newspaper, and I did. It was obvious now: there were no assassins hiding in the School Book Depository.

At the same time the president's death was announced, another major event occurred that totally changed our presumptions about the assassin. I knew nothing of it until I left Zapruder's office.

OSWALD, THE MISSING EMPLOYEE, upon leaving the building had walked unmolested for a few blocks uptown and caught a public bus that would pass his rooming house in Oak Cliff. Although she believed he did not see her, Mrs. Mary Bledsoe, a passenger on the bus who had seen the president earlier on the motorcade but was yet unaware of his assassination, recognized Oswald as the young man to whom she had rented a single room for a week in September. She had refused to give him additional days because of her unfavorable impression of him. Mrs. Bledsoe later testified to the Warren Commission that she looked away from him on the bus and did not want him to see her. He boarded the bus looking like a "maniac," she said, with a face "so distorted."[4] Already the downtown traffic was congested, and since he presumably was in a hurry, he quickly got off and hailed a cab to take him to his rooming house, asking to be let off a few doors beyond his room at 1026 North Beckley Avenue.

Rushing back to his eight-dollar-a-week room, Oswald ignored the housekeeper's casual greeting, went into his small room, picked up a light jacket and pistol, and departed, walking toward busy Jefferson Boulevard a few blocks away. On the way Dallas police officer J. D. Tippit, having heard only a brief dispatcher's report of this possible suspect, stopped Oswald several blocks away at Tenth and Patton streets for questioning. After a few words Oswald shot and killed Tippit at about 1:15 p.m.

Nearby residents who saw it happen used the officer's phone to report that the killer fled. As police sirens sounded, shoppers and retail store employees along store-lined Jefferson Boulevard saw Oswald's furtive actions and further alerted police. Oswald ducked inside the

Shocking news arrived that a Dallas police officer had been shot to death in Oak Cliff. Could there have been a connection with the assassination? We didn't know. Darryl Heikes, photographer, *Dallas Times Herald* Collection, the Sixth Floor Museum at Dealey Plaza.

Texas movie theater where, after a brief struggle, officers arrested him at about 1:35 and took him to the police station. This occurred at approximately the same time that Cronkite announced President Kennedy's death. Oswald, taken to the police station, now claimed the major attention of journalists who crowded into this site to cover the remaining story.

Even now—as I write these words—speculation continues as to where Oswald was going. There seems to be no easy answer. After having left $170 that morning for Marina and the children, he had only $13.87 left. He had no waiting comrades to help him flee to parts unknown. There were no major transportation outlets in Oak Cliff.

With fellow employees inside and below him in the building and hundreds of onlookers outside, not to mention the nearness of so many federal agents and police officers, how did Oswald expect to escape? In his own mind, he must have expected to be arrested at the scene and tried in a criminal court with attendant worldwide publicity.

Suspect Lee Harvey Oswald was arrested inside a movie house in Oak Cliff after a scuffle with officers. The nearest officer, barely escaping Oswald's effort to shoot him, was M. N. McDonald, now showing a long scratch along his face from the struggle, interviewed here by Jim Ewell, police reporter for the *Dallas Morning News*. Tom C. Dillard Collection, *Dallas Morning News*, the Sixth Floor Museum at Dealey Plaza.

That early morning, as we later learned, he had left nearly all his cash and his wedding ring on a dresser next to his sleeping wife, Marina, who spurned his final plea to return to him as a husband and father and resume their lives together. He had kissed his two sleeping children good-bye.[5] The fact must be that after fleeing from the depository, he had no viable plan as to where he would go. For him

Sometime later McDonald, principal captor of Oswald, signed this picture for
me in which he holds Oswald's pistol. Darwin Payne Collection.

his deed was a suicidal mission. He knew that if caught or slain, as he
surely expected, he would be killed in a clash with officers or arrested,
found guilty, and executed after a trial, and go down in history as an
important figure.

Elsewhere that noonday, US district judge Sarah Tilghman Hughes
had been at the Trade Mart luncheon, little suspecting that Johnson
would later ask for her to give him the presidential oath of office on
Air Force One as it revved its engines to return to the nation's capital.
The judge had left the luncheon when she heard Erik Jonsson's

shocking announcement that the president had been shot. Someone in the crowd shouted, "Those damn fanatics, why do we have them in Dallas?"[6] Judge Hughes departed in grief in her own car.

Short, feisty, liberal, feminist, and smart as a whip, she was appointed by Kennedy in 1961 to be federal district judge for the Northern District despite the initial reluctance of his brother, Attorney General Robert Kennedy, and opposition from the American Bar Association because it considered her too old at age 67. A Baltimore native, Hughes, born in 1896, had been an avowed leader for women's rights ever since she started her career in law enforcement as one of the first female police officers in Washington, DC.[7]

Without much thought about it, Hughes had figured Johnson might choose to go to his LBJ Ranch in Central Texas for a swearing in, or perhaps leave immediately for Washington, DC, where it could be done there. At Love Field, Johnson, already inside Air Force One, was pondering the matter. He made calls to Kennedy's brother (and attorney general) and to other leading figures, and finally to Deputy Attorney General Nicholas Katzenbach, who advised that anyone, even a justice of the peace, could do the job.

There were other federal judges in Dallas, including T. Whitfield Davidson, a cantankerous segregationist Democrat, and Joe Estes, also a Democrat. But Johnson wanted Hughes. But where was she? Nobody knew. She wasn't answering her phone at home. "Find her," Johnson emphasized.[8]

Finally, Barefoot Sanders, US attorney in Dallas and Hughes's good friend, reached her by telephone at her home. He asked her how long it would take for her to get to Love Field. "Ten minutes," she said, "but what about the oath?"[9] She decided she could swear him in without it, although by the time she arrived the exact text had been found in the Constitution: "I do solemnly swear (or affirm) that I will faithfully execute the office of President of the United States, and will to the best of my ability, preserve, protect and defend the Constitution of the United States."[10]

White House photographer Cecil Stoughton snapped the famous picture over her shoulder showing Lyndon B. Johnson affirming the oath. As soon as they were done, the new president said, "Now let's get this plane back to Washington."[11]

Having embraced with a hug the president's widow, whom she had never met, Hughes got off the airplane along with Stoughton, Dallas Police Chief Curry, and Westinghouse reporter Sid Davis.

Chapter 8

At the Assassin's Room

WALKING BACK TO THE newspaper gave me time to think. I still didn't know how many in the limousine had been hit. I knew that our president was dead. I knew that our governor was seriously wounded, perhaps himself now on his deathbed. I knew by now that our fellow Texan, Lyndon B. Johnson, was president and uninjured, but I knew nothing about the swearing-in ceremony on Air Force One.

As I entered the newsroom, I encountered a tempest of frenetic activity, but the shouting I had been a part of at first news of the shooting had ended. The image of top news executives, editors, and reporters, their faces marked indelibly with deep frown lines, was a different, never-to-be-forgotten sight. Now there was concern about putting together all the pieces of news.

At city desk, senior executive editors who usually were inside their own offices, away from deadline turmoil, surrounded Smart. Executive editor McKnight sat at a city desk typewriter, pounding keys. Executive sports editor Blackie Sherrod, famous for his witty way with words, sat next to him with his sleeves turned up, probably

Editors at the *Times Herald* were working hard as the day constantly
changed. At center is City Editor Kenneth Smart. Looking over his shoulder
is Managing Editor Hal Lewis. Andy Hanson Collection,
the Sixth Floor Museum at Dealey Plaza.

suggesting a word or two here or there as well as providing moral
support. Managing editor Hal Lewis and news editor Dameron were
busily involved, and copyeditor Bill Sloan, my good friend, was there,
as was another veteran copydesk man, Charlie Stone. Other copydesk
veterans also were working.

Chambers, too, was vitally interested, but probably repressing
urges to be more intimately involved since it had been so many years
since he had been reporter. Last-minute news continued to come from

our reporters and wire service reports from various locations—the Trade Mart, Parkland Hospital, the police station, Dealey Plaza, and others. Associated Press and United Press International copy spilled out constantly from their machines. Photographers were rushing from the darkroom to show their damp prints.

Waiting on our desks was our first version, bearing the huge front-page headline "PRESIDENT DEAD." The two dark, foreboding, and unimaginable words appeared in a typeface so large that it was never used for a news story except perhaps something such as "WAR IS OVER." Immediately below, a sub-headline added, "Connally Also Hit by Sniper."

The top story, bearing George Carter's byline, had been put together in bits and pieces, often without the transitional phrases that McKnight and Sherrod were adding. Carter's story opened with a single sentence: "President John F. Kennedy died of assassin's bullets in Dallas Friday afternoon," followed by this sentence: "The President and Gov. John Connally were ambushed as they drove in the president's open convertible in a downtown motorcade."[1] This initial story, hastily put together under great pressure, filled virtually the entire page with a heartrending six-column photograph showing the president and Jacqueline greeting the ecstatic crowd at Love Field only a couple of hours earlier.

Carter continued to listen to the police dispatcher from his press room post, but as more material flowed in, his byline alone was not appropriate. Too many others had contributed since then, including me.

Keith Shelton recalled that these working pages were replated every time major information came in. Outside the building customers lined up to buy papers as they came off the presses—a nickel for each one. "Lots of people were watching television," he acknowledged, "but they were still looking to the newspaper as the first source."[2]

Unavoidably, our first story revealed the complications of minute-to-minute reporting of such events. The fifth sentence in our main story stated without details: "A man was arrested and taken to the sheriff's office." This individual, it quickly was determined, was merely a bystander. Further down in the first column, this sentence appeared: "Police issued a pickup order for an unknown white male, about 30, slender, 5-10, 165 pounds, armed with a .30 caliber rifle." Without his name, this described Oswald as the only depository employee missing. And this same story reported that "six or seven persons were believed hit by [a] sniper's volley."[3] This gross exaggeration left open the question of whether a single Secret Service agent had been killed.

The front-page photograph of the jubilant crowd greeting Kennedy and Mrs. Kennedy at Love Field was taken by Eamon Kennedy but erroneously credited to Willie Allen, who was elsewhere. It covered six of the eight columns and continued with the same erroneous credit line for every edition.[4]

The only other story on page one was written earlier by Jim Lehrer, detailing advance security arrangements, but now amended with new information. Its headline was now in past tense: "Secret Service Checks in Vain." As details continued to take up space on the front page, Lehrer's article was moved inside to page 17.

More information arrived from various sources—eyewitnesses, Secret Service agents, Sheriff Decker, White House Assistant Press Secretary Malcolm Kilduff, and the wire services. The huge, whirring presses briefly paused so additional news could be inserted on the front page and three designated pages (17, 18, and 19) rather than spread willy-nilly throughout. Other sections in the paper, such as sports, entertainment, women's news, and business, were untouched.

A copy of each new edition was placed on every newsroom desk. A second headline, "CONNALLY SHOT," in the same huge type as "president dead," now appeared immediately below it. A smaller headline (called a kicker), saying "JFK Ambushed in Dallas," was centered now above the top line. New information included the discovery of the rifle and the three expended shells on the depository's sixth floor facing Elm Street, this information perhaps coming come from a police spokesperson or from Joe Sherman or me. The rifle was described

Eager customers at a Love Field newsstand scrambled for papers with the
latest information. Our first headline, "PRESIDENT DEAD," soon had
an equally large line just under it: "CONNALLY SHOT." Andy Hanson
Collection, the Sixth Floor Museum at Dealey Plaza.

incorrectly as a "high-powered World War II surplus weapon with a
telescopic sight." Simply stated was "unconfirmed" speculation that a
Secret Service agent also had been killed but the Secret Service could
neither confirm nor deny. The lede story, double-columned in bold-
face type, continued on page 19, where eyewitnesses' comments about
the president's arrival at Parkland Hospital appeared.

On this same page, a two-column headline, "JFK, Patrolman Killing Linked," with accompanying story quoted "high-ranking officers"

as saying the killing "might" be connected to the president's death. It identified the slain police officer as J. D. Tippitt (misspelled instead of the correct "Tippit") and reported that an unnamed male suspect was captured and arrested in the Texas movie theater on Jefferson Boulevard after the "youth" put up a fight and pulled a pistol on the officers who subdued him. He was rushed to the police station. One detective said the "general description" of the suspect "matched that of the man who eyewitnesses said shot the president." Without naming him, it described the suspect as "about 25 years old with his blond hair cut short."

As more details about his arrest unfolded, the presses were halted and the "JFK Ambushed in Dallas" line above the major headline became "Suspect Arrested." The suspect, identified as Lee Harvey Oswald, was described as a thirty-day employee of the depository and a "suspect" in the fatal shooting of Tippit. A vice president of the depository was quoted as saying Oswald had been at work that day and that the sixth floor was "easily accessible" to him.

A small story at the bottom of page 17 should have been a principal ingredient of the main story. "Oswald Had Asked Soviet Citizenship" was the astonishing headline. The item, credited to the *Fort Worth Star-Telegram*, described how Oswald, a former Fort Worth youth and ex–US Marine then living in the Soviet Union, turned in his US passport in October 1959 to the American embassy in Moscow and applied for Soviet citizenship. Separately, but at the top of the page, appeared a large photograph of Oswald between a uniformed police officer and a detective as they escorted him into the police station.

CONSIDERING THE EXTREME time limitations, our final edition contained a remarkable amount of vital information, a testament I think to our staff's journalistic prowess. The three inside pages contained a flood of stories under separate headlines and photographs. The photographs now included a five-column close-up of Oswald with a bruise around his eye, giving evidence that he indeed had resisted arresting officers. The excellent photograph's caption went only so far as to say that "Lee Oswald, center, is being questioned in President Kennedy's slaying." These inside pages also contained a photograph of three officers with uplifted rifles at the School Book Depository, an agent inspecting a grassy spot where an errant bullet was thought to have landed, a broad view of the depository showing a crowd of officers outside its entrance, and a four-column formal photo of President Kennedy at his White House desk.

Headlines on these inside pages summarized details gained over some two quick hours of hard and desperate journalistic work: "Secret Service Checks in Vain," "Slaying of President Brings Dallas to Halt," "It Might Have Been Backfire," "Oswald Had Asked Soviet Citizenship," "Candid Snapshot: Picture of Death" (a reference to eyewitness Mary Ann Moorman's Polaroid photo), "Wave of Unbelief Sweeps over Trade Mart Crowd," "JFK, Patrolman Killing Linked," "Dallas Policeman Recounts Instant Assassin Struck" (with byline by Dallas Police Officer B. W. Hargis), "The Crowd Waited; 'They've Been Shot'" (an account by *Times Herald* editorial page editor A. C. Greene about the reaction at the Trade Mart), "Lensman Heard Shots, Saw Gun" by Bob Jackson, and "I Saw Him Die," with a byline by Peggy Burney, the Jennifer Juniors employee and cousin to women's editor Vivian Castleberry.

These detailed news accounts further convinced me of Oswald's guilt. There was ample evidence in his rejection of American citizenship and his lengthy stay in the Soviet Union to show his dedication to Marxism and Communism. This represented an astounding turnaround in my conviction that the extreme right wing in Dallas had been guilty. And others, journalists and normal citizens alike, I quickly learned, felt the same surprise.

I still considered that Oswald might have been one of several conspirators. It seemed impossible to imagine that the man who had slain the president could have rushed so quickly from his sixth-floor perch to the ground floor without being seen by fellow employees as he fled the building. There were, admittedly, unanswered questions and inconsistencies in our news stories. One woman was quoted as seeing a man who appeared to be a Secret Service agent fire a shot at a man. "I thought I saw someone in the motorcade in street dress shoot back at a person running up the hill," the woman said. Her belief about seeing a man running up the hill would lead to countless conspiracy beliefs (continuing to this day).

Our first edition story told of the arrest of a suspect outside the depository when workers inside the building attracted an outside police officer's attention by tapping on a window and pointing to a man in horn-rimmed glasses, plaid coat, and raincoat. "The officer immediately arrested the man for questioning and placed him in a roomful of witnesses in Sheriff Bill Decker's office across the street from the depository," the story stated.

"With the young man protesting, the crowd all along the way jeered at him as he was escorted across the street. One woman said to the man: 'I do hope you die.'

"Another screamed hysterically, 'Is that him? Is that him?'

"An unidentified photographer shot a picture of the arrested man and then said bitterly, 'I hope you burn.'

"Officers on the case would not explain what connection the man might have with the shooting nor would they identify him."

The crowd's behavior toward this man, whom they had no way of knowing was completely innocent, was understandable. Similar emotions had been running through my head—a deep feeling of hatred for an individual who could take the life of our president.[5]

With Officer Tippit's death, the city seemed to be falling apart. What else could occur? No one could say, but no one expected more than perhaps an Oswald confession and a trial held in Dallas County. But surely the worst of the city and national nightmare was over.

ALL AFTERNOON I HAD BEEN worrying about my wife. That is, I should say, *while* working! I wondered—improbably and naïvely—if she had heard of the earth-shaking events. Surely she had. But as a fourth-grade teacher, she (and other teachers) were insulated from the day's news. Of course, though, she had to know about it. But when had she found out? And how was she taking it? The Western Union wall clock showed that it now was about 5:00 p.m. This meant that she should be home from school. I dialed home—our second-floor apartment just across the Houston Street viaduct in Oak Cliff.

Pat had heard the news almost as soon as it happened from a fellow fourth-grade teacher, Eleanor Cowan, a devoted Democrat and ardent Kennedy supporter. Eleanor had gone into the school's visual aid room during her lunch period to watch the president's speech. Beginning with the president's arrival, she had listened quietly in her classroom on her transistor radio to the motorcade's progress. Shocked, she hurried to the teachers' lounge at lunch hour to tell Pat and the other teachers. As Pat told me, many teachers broke down and cried at the news, including those who previously had held no special fondness for the president. Their principal advised teachers to tell students of the president's death in the best way they could.

One small boy in Pat's class announced to a few of his classmates sitting nearby that he was glad. No doubt he had heard his parents lambasting the president in a hateful way. Pat did not reprimand the boy. It was his parents to blame, not the boy, she said.

The day certainly was not over. McKnight wanted to see me. Uncertain what this editor might want, I hurried across the room to his office. An FBI agent, sitting there with him, asked me for more information about the Public Affairs Luncheon Club, the envelope holding the anti-Kennedy resolutions, and the incident that had occurred during Wallace's speech. I had almost forgotten that I had told Bates about my suspicions and suggested that someone look into a possible connection. The agent listened with interest.

But he told me that the book depository whose envelope I had been given had been checked out. It was from a different and unrelated depository. There seemed to be no connecting evidence. They would look further into the matter to be certain, he said, and he appreciated my help. As I left the office McKnight also thanked me. It had been, he said, a very good lead and one that might have been fruitful.

I was slightly disappointed that my information had not led to something more relevant. The afternoon's excitement had been such, however, that this news made little emotional impact on me. The alleged Marxist assassin certainly was not a right-wing fanatic.

BACK AT MY DESK Ken Smart approached, walking quickly with a serious expression that told me that I was about to be sent out of the office. I was right.

He handed me a slip of paper with an address written in pencil: 1026 North Beckley. "Oswald is our 'boy,'" he said. "Go to this address and find out everything you can about him." Getting the address had been a real coup, he implied, and he wanted me to get there immediately. Of course!

I knew Beckley Avenue. It was a major thoroughfare in Oak Cliff on the other side of the Trinity River but no more than a few miles away. I didn't remember if it would be North or South Beckley at that point. So, checking the city map that I always kept in my car, I started at North Beckley, intending to follow it if necessary until it became South Beckley. I couldn't miss it that way. I wanted to get there before it was jammed with too many newsmen and cameramen. Their numbers in the city were continuously expanding. Surely others would be there soon.

No matter what I found there, I felt confident of what lay ahead for me.

If any interviews awaited, as I felt certain they would, I would ask every question I could imagine, record every detail. Even the smallest tidbit might become an important part of the bigger story. (In years ahead and to this day I am occasionally asked if I recognized then how historic these moments were. Of course, I did! At every step I fully realized, as did every journalist, that we were in the process of seeing history made.)

With the address in my notebook beside me in the front seat of my 10-year-old Oldsmobile, I followed Commerce Street through Dealey Plaza and under the Triple Underpass where the presidential motorcade had been headed earlier on the adjacent Elm Street. The sun was dipping beneath the horizon. Now, though, a gigantic heap of lovely floral arrangements had appeared magically on the Dealey Plaza grass. I was heartened. Dallas citizens had responded immediately and as best they could to this most tragic day in the city's existence of more than a century and a half. Nothing would ever surpass it in tragical dimensions.

I drove across the long Commerce Street bridge, passing over the Trinity River and its wide floodplain between earthen levees (placed in the early 1930s to protect the city from floods). Upon crossing the bridge (or viaduct, it was called), I was at the northern tip of Beckley. I followed it southward through an area of small businesses.

At the point where North Beckley crossed another major street, Zangs Boulevard, a busy intersection with an electronic traffic signal, I found what I was looking for—the second house from the traffic signal on the eastern side of North Beckley. The red-trimmed one-story brick house that was 1026 North Beckley had a sign on the front lawn: "Bedroom for Rent." (Somehow, it failed to occur to me that this house, separated by Lake Cliff and its surrounding park, was only two long blocks from our own apartment on Blaylock Drive.)

I was by no means the first journalist there. I realized this when I saw several news wagons parked across the street at a service station closed for the day. Just how Smart obtained the address I didn't know—probably from one of our reporters at the police station. Plenty of others certainly had it too, but most of the newsmen, both local and visiting, were at the downtown police station. Images of its busy and narrow third-floor hallways, packed with journalists, were being televised live across the nation from that location.

As I walked to the front door, I could see through the windows a beehive of activity—interviews being conducted by broadcast journalists under bright lights and reporters taking notes from individuals. I saw no need to knock or ring a doorbell, so without ado I opened the front door and walked in. Despite the activity, the atmosphere seemed calm. No police officers or federal agents were there, just reporters and a few photojournalists were scattered about in a well-furnished living room and dining room that opened further toward the back of the house.

Its modest front was deceptive, for as I soon learned, the dwelling was a rooming house extending far to the rear.

Greeted inside by no one, I looked for my first likely interviewee. My initial target was a lone man in his 30s wearing khaki pants and a worker's shirt, obviously not a reporter or detective or federal agent. I identified myself and he readily gave me his name as Bob Palmer. However, he was reluctant to say anything other than he really had not known Oswald. Most of those who lived there, he said, kept mostly to themselves.

Having struck out with him, I edged into a handful of newsmen who were talking with another man and a voluble middle-aged woman who seemed to know something. She was the housekeeper, Mrs. Earlene Roberts. The man, owner of the house, was Arthur C. Johnson, probably in his 50s. He and his wife, Gladys, nowhere to be seen, had lived in the house for seventeen years.

Mrs. Roberts was clearly the more talkative. Had she seen Oswald this day? Yes, she had. He had stopped by briefly that very afternoon not long after the president had been shot. She had had no thought of any connection with the assassination.

With this, Mrs. Roberts became "hot copy" for the several television journalists. They encircled her with their bright lights and began asking more questions. I bided my time, figuring that I could catch her shortly afterward with my own questions. I needed more details than the photojournalists would get. Meanwhile, I returned to the owner, Mr. Johnson. I asked if he would show me Oswald's room. He nodded to nearby French doors opening to it. A couple of other reporters joined us. In fact, Oswald's small room was just adjacent to the living room where we stood. I estimated it to be about five by twelve feet. It had no outdoor entrance.

Officials with a search warrant had arrived at about 4:45 p.m., Mr. Johnson said, and had taken Oswald's few belongings. I regretted

Before his arrest, Oswald, now living alone, had stayed for weeks at this rooming house, 1026 North Beckley. That afternoon I interviewed many who lived there and learned much about his unusual demeanor. Nat Pinkston Collection, the Sixth Floor Museum at Dealey Plaza.

that they had done such a good job, for the room was very bare. I knew that Oswald's belongings were essential for their purposes. The men had included William F. (Bill) Alexander, hard-nosed assistant district attorney and chief prosecutor for District Attorney Wade.[6] Justice of the Peace David Johnston and Dallas police detectives F. M. Turner and H. M. Moore were with him. They had found and taken away an empty pistol holster, a few items of clothing, shoes, a shaving kit, a city map of Dallas with pencil marks identifying the School Book Depository, an address book, paperbacks of two James Bond novels and another entitled *A Study of the USSR and Communism*, a pair of binoculars, several pamphlets and handbills, a certificate of undesirable discharge from the US Marine Corps, and a few letters and documents indicating a tie to Communism.

I scribbled down notes describing inconsequential things about the room and its pitiful contents. The walls were light blue, perhaps baby blue. An uncovered mattress, rumpled sheets, blanket, and bedspread were scattered on top of the twin bed. A tiny air conditioning unit was in the window. An old-fashioned dresser with an attached mirror rested on one narrow wall. Just inside the entrance stood a wastebasket holding a tiny and empty container for chewing gum and a can of shaving dream. A space heater and vanity dresser with lamp and flimsy white window curtains completed the room's furnishings.

In this very room, so similar I supposed to hundreds of others in inexpensive rooming houses throughout the country, the murder of the nation's president had been envisioned—a crime that would impact the entire world. I had no doubt about that. I tried hard to visualize the thoughts that could have passed through an assassin's mind in such a prosaic setting. But I couldn't. I still knew so little about him. Becoming clear, however, was the fact that he had been a most unusual person. As my interviews would progress, the picture of an aloof roomer who mostly stayed to himself became evident.

As to Oswald's connection with the assassination, Mr. Johnson said he knew nothing except what he had heard this afternoon on the news media. Oswald had rented this room under a different name, O. H. Lee, having taken it in October about six weeks earlier. (One of his previous residences was just a few blocks away, where he had lived with his Russian-born wife, Marina, and their two children in a duplex.) He was the quiet type, Mr. Johnson stressed. None of the other tenants had been able to communicate freely with him and, in fact, nobody even tried after it became apparent that he wasn't interested.

How about his hours? Did he stay out late at night? Have many visitors? Odd visitors? Non-English-speaking visitors?

No, no, not at all, answered Mr. Johnson. As a matter of fact, Oswald's hours had been very regular—just like any other working man's hours. He came home early in afternoons and stayed to himself, occasionally watching television in the living room with a few other tenants but making little conversation.

I was trying to pull from Mr. Johnson the very detail that might be temporarily lost in a forgotten corner of his mind, something that

I might pull from him if only I could think of the right question. Then he responded with new information that intrigued me and other reporters who overheard it. Oswald frequently used the telephone in the hall, and they could hear him talk as they watched the nearby television screen. He wasn't speaking in English. They had no idea what language it was, but it was either German or possibly Russian, Mr. Johnson believed. Certainly, though, he was a native English speaker. My guess was Russian. At least someone would have recognized a few German words, but his book on Communism suggested the Soviet Union.

Who could he have been talking to? Nobody knew. Was it possible to guess what he was talking about? No.

Most of the other reporters drifted away. They had other angles to cover—Oswald in the police station jail, stories to be written or put on the air as soon as possible. Television and radio journalists needed their film or audio tapes to be processed in a hurry. But I had plenty of time. So I stuck with Mr. Johnson.

"I didn't pay much attention to him," said Mr. Johnson.

"Did you ever talk to him at all, about anything?" I persisted.

"He'd shoot the bull some. We'd hurrah back and forth sometimes," Mr. Johnson said, doing his best to respond. "Actually, though, he'd hardly speak to you," he conceded.

Just what they shot "the bull" about those few times wasn't clear. It was no more than a few words that had no real meaning at all, Mr. Johnson insisted. Finally, it became clear that Mr. Johnson was trying to help me, but there just wasn't much else he could say.

I switched to another line. What were the circumstances when Oswald rented the room? How much did he pay for his room?

The rent was eight dollars a week. "He just walked up one day, asked how much it was, and said he would take it."

How about references?

"Well, we're in the habit of getting relatives' names, but Mrs. Roberts said he told her it didn't make any difference. He wouldn't give her any."

Did he have a gun?

"I never saw a weapon myself but they found the holster to a .38 pistol here in his room," he said. "They," he explained, were the officers who had been by earlier in the afternoon gathering up Oswald's belongings. I asked him if he had ever seen Oswald mad or anything indicating a short temper. He pondered the question. At first he said no, then paused, apparently weighing something in his mind. He decided to tell it, no matter how trivial.

"The closest I ever saw him come to getting mad was four or five nights ago when we all were watching television—him too. One fellow got up and switched the channel to another station without asking others. He [Oswald] didn't say a word but I looked at him and it looked like it made him mad as fire."

While I was thankful for the incident as a means of measuring Oswald's temper, it was not something I could get much mileage out of. But I recorded it in my notebook, just as I was writing down everything else.

Perhaps, I suggested, a key to Oswald's personality or interests could be found by the television programs he watched. But Mr. Johnson couldn't remember the program that had been on before he did the slow burn. One thing he did remember, though. Oswald went to bed before the local ten o'clock news broadcast. But so did so many of the others. They had early wake-up calls for work. "As a matter of fact, he'd go to bed at nine or ten o'clock," Mr. Johnson said.

As he talked of Oswald, Mr. Johnson never once mentioned him by name. It was always "he" or "him." Only today had he learned that his tenant's real name was Lee Harvey Oswald.

My interview was slowing down. The only hard news I had was that he had been a loner and caused no trouble. He had regular habits, paid eight dollars a week for his tiny room, had been living there only a short time, and made unexplained telephone conversations in a foreign language, possibly Russian or German. I had no idea whether Oswald was married, but the calls certainly indicated a close connection with someone. The possibility that he was communicating with a collaborator arose, but speaking openly with such a person where he could be heard, even in a foreign language, made it unlikely.

Those telephone calls were strange indeed, though. An explanation was needed—very much so. But Mr. Johnson didn't have it. I did learn that a significant addition above the garage some years before had added enough extra space so the house could accommodate seventeen short-term roomers in addition to being the couple's own domicile. The rooms basically were for single white men, mostly construction workers, who could eat simple breakfasts or evening meals at the house. The neighborhood itself was rather mixed with middle-class houses; small businesses, such as a washateria a block down the street, a snack bar two blocks away, and the service station across the street; apartment houses; and another rooming house or two not far away.

Only a few reporters remained. I turned to the now-available Mrs. Roberts, free after most reporters had departed. I had her virtually to myself. She was a pleasant, easygoing woman, 58 years old. Short and a bit dumpy, she wore clothes appropriate for her job, keeping house. Her eyes twinkled behind her glasses. I think she was somewhat pleased to be interviewed, having overcome her initial shock about what had happened and now finding herself to be an object of interest. My first question was when she last saw Oswald.

She repeated with some elaboration that earlier comment I had heard. "He came in today at about 12:30 or one and I said to him, 'My, you sure are in a hurry.' He never answered. He just went right on to his room and left wearing a short gray coat. The last time I saw him he was standing outside, waiting on a bus, I guess."

His failure to respond hadn't bothered her. "It wasn't unusual," she said.

Oswald always ate at night in his room. "He kept milk in the kitchen refrigerator. Usually, he'd have cheese and cold cuts and cereals. Some bananas were left in his room today." He was clean but by no means well-dressed. "Usually, he wore khakis," Mrs. Roberts said.

Already I was considering my story and what kind of information I needed to include as the small touches that add much to a personality piece, whether about a distinguished citizen, banker, hoodlum, or presidential assassin. Oswald was beginning to seem quite normal.

Then she said something about him that would stick in my head for days. It was what I considered at the time a perfect quote to describe an accused assassin.

"I just took it for granted that he didn't care for people," she said. She had accepted him on his own terms. She had continued to be friendly with him but had not expected much if anything in return. "I said to myself he was a kind of peculiar man," she added, still doing her best to amplify his enigmatic personality.

Had she seen any guns or rifles or other weapons in his room at any time?

"No, I never saw any. I have the room next to him," she said, toward the kitchen. "If he'd had a gun, I'd have hit the front door running."[7]

A rather distinguished-looking woman, dressed as if she had a downtown office job, approached. Guessing that she must be Mr. Johnson's wife (Gladys Johnson), I left Mrs. Roberts for a moment to listen to the questions being posed by another newsman. I gathered that she was commenting with little pleasure. It appeared that Mrs. Johnson was about ready to order the dwindling bunch of reporters out of her house. But under probing, she was telling what she knew about Oswald.

"He was a quiet kind of person," she said, agreeing with other observations. "I never saw anybody conduct himself quite like him. No, I never would have suspected that he would do a thing like that," she said, answering the common question as to whether she could imagine him as an assassin.

As frequently as the question was asked, and as important as it could be, there was hardly anything else an individual could say in response. It is hard to conceive of anyone being a killer, much less a person killing a president with little or no motive. And as I had observed in my newspaper career of just a few years, even admitted murderers usually resemble nothing more than ordinary people one sees on the street.

I asked her what she knew about the telephone conversations in a foreign language.

"I'm sure it was Russian," she said. "He never spoke English on the phone." And while she had no idea with whom he talked, Mrs. Johnson somehow noted that he dialed or received calls with a BLaylock telephone prefix. I recognized BLaylock as the prefix for suburban Irving.

Those conversations sparked curiosity. If it indeed was in Russian, it was hard to conceive of a Dallas right-wing extremist speaking conversational Russian with friends who detested Communism.

Could it be that ultrarightist stories about ominous Communist intentions in the United States could have some credence? A president had been assassinated. What would happen next? Some fifty years earlier in Europe, a world war had started from the slaying of the Archduke Franz Ferdinand of Austria, leader of a small nation. Still fresh on my mind, too, was the movie *The Manchurian Candidate*, in which Russian Communists brainwashed an American military officer to assassinate a newly named candidate for the presidency.

Returning to Mrs. Roberts, it appeared that she knew more about Oswald than anyone in the house. According to the house records, she told me, Oswald had moved there on Monday, October 14, just six weeks earlier. "He had one little satchel and a few clothes on a coat hanger," she said. He had shown up on foot. He had no car, an oddity for most men of his age.

Mrs. Roberts bristled a bit at one of my obligatory questions, intending to uphold the virtue of her tenant as well as the house when I asked if women visitors ever came to see him. No, never, she declared.

My questions had become quite random—aimed in any direction that entered my mind. The officers who had come earlier in the afternoon to take Oswald's belongings had found a holster for a pistol, I said. What else had they found?

"They took all of his clothes. And they picked up a map of some kind. It looked like a map of Dallas."

What else?

"He had a few western magazines and he had one book in a foreign language. It was about an inch thick."

Later, I wondered about the western magazines. Had Mrs. Roberts been mistaken? Western magazines seemed incongruous with a man who spoke Russian and apparently had been politically inclined to assassinate a president.

Everyone in the house except Oswald was the "friendly kind," said Mrs. Roberts. "He just didn't talk," she stressed.

Mrs. Johnson, standing nearby and listening to us, interjected a matching thought.

"If he met you he would speak to you only if you spoke twice," she said. "He was nice and polite when he did speak, I will say that."

More reporters had entered the house now. Its location was becoming known even to the out-of-town press who didn't have the advantage of the local press's contacts.

I looked across the room to see who was there and recognized one reporter. He was Jim W. Jones of the *Fort Worth Star-Telegram*, a tall blonde-haired man whom I had known in Fort Worth. We nodded, smiling, and continued with our separate interviews. Jim was interviewing Mrs. Johnson; I stuck with Mrs. Roberts.

I then returned once more to the tiny room Oswald had lived in for the past six weeks, searching for more clues to his identity and for bits of color. But there was nothing more there; only so much could be found to describe a common, plain, small room that held no hints of its occupant's identity.

I had thought of more questions for Mrs. Roberts, but the harder I searched, the simpler they got. Did he drink? I asked.

"He never drank," she responded quickly.

What time did he come in each day from work?

"Around 5:30. He never brought a friend here. He was always alone."

It was probable that Oswald had ridden the bus to work every day. But he could have walked here after the shooting, because the distance from the depository was only a couple of miles. But then Mrs. Roberts abruptly gave me an interesting bit of information. I felt a bit embarrassed that it had slipped by me for this long. Neither she nor the others had known him by his real name. She had learned it only today. "He was registered here as O. H. Lee," she said. He had obviously reversed Lee Harvey Oswald initials to O. H. Lee. "But the police name for him was Lee Oswald," she added.

He had obtained this room six weeks before the presidential visit. The motorcade route had been displayed the day before by the *Times Herald*. No location could have been better than the depository for an assassin's quick exit from downtown. A person escaping in the other direction would have encountered busy traffic on the downtown streets. But leaving the depository via the long viaduct to Oak Cliff would be a faster escape.

Mrs. Roberts was enjoying my questions. She was at that point where she began to volunteer extra information rather than sitting back and waiting for the next. I believe I had sufficiently impressed her that I was interested in any detail—no matter how trivial. As a result, she leaned over to me and whispered information that she apparently wanted me alone to hear. I had become her friend!

Smiling mischievously, she said, "There was one funny little thing about him that we made fun of. When he'd go to the bathroom he'd twist his rear in a funny way just as he was going in. So we called him 'the butt twister.' That's what we called him behind his back."

The name was related to the popular dance around the nation at the time—the twist.

Mrs. Roberts hardly paused after her "butt twister" description and said that Oswald was fidgety. "He'd watch television five or ten minutes and then get up and be gone." I asked her to tell me once again the circumstances about him asking if he could rent a room.

"I said yes and showed him the one at the back and that one," pointing to the room that he had accepted. "I told him that before I take you in, you don't drink here." He agreed not to drink. "Give me the name of a close friend or relative," she told him. "But he wouldn't do it, even when I insisted it was necessary. He just said to me, 'Oh, it doesn't matter anymore.'"

The image of a disillusioned man, embittered by some experience that had made him lose any desire to live, passed through my mind. What else could it have meant? I wondered if Mrs. Roberts had been mistaken about that remark. No, she hadn't.

She repeated once again her memory of Oswald rushing in shortly after noon and picking up a "short, gray zip coat." Afterward she saw him waiting outside at a bus stop. Probably, I imagined, he had forsaken the idea of taking a bus because of the need to escape before he was discovered missing from the depository. The police surely would be looking for him. (Later it would be learned that he had given up on his idea to catch a bus and had set out walking toward Jefferson Boulevard.)

It was time to go back to the *Times Herald*, but as I left I stopped at a table where Mrs. Johnson was engaged in another interview. I heard additional information about that "foreign language book" Mrs. Roberts had seen in his room. She said there was a second book there about Communism. Then in the living room I saw the reticent roomer named Bobby Palmer with whom I had first talked some two hours earlier. Perhaps he had warmed up by now and would talk more freely. He did, just barely. "A lot of us, four or five, would sit and watch television at night," he said. "He didn't join us often, but he did sometimes. I was never able to carry on a conversation with him, though. He was just standoffish."

Then I gave him the inevitable question. Could he imagine him assassinating the president?

"I can't believe anyone could do it," he answered carefully.

As obvious and painfully apparent as this question was, I felt that I had to ask it. While perhaps ninety-nine out of a hundred could not conceivably imagine Oswald murdering Kennedy, what if one person *could* imagine it? Why would that one person have thought so? The answer might provide an important link to his personality.

BY NOW, ABOUT 6:30 P.M., it had become dark. I returned to the newspaper to write what I had learned. That, I knew, was precious little, but such details should be of significant interest. There wasn't much traffic to interfere with my thoughts. Anyway, there would have been no time to stop at our nearby apartment. Time was precious. The Saturday edition awaited.

Normally, the newsroom was dark at night. This night all lights were on. I saw what must have been every member of the news side working feverishly at their typewriters and telephones. In society, sports, business, and all departments, reporters were striking their typewriters, talking together or on the telephone, or just scurrying about. In the middle of the next-door break room was a huge table covered with sandwiches. Two huge pots of coffee sat on another table.

The sight of these sandwiches and coffee boosted my spirits immediately, as it had always done on election nights when we stayed late. It was such a small thing, yet it meant a lot. I had not eaten all day— not a sandwich or snack of any kind. It would have been out of the question to take away time for eating.

Our harried reporters and editors looked as if they had been up all night. Collars and ties were loosened (we all wore suits these days), and whiskers were taking on two-day lengths. Women and men alike appeared exhausted from the ordeal of having the president assassinated in our city, working hard on stories about it, and hearing of Officer Tippit's death, Oswald's arrest, charges filed against him for murdering Tippit, and his arraignment a few hours later for the president's assassination. Work now, of course, also was preparing for Saturday's small newspaper that would have an early deadline so we could work on the huge Sunday morning edition.

We knew that Oswald was being questioned at the police station. His Russian wife, Marina, their two young children, and his mother from Fort Worth also were there.[8]

I feared that city editor Smart would ask me to turn my notes over to another, more experienced writer, Ben Stevens, who already was working on a story about Oswald based on wire reports describing his rejection of US citizenship and his defection to the Soviet Union. Higher-ranked executives, including McKnight and Sherrod, were sitting near Smart. I was surprised to see Blackie there because his somewhat impressive assistant managing editor title capitalized on his recognition as a sportswriter. Never had I seen him participate in straight news coverage. But here he was, still in the middle of things, inspecting a stack of photographs taken that day by *Times Herald* photographers.

Smart was eager to hear what I had. He pointed to an overflowing folder of additional materials that Associated Press and United Press International news services had provided. Nodding to rewriteman Stevens, sitting across the desk from him, he said Ben had been collecting wire copy for a single Oswald story. The two of them, who had attended the same high school in suburban Carrollton, listened intently as I told what I had learned about Oswald's Dallas life, his reluctance to engage with others, his telephone conversations in a foreign language, his hurried visit to his room on North Beckley shortly after the shooting, and other random bits of information. I assumed now that I would be turning my material over to Ben for his profile from wire copy and my new information. But Ken turned to Ben: "I think Darwin's got the story. Why don't you give him your wire copy so he can combine it all?"

Ben agreed. I thought he might be irritated to lose the story, but he—an always friendly colleague—showed no trace of it as he turned over his stack of wire copy. I took off my coat, grabbed a sandwich and Coke, and sat down at my desk to read the wire copy before beginning to write. Ken said to make the story as long as I needed it to be.

The wire copy about Oswald was amazing. How the Associated Press and United Press International had learned so much so speedily about Oswald's intriguing past was beyond me. But, after all, they did maintain files on past stories. I saw that Oswald was not as unknown as I had imagined. He had generated national news when he defected to the Soviet Union and when in 1959 had walked into the American embassy office in Moscow to give up his US passport with intentions of becoming a Soviet Union citizen. This intriguing aspect of his life had been mentioned briefly in our final edition, but I somehow had missed everything new after I went to his room on North Beckley.

His unusual life had been quickly picked up by American reporters in Moscow. They had written stories especially for the AP and UPI that appeared throughout the United States. He had told reporters of both his admiration for the Communist way of life and his intention to become a citizen of the Soviet Union. The wire services had no difficulty in retrieving and reprinting those original stories. For me

A defiant Oswald, refusing to admit guilt, displays his "power salute" as he arrives with detectives at the police station after his afternoon arrest at the Texas movie theater. Bill Winfrey, photographer, Tom C. Dillard Collection, *Dallas Morning News*, the Sixth Floor Museum at Dealey Plaza.

the background material provided solid information to weave into my profile. Such information obviously would appear in some of the other stories, but I had much new material. I would credit the wire services, though, for their material.

I would have included in my story, but had not yet learned, the circumstances preceding Oswald's arrival at 1026 North Beckley Avenue some six weeks earlier. Having spent the weekend with Marina at the Irving home of her new friend, Ruth Paine, upon returning to Dallas that Monday morning in October, he had retrieved his meager belongings from the rooming house on Marsalis Avenue, whose owner had rejected him, then walked to Beckley to secure his new room.

Between sandwich bites I transcribed my shorthand notes. Hands on the Western Union clock were approaching midnight. Some reporters were still out. Others remained in the newsroom, trying to finish stories for Saturday's paper. The work of others was over for the moment, yet they stayed, huddling in small groups, talking over what they had experienced on this workday. It appeared that this could go on all night, and I learned later that many indeed spent the entire night there. Not only was there the duty of writing local stories, but the wire services were also pouring out a deluge of the latest.

My Oswald story, I knew with Smart's encouragement, didn't have to be short. No detail could be too insignificant. Years from now, I thought (rather ingloriously), historians and students likely would examine the first newspaper articles written in search of some forgotten tidbit that might possibly provide fresh insight into the historic event.

It had been a few hours earlier that I had struggled to write a proper lede about how Dallasites so passionately welcoming the president and Jacqueline. But oddly enough, on this night an appropriate lede seemed within easy reach about the man who had assassinated her husband.

The words flowed easily. The added wire copy background described what I considered to be a fascinating portrait. Since my deadline would not occur until 8:00 in the morning for our thin Saturday paper, I took my time. No matter how long it would take, I wanted to do a good job. I wrote my first draft triple-spaced as always on single sheets with two carbon copies. But I didn't intend the first draft to be the only draft; I would take time to make improvements before going home.

My first lede went like this: "Lee Harvey Oswald's life history is one of a perplexed, confused man." Nope, too simple, I thought. I added another aspect to it, one that pleased me. So my new opening was this: "Lee Harvey Oswald's recent years show a perplexed man who took bizarre steps to change the course of his life. The 24-year-old admitted Marxist, who married a Russian, gave no indication of this in his day-to-day life. To his fellow roomers at 1028 North Beckley, he was 'peculiar' and 'stand-offish,' but not what you would call eccentric. He was a man they couldn't get to know."

The completed story was some sixty column inches long, or about fifteen triple-spaced pages. It took me about two hours to finish.

I folded my "masterpiece" and placed it in the basket at the left edge of Smart's desk, where completed stories were placed for evaluation. The other two carbon copies went into separate baskets, one for the Associated Press in the adjacent room and another for the *Times Herald*'s records. Why the AP? It leased space in the large office next door. In our working agreement we supplied AP with copies of all local stories.

A few minutes later Ken approached me with my story in his hand. "What's your basis for this part about Oswald being an 'admitted Marxist'?" I unfolded for him the wire service stories that unanimously agreed on Oswald claiming to be a Marxist. He had no more questions.

My workday and that for most of our reporters had lasted about fourteen hours. So at long last, after a day that seemed never-ending, I called Pat to say I was heading back to our apartment. I grabbed my coat from the rack, took the elevator, and drove across the viaduct to our apartment.

When I arrived, far after midnight, I found Pat still awake. What else could I have expected? She had been alone since her school day ended. I had been concerned for her during such a frightful time. While I had been busy, she had done nothing after school but watch the constant flow of horrifying news, hearing from me once, possibly twice, and talking on the telephone with her parents in Houston, my own parents in Dallas, and her friends.

She was okay but understandably still reeling from being so close to such an event. She had no idea just how close, for she was shocked to hear that the accused assassin lived little more than a couple of blocks from us on the western side of Lake Cliff Park. We must have driven past his rooming house a couple of times or more a day.

Marina Oswald would testify that in happier times she and her husband sometimes walked to the lake from their duplex a few blocks away at 214 West Neely Street with their daughter June, now nearly two.[9] Could we possibly have seen the Oswalds? The eastern side of the lake was immediately across the street from us.

On this sad, sleep-deprived, post-midnight hour, we were no different from millions of Americans. Long after we turned out the lights, we lay awake discussing our thoughts. It seemed, we agreed, that the assassination felt like a death in our own family. The depth of our feelings of personal loss was surprising to us. Finally, at long last, at an uncertain hour, we fell asleep. Another big day awaited. because it considered her too old

Chapter 9

"This Case Is Cinched"

N EXT DAY, AFTER SLEEPING LATE, I returned to the newsroom eager to see how my profile was displayed in our Saturday edition. I hoped and expected to see my byline with a favorable placement. The story was there, all 1,800 words, well displayed at the top of an inside page under a five-column headline: "Oswald: A Study in Fantasy." But there was a huge disappointment—no byline! And the presses were already rolling!

I was acutely aware—immodestly aware—that future researchers who looked up *Times Herald* accounts of the assassination would not see my byline. Smart was already at his desk, checking the early pages for corrections. I didn't complain or mention to anyone my disappointment. Only the most veteran reporters would complain about not having a byline. As I watched Ken studying the edition's first pages, he glanced at me, turned toward me, briefly apologized for the omission, then wrote down "By Darwin Payne" as an insert and sent it to the back shop for the next stop of the presses. I felt much better and waited for copies to arrive with my byline. I saved two or three of them (which I still have).[1]

With my disappointment resolved and my next assignment my regular Saturday evening at the police station, I returned to our apartment to watch the news. I was able to catch up with what I had missed: images of the police station's third floor where a restless flood of reporters from throughout the nation and world clambered for space and action. I would be at the same place beyond the midnight hour, relieving our afternoon reporter.

Driving there through remarkably quiet downtown streets, I arrived shortly before 5:00 p.m. and parked a couple of blocks away, assuming that the small police underground parking spaces for reporters would not be available. I had expected to see civilian crowds mingling outside the building, just as at Dealey Plaza. After all, inside the station the accused assassin of our president was being held for questioning. The eyes of the world were concentrated on what was happening in the homicide bureau where the accused assassin's interrogation was occurring.

As I drove near, though, I was astonished that surrounding streets were eerily devoid of traffic, shoppers, or spectators. Something else that surprised me was the number of network television trucks in "no parking" zones across from the police station. Thick cables extended from them through the station's partially open windows so live coverage could reach the nation. So that's where the spectators were—watching the constant flow of assassination news on television.

Chief Curry, I would learn, also had been astonished to see television trucks whose drivers simply ignored very apparent "no parking" signs. He didn't know who, if anyone, had given them permission. Evidently, no one. Their television cables extended into the third floor where the action was.

What especially concerned me personally was the fact that, if asked for one, I did not have a press card. A press pass had never been issued to me, not by the *Press* or *Times Herald* or any city, state, police department, or other governmental agency. In my four years as a reporter I had never been asked to show press identification at any news event. Nor had I ever seen a fellow reporter display one. (My one-day-only tag for riding on the 1960 Kennedy campaign bus from Fort Worth to Arlington didn't count.) However, under these circumstances, I feared that an identifying press pass would be required to satisfy security measures. If one was ever needed, this surely was that time. My concern accelerated as I approached the police station entrance. Without press credentials I felt sure that I wouldn't be admitted.

I WAS WRONG. As I entered the first floor, no one was even there. Nor were there barriers at the elevator. I simply pushed the third-floor button and up I went. My concerns disappeared. Even though I had been watching the same images on black-and-white television all afternoon, the opening elevator door, also without security, presented a shocking scene. Revealed was a mass of weary, harried-looking journalists such as I had never seen. They filled the narrow hallway side to side, waiting for the next police appearance or whatever, perhaps a confession from Oswald. Cigarette butts, empty soft drink bottles, and other debris covered the floor. Television cables, huge stationery cameras, floodlights, and their handlers were centered at the broader space in the open area in front of the elevator. This was jungle journalism such as Dallas detectives and local reporters never before had seen. Nor had the participating journalists. District Attorney Henry M. Wade estimated the total number of reporters and photographers at about three hundred.

National television showed the mob and space I now was a part of. Specialized detective offices lined both sides of the hallway—homicide and robbery, burglary and theft, auto theft, juvenile, and a few others. The press room was at the north end, the chief's office opposite on the south end. Two uniformed officers stood at the entry to homicide and robbery, protecting it from press intrusions.

I wasn't the only one taken aback at the scene. One detective said reporters were packed together so tightly that he had to push his way through to reach the homicide office. Once there he could open the

Reporters and photographers from around the nation and world soon arrived at the police station's third floor, where Oswald was interrogated in the homicide office. *Dallas Times Herald* Collection, the Sixth Floor Museum at Dealey Plaza.

door only with physical exertion. Captain Glen King, public relations officer, described it this way: "Every time a police officer stepped into the hall he had to fight his way through microphones, cameras, floodlights, a maze of cables and wires, and questioning reporters."[2] Secret Service agent Forrest V. Sorrels said, "You would almost have to be there to see it, to actually realize the conditions. . . . It was almost indescribable."[3]

I could see that most of these reporters weren't from Texas. Some, I saw, were speaking with heavy foreign accents. The largest contingent must have been from the nation's major newspapers. The *New York Times* had wasted no time in sending half a dozen additional reporters to Dallas to join Tom Wicker as soon as shots were fired at Dealey Plaza.

Millions of viewers were seeing the third floor this night, live on television! One or more of my relatives claimed to have seen me moving through the crowds of reporters and photographers. I had found myself a stranger in a police station that had been very familiar to me.

I plunged through the crowd and headed for the familiar and simply furnished press room where local reporters hung out. There, on the worn sofas and chairs, I perhaps would find a few familiar Dallas or Fort Worth faces.

On the way I saw a welcome friend, Wilborn (Bill) Hampton, a fellow journalism student at the University of Texas at Austin now working for UPI. As we talked three youths, possibly in their late teens, approached us. One of them was wearing what appeared to be a legitimate US sailor's uniform. He said he was here to interview reporters and send a story to his high school newspaper in California. What in the world, I wondered, were three teenagers doing in this hallway so packed with professional journalists that one could hardly breathe? Not wanting to get bogged down myself with them, I slipped away into the crowd.

I realized how senseless it had been for me to worry about being stopped at the door for lack of a press pass. Obviously, there was no security. Little did I realize that in the crowd this same evening was Jack Ruby, as he had been the previous evening. I had never heard of Ruby.[4]

At the press room, *Times Herald* reporter James (Jim) F. Koethe was waiting for me to relieve him. Thus far, he told me, police had been linking Oswald with more and more evidence that tied him to the assassination and Tippit's murder. Jim was a bit of an adventurer, having a particular interest in tales of lost treasures in Texas, a subject he frequently wrote about. He, thankfully, wanted to stay with me for a while to employ a strategy to guarantee a telephone would be immediately available to us when news broke. There were no more than three, possibly four telephones in the press room. All reporters were desperate to find the nearest telephone with each new development.

Jim suggested that when two reporters worked together, one of us would be the leg man and the other the telephone man. Whenever a police spokesman or official stepped outside the homicide office with news—or certainly when Oswald was brought through the hall—as leg man I would race with others to get the news. Jim, as telephone man, would stay in the press room with the others gone, then grab and hold a phone so I could return and call the office immediately with whatever I learned. (I note that our exclusive use of the word *man* reflected the fact that the only woman reporter said to be directly involved in the assassination coverage at the police station was Peggy Simpson of the Associated Press.)

How did the other reporters find a telephone? Some barged into bureau offices along the hall, all of which, except now for homicide and robbery, were open. In some instances cordiality evolved quickly between reporters and detectives. Some detectives willingly offered telephones. Numerous long-distance calls, made without the knowledge of responsible City of Dallas officials, were charged to the city.

Hostilities sometimes arose. In one office a reporter tried to hide a telephone for his exclusive use under an absent detective's desk. Many desperate reporters, finding no telephones available anywhere in the building, had no choice but to go outside to their hotel room, hopefully nearby, or find a street telephone booth.

Jampacked with journalists from across the nation, western Europe, and elsewhere, the hallway did not seem to offer much room for enterprise reporting. A lone out-of-town reporter who was away from the homicide office would risk missing an anticipated report if he or she stepped out for lunch. What if Oswald confessed guilty to the crime during a thirty-minute break for food? That would be unfortunate indeed. And a confession from Oswald was what we were waiting for. If it came as we expected—certainly our local reporters did—we would explore its ramifications and then wait for his trial in Dallas or elsewhere in Texas.

On this third floor the wider area adjacent to the elevator had become the site for the mounted television cameras. These big cameras were connected by the huge cables with the outside network trucks, providing live coverage. Network newsmen, standing in front of these cameras, microphones in hand, were poised to ask questions when an important official arrived at the third floor or stepped out of the homicide office. This placement simplified everything for any spokesperson. I realized—no secret, of course—that whenever an official stepped here to make a statement, he was speaking to the nation. Newspaper reporters, taking notes, could not relay this news to their readers until their next edition. The television broadcasters simply faced the cameras to talk to the nation of the latest development. Radio broadcast reporters had similar advantages but without accompanying pictures. Newsmakers most often responded to questions from the television journalists. Print journalists, standing with pad and pencil, were frequently ignored.

Interviewed by the Warren Commission four months later about the impact of journalists, J. Lee Rankin, general counsel, asked Chief Curry if he recalled giving any interviews that weekend to "newspapers." Curry responded: "I don't recall giving any interviews to newspapers."[5]

What a statement! At an early point I and others realized that print journalism had lost its historical stature as the basic source of information for the American public. Newspaper and print reporters had the usual advantage of one-on-one interviews with detectives, police chiefs, judges, county officials, mayors, city managers, or other sources. Newspaper reporters needed and wanted deeper information that could be attained only with their lengthier interviews. But that role for them was ending.[6]

Dan Rather said live television news coverage is "what sold the nation—including many former critics—on electronic journalism." As a result of his stellar work during this assassination weekend in Dallas, Rather would be promoted to CBS-TV's White House correspondent.[7]

Communication between out-of-town reporters and their far-away newsrooms was difficult in these momentous days. Some help came in the form of a large blackboard inside the press room, evidently placed there by the police's public relations office. Telephone calls to the press room would be picked up by the person nearest the phone. There was no telling who might be on the other end. I somehow remember one message scribbled in chalk on the blackboard: "Herbers, call the Times newsroom."

City Manager Crull, Assistant Police Chief Charles Batchelor, and Chief Curry, although seeing the problems that the massive press numbers could inflict upon the investigation, nevertheless determined at a meeting on the afternoon of the twenty-second to accommodate its representatives as much as possible. The enormity of the crimes and the public's interest in being informed compelled it, Captain King later told the American Society of Newspapers Editors.

SHORTLY AFTER KOETHE and I agreed upon our strategy, loud shouts from the hallway signaled that something was happening. It was 6:15 p.m. I sprang from my sofa seat and joined the stampeding mob toward the homicide office, leaving Koethe in his chair with an unchallenged telephone.

Chief Curry, stepping out of the homicide offices, was accompanied by a tall, impressive-looking man who was familiar to me. I recognized him as H. Louis Nichols, an attorney whom I had seen many times at city council meetings as he represented the city of Dallas in zoning changes. Curry properly introduced him, though, as president of the Dallas Bar Association. Nichols, he said, had just visited Oswald in the upstairs jail and was willing to respond to questions.

Nichols said he had felt an obligation to see if Oswald had an attorney or needed help in finding one. He had been under arrest without representation for more than twenty-four hours, undergoing questioning by skilled interrogators. He had already been arraigned in an appearance before local Justice of the Peace David Johnston, yet he had no legal representation. Many had called about this, including my University of Texas friend Greg Olds, president of the local American Civil Liberties Union.

Nichols, poised and relaxed as he described his visit, addressed especially the network correspondents with their microphones and bright lights. He had not known that Curry would ask him to speak to the press afterward.

"When I heard about this I decided to come down and make inquiry to see if he [Oswald] wanted counsel," Nichols said. "I've just visited with him and he said his first choice is a lawyer in New York named John Abt. If he couldn't get Abt, his second choice would be a lawyer who was a member of the American Civil Liberties Union." Oswald told him that if he was unable to get Abt or an ACLU attorney, he might request his further help. Nichols asked Oswald if there was anything else he could do. "He said no. I satisfied myself that he is not being denied counsel, so I left."[8]

Nichols's appearance only whetted journalistic appetite. Because he was an attorney not associated with the police department, reporters wanted his objective view of the prisoner and his treatment. Was there evidence that Oswald was being mistreated? Did have any marks on his body? Did he appear desperate for help?

A dozen of such questions were being shouted at one time. Nichols first answered the loudest one. Had he discussed the shooting with Oswald? The answer was no. Further questions came without pause. Had he seen any abnormalities in Oswald or in the way he was being treated? He seemed "perfectly rational," said Nichols. Who would ask Abt to represent Oswald? Oswald's family, Nichols responded. The accused assassin did not appear defiant, said Nichols, still standing in the bright lights.

"When I saw he desired no services," Nichols said he ended his visit. But questions continued. Did he think Oswald could get a fair trial in Dallas? "Probably," Nichols responded. And then a final question—how about Nichols himself representing Oswald? Nichols answered quickly that he did not practice criminal law.

So as Nichols broke away from the bright lights, a few persistent questioners followed him, hoping for more. But most newsmen needed to find telephones, swarming into every open office along the hall, grabbing the first telephone they could put their hands on, often under the noses of the detectives working in those offices. Luckily, few detectives other than homicide and robbery were working on this late Saturday, so their telephones were available to the first ones to come.

Back in the press room Koethe waited for me, holding a telephone already open to the city desk. I relayed this new information for Sunday morning's central story. Our last deadline this night would be an hour after midnight, so there was plenty of time for more news. (On Sundays only, the *Times Herald* was a morning paper with deadlines similar to those of the *Morning News*.)

Soon after Nichols's departure, shouts again cascaded through the hallway. "What's happening? What's going on?" From further up the hallway came spontaneous cries: "They're bringing in Oswald."

I AGAIN JOINED the rush. Those many already ahead of me had the best view as three accompanying officers pulled and shoved the handcuffed, T-shirt–clad prisoner through the surrounding reporters toward the homicide office. Dozens of questions, directed at Oswald, sprang out. "Did you do it?" "What do you have to say?" I couldn't clearly hear Oswald's replies amid all the turmoil, but he denied guilt as the officers escorted him through the clamoring journalists and down the hall toward the homicide office.

All he wanted now, he said, were some "basic human rights such as a shower." These last words I heard as he disappeared into the homicide office. Under such shared difficulties, a gentleman's agreement had developed among the reporters in which those closest to Oswald repeated for others the few words they heard.

Captain Fritz had found a photograph—soon a famous one— showing Oswald at an outside stairway where he and Marina had lived at 214 West Neely Street, a few blocks south of 1026 North Beckley. His aggressive pose showed him holding a rifle under his arm, a pistol in his holster, and the socialist newspapers *Militant* and the *Worker*. (Oswald claimed that he was not that individual, arguing that a photograph of his face had been substituted on the original. Later Marina said she took the picture at her husband's request behind their duplex on West Neely Street. Oswald denied ever having lived on that street.) Detectives would escort Oswald to and from the homicide office sixteen times (eight round trips) during his less than two days at the police station.[9]

I was sitting in the press room with another local reporter when a crew-cut detective handed us a just-released "beef sheet" (the term for a police crime report) about the assassination. The report followed the typical format, normally a single page.

The detective waited for us to send its information to the city desk, but it contained little that was not already known. He jokingly suggested that he might go downstairs and reproduce dozens of copies of it, then sell each for a dollar, a feat he imagined would make him a rich man. Eventually, the report was reproduced by various media. This same friendly detective, although not involved in the Oswald investigation, also gave us better information he had taken from Oswald's address book. It had the name of FBI agent James Hosty, who before the assassination had irritated Oswald by questioning Marina. The book

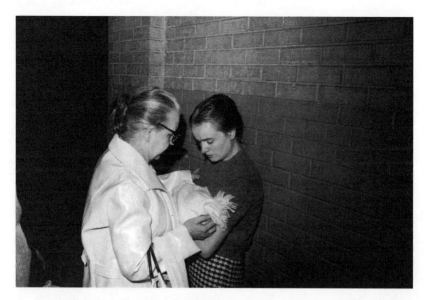

Oswald's Russian-born wife, Marina, arrived at the police station with their
one-month-old daughter, Rachel, accompanied by Oswald's mother,
Marguerite. Darryl Heikes, photographer, *Dallas Times Herald* Collection,
the Sixth Floor Museum at Dealey Plaza.

contained Hosty's address, home telephone number, the license plate
number of his car, and several FBI calling cards—for what purpose
one could only surmise.

I wandered up and down the hall, exchanging words with
local journalists in the crowd. I saw Seth Kantor, the Washington
correspondent who had worked with me on the *Fort Worth Press*
and with whom I had talked on the Kennedy campaign press bus.
Now he represented Scripps-Howard as its capitol correspondent.
Seth, familiar with Dallas, had taken a hotel room at the multistory
White Plaza across from the police station where he perhaps knew
Fritz lived.[10]

An hour after Oswald was taken into the homicide bureau, he was
returned to his jail cell, once more making the short trip through the
dense crowd of shouting newsmen. Still defiant, he cockily denied
connections with the crime.

On Saturday afternoon Police Chief Jesse Curry revealed to the press
that a photograph of Oswald taken by his wife, Marina, showed him posing
proudly with rifle and pistol. Lyndal L. Shaneyfelt Collection,
the Sixth Floor Museum at Dealey Plaza.

Except for his interrogations, Oswald was kept in this private cell in the small
temporary police jail on the fifth floor. Two officers always watched him. He was
permitted to use a telephone. Allison V. Smith, photographer.

"I don't know where you people get your information. I haven't
committed any acts of violence," he shouted. This high school drop-
out who had filled book orders at the depository did not appear to
be intimidated and was matching reporters shout by shout. He was
surprisingly strong in that respect, so unlike murder suspects we had
seen lurking out of Fritz's office.[11]

Later another surge of activity burst forth as reporters surrounded
another news source, Captain Fritz, standing outside his door and
ready to talk. This time I was close enough to hear everything.

"Are you close to a solution?" someone asked him.

"Yessir," was his response.

How about that rumor that he had an incriminating photo of Oswald with weapons?

True, Fritz readily admitted. The incriminating rifle had been traced back "far enough to be sure" that it belonged to Oswald. This was electrifying news. If true, it would be a vital clue in the forthcoming murder trial. Fritz put it this way: "This case is cinched."

There were many other short interviews that night with key investigators, mainly Dallas detectives. Bits of information about the investigation popped up, but it wasn't until Chief Curry appeared outside the homicide bureau door that he brought reporters up to date on what they had learned in this first full day of investigation.

"Basically, the case is closed. We had a good case this morning and we have a better case tonight," he stated firmly.

Curry, a large, square-jawed man who reached his leadership position by coming up through the ranks after beginning as a traffic officer in 1936, gave a convincing case against Oswald.[12] Reporters and news photographers surrounded him as he made important announcements. I was shocked to see a visiting reporter with enough nerve—or disrespect—to prop his notebook on Curry's back while taking notes. The chief didn't display any irritation or surprise. And I think it must have been at this time that I saw a news photographer lie down on the floor just under the chief's legs so from there he could take a unique picture of the inquiring reporters.

City Manager Crull later said that the outsiders' behavior also embarrassed local newsmen as they crowded, pushed, and attempted to take over. According to Captain Fritz "these people" looked "unkempt" and "acted more like a mob" than local news reporters. Homicide detective James R. Leavelle was more explicit: "If you ever slopped hogs and throw down a pail of slop and saw them rush after it you would understand what that was like up there—about the same situation."[13]

Oswald's rifle, Chief Curry said, had been traced to a Chicago mail order house. Handwriting on the order matched Oswald's, according to FBI analysis. The rifle cost $12.78 and was sent through the mail to A. Hidell, a pseudonym Oswald used at Dallas's Terminal Annex post office. A ballistics test the next day was expected to prove conclusively that the weapon was the same as the one used in the assassination.

Curry also confirmed existence of the damning Oswald photograph. How surprising to think that an ordinary individual would pose for such a picture. According to Marina Oswald's later testimony, Oswald had insisted that she take his picture. (The outside stairway leading to the Oswalds' second-floor duplex is still there, generally accessible to those very few who know its location. I have even posed for a personal picture at the same spot as Oswald, but not holding weapons.)

By now it was evident that Oswald was not some wild, deranged person who shot the president out of delusions. He was no John Wilkes Booth, with his hatred of a president, no Charles Guiteau, no Leon Czolgosz. Rather, he must have acted upon a calculated plan based on ideological principles. The incriminating photograph suggested Oswald's thoughts about using violence to support his Marxist convictions.

Questions continued to be shouted. Would Oswald be transferred to the county jail? The usual procedure, once charges were filed, was to transfer a prisoner from the police jail to the more permanent eight-story prison in the Dallas County Criminal Courts Building across the street from Dealey Plaza. And if his trial were held in Dallas County, the courtroom would be in the same building. If found guilty, he would be transferred to one of the state penitentiaries. Courtrooms and the sheriff's office were on the lower floors.

Curry steadfastly declined to be specific about the time of transfer, which was obviously for security reasons even though he did not say so. He recognized that visiting reporters crowding the narrow hallway were far from home without rest breaks and possibly without places to sleep. They wanted both but could not miss important developments, which might come at any time. Foremost of these would be an announcement that Oswald had confessed.

This was especially the opinion of local reporters, cognizant of Fritz's well-known ability in gaining confessions. There was little indication of that now, however, given Oswald's steady denials. As the evening grew longer and the questions about the transfer's time persisted, Curry hedged. "You'd better be here around 10:00 a.m.," he said.

Still not satisfied, newsmen pressed for more specificity. Curry begrudgingly assured the dwindling crowd that nothing of *importance* would happen before that time. This was taken as assurance that Oswald would not be transferred *before* 10:00 a.m. Curry clearly did not mean that he would be transferred precisely at that time; he implied only that Oswald would not be transferred prior to that time. (Afterward, many critics would unfairly criticize the chief for saying that he had announced 10:00 a.m. as the time of transfer.)

The transfer time was especially important to television reporters and their crews with limited capabilities. They and the print journalists would have two opportunities to see and film Oswald—his departure from the police station or his arrival at the county jail entrance across from Dealey Plaza. Ironically, the county location meant that Oswald, if housed there on the west side, would have a view of the assassination site and depository.

Despite Curry's advice that it would not be necessary to arrive before 10:00 a.m. next morning, some newsmen still stayed, fearing that Oswald might be whisked away earlier, possibly this very night. But the chief's seemingly honest answer about nothing happening before that time satisfied almost all the exhausted reporters, and they departed with some confidence.

My own assignment was to remain until 2:00 a.m., so I would stay until then. For the next morning's transfer, *Times Herald* reporters would return to both locations.

Reserve Police Captain C. O. Arnett, guarding the door to robbery and homicide, said fourteen police reservists had been activated next

day to assist with the transfer. Once at the county jail, Oswald would
be under Sheriff Decker's authority.

AFTER CURRY'S LAST APPEARANCE that night, I drifted with
a couple of other local reporters alongside Deputy Police Chief M.
W. Stevenson as he strolled to the administration offices opposite
the press room. He was relaxed and cordial, pleased, I think, to visit
privately with us.

Yes, he acknowledged, he had seen Oswald interrogated. "Nothing
seems to affect him," he said. "We've shown him the pictures under
that stairway and even that didn't shake him too much." I asked for
Oswald's explanation. "He claimed they were faked," Stevenson said,
"that he had had some experience as a photographic technician, and
we had transposed his face onto somebody else's body to try to get
him to talk."

Oswald, he said, was being kept in a one of the temporary jail cells
on the fifth floor between empty cells. An officer was stationed there to
observe him, but Oswald was not so isolated that he couldn't see cell-
mates around him. "And as far as I know he's been eating all his meals,"
Stevenson said. Aside from interrogation sessions or standing on police
lineups, he was brought on the private elevator to the homicide office.
Each time, held securely by two detectives, he had to pass through the
aggressive crowd of third-floor reporters to the homicide office.

We talked on. Chief Stevenson, relaxed as he sat on top of his desk
in his large office, spoke freely of small details. But he added nothing
new to the basic case against Oswald as reported by Fritz and Curry—
nothing worthy of stopping the presses.

Oswald's principal interrogator, Captain Fritz, was born in 1895 in
Dublin, Texas. As a young man he made a living trading horses and
mules in West Texas and New Mexico, eventually enrolling at Tarleton
State College in Stephenville after he sold three horses to pay tuition. In
1921 he joined the Dallas Police Department as a beat officer. He became
a detective, advancing through the ranks to captain in 1934 as organizer
of the homicide and robbery bureau. Through the years he gained a

good reputation as an excellent, low-key interrogator who generally began with a friendly effort to win a suspect's confidence. He sometimes brought vagrants from the streets to jail to see that they had a shower and hot meal before releasing them. (The reader will recall Fritz when he was responsible for the safety of President Franklin D. Roosevelt on his 1936 visit to Dallas.)

With the assassination occurring in Dallas, it was local police who had primary responsibility for developing evidence. (Assassination of a president was not then a federal offense.) As Fritz interrogated Oswald, the Dallas County district attorney's office was gathering evidence, much of it from the Dallas Police Department, for Oswald's trial. Secret Service and FBI agents were understandably playing key investigative roles as well.

Prosecution in a state criminal district court probably would take place in Dallas, surely led by District Attorney Henry Wade, a former FBI agent who had been the county's district attorney since 1951. Born in 1914 in Rockwall County, adjacent to Dallas County, Wade was elected Rockwall's district attorney in 1938 after graduating from the University of Texas law school. During World War II he served in the US Navy aboard aircraft carriers *USS Hornet* and *USS Enterprise*. After he lost in a runoff to be Dallas County's district attorney, the winner hired him as an assistant district attorney, perhaps an unfortunate decision, for in the next race Wade campaigned again and won the position.[14]

Wade's office in the Criminal Courts Building was always open to local beat reporters, who could simply walk in to see him without making advance appointments. When I later covered the courthouse, he sometimes would descend from his upper-floor office and join three of us for a lunchtime game of dominoes. An excellent prosecutor, he was expected to lead in Oswald's trial, aided by chief criminal prosecutor Bill Alexander.

Chief Curry, Wade, Alexander, certain homicide detectives, the Dallas County Sheriff's Department, FBI, and the Secret Service all participated at times in the interrogations led by Fritz. Sometimes a

Texas Ranger was there, and at least once a US Postal Service inspector participated because Oswald had rented a post office mailbox under the false name of O. H. Lee. These crowded interrogations made Fritz's job more difficult.

Oswald had been charged with both the assassination and the murder of Officer Tippit, but additional significant news, generally expected, would be a confession of guilt. If so, surely it would unveil startling details for understanding his reasons for the assassination and whether others might have been involved. It certainly would introduce a new phase to a story already destined to extend far into the future.

FRIDAY EVENING, WITH THE PRESS continuing to ask questions tinged with criticisms of police procedures, Curry, Wade, and Fritz had agreed to make Oswald directly available in the downstairs police assembly room. I was not present; I wish I had been but I was busy writing my profile of Oswald at that time. Following is what happened according to all reports. In short, it was deemed a disaster.

In this crowded room the nearest reporters stood surprisingly close to Oswald, who again exhibited unusual strength in insisting that he was not involved in the assassination. After only six minutes—with an eager press ignoring stated ground rules for restraint, reporters yelling questions from every corner, television cameramen jockeying for their best positions, and fears that journalists were about to overrun the suspect—law officials called a halt.

Among the "reporters" present was nightclub owner Jack Ruby, known to many officers present that evening. Ruby was likely armed with the .38-caliber pistol he typically carried. Recognizing District Attorney Wade, Ruby managed to pull him aside for a quick interview with local KLIF disc jockey Russ Knight, familiar only to Wade as a colorful radio personality known as "the Weird Beard."

While the number of reporters at this midnight press conference was estimated to be as many as a hundred, Justice of the Peace David L. Johnston, who shortly before had arraigned Oswald for assassination, estimated that at least fifty or sixty of those present were officers

Oswald, center, is surrounded at a midnight press conference by reporters who have violated police guidelines to avoid close contact with him. The encounter was shut down after only a few minutes. *Dallas Times Herald* Collection, the Sixth Floor Museum at Dealey Plaza.

District Attorney Henry Wade, left, responds to reporters after the unsuccessful "midnight press conference." *Dallas Times Herald* reporter Jim Lehrer is at the right. *Dallas Times Herald* Collection, the Sixth Floor Museum at Dealey Plaza.

of the law, not reporters and photographers. Johnston said he saw and recognized police officers in uniform, detectives, federal agents, District Attorney Wade and two of his assistants, two or three private attorneys, one or two deputy sheriffs, and three or four police stenographers. In his opinion the numbers of the press did not overtly violate the conditions that Chief Curry had insisted upon.

Unknown to me, one of my University of Texas journalism colleagues had been making waves by telephone. Prior to this mad press conference, Joe Goulden, the former *Daily Texan*'s managing editor I had admired so much and who now was with the *Philadelphia Inquirer*, reached the homicide and robbery office by telephone, found Assistant District Attorney Bill Alexander, and asked, "What's going on down there? We're not getting anything straight. It's all garbled. Is Oswald going to be charged with killing the president?"

Alexander responded, "We're getting ready to file on the Communist son of a bitch." Goulden said he couldn't use "Communist" in his story for fear of libel unless it was in the official charge. "Well, how about if I charge him with being part of an international Communist conspiracy? Could you run with that?" Goulden was fine with that, saying "you got it."[15]

I had no knowledge of it then, but my University of Texas friend Greg Olds, now president of Dallas's American Civil Liberties Union, had visited the police Friday evening to inquire about Oswald's legal representation. Was the suspect being interrogated without an attorney? Being mistreated? (Oswald actually was a new member of the ACLU, having mailed a two-dollar check to the national office on November 4 for his dues.) Assistant Police Chief Glen King advised Olds that Oswald had been told of his right to representation but he had not requested an attorney. Since he was already at the police station, Olds went to Oswald's midnight press conference too. No one asked for his identification. Neither had anyone else been screened.[16]

WITH CURRY'S EARLIER DEPARTURE, I went down to the basement parking area where Oswald's transfer next morning would originate. This was where short-time prisoners of a few hours or days gained their freedom. A few newsmen had found their way to the area, probably fearful that an earlier transfer of Oswald might take place.

I saw there a familiar *Times Herald* advertising salesman who was with an attorney bailing out a client after a charge of drunkenness. We talked amiably for a while, and I suddenly had an idea. No reporter had seen Oswald behind bars. Other than Oswald's own complaint about his need for a shower, no one had described how he was faring. Was he sleeping, reading, wailing, shouting out to fellow inmates, refusing to talk to anyone, denying to fellow inmates any role in the assassination? If I could learn about his actions from a jail mate, it would make an interesting story.

I told my friend of my idea. Could we ask the lawyer's client, now being released, about Oswald in jail? Had he seen him? Had conversations with him? Noticed how he was spending his time behind bars? The ad salesman heartily concurred, and so did his attorney friend.

When the now-free inmate emerged and I was able to talk to him, my hopes sank. I had wanted at best to meet a businessman who had had one too many drinks, been arrested for DWI, and was now sober. But the client appeared to be a seedy, red-faced man in scruffy clothes who was either still drunk or suffering from a heck of a hangover. That the police would release him in this condition was unexpected.

His lawyer asked the first questions. "Hey, did you see Oswald in there?"

"Who?" He didn't catch the name.

"Oswald!"

Still nothing.

"You know, the guy that shot the president. They've got him in jail up there."

The former mumbled some words in the negative. He had seen a few other fellows in jail all right, but he hadn't seen anybody being treated special. I asked other questions, trying to spark some remembrance. But nothing worked. We couldn't even determine that the released prisoner knew that the president had been assassinated.

My hopes for an exclusive eyewitness report on Oswald in jail collapsed.

Chapter 10

My Call to Chief Curry

RETURNING TO THE press room, I anticipated nothing new at this late hour. All but a handful of the visiting reporters, having taken Curry at his word and needing a good night's rest, were gone. So were most of the detectives and the night police chief. Even our reporters, except for a few on the city desk and copy desk, had gone home as usual on this late Saturday night. Despite solid evidence linking Oswald to the crime, there was one missing ingredient. A few onlookers had seen the rifle barrel extending from the window. But as far as we knew, no one could positively identify Oswald as the shooter.

I chatted as I regularly did on late Saturday nights with veteran reporter John Rutledge of the *Dallas Morning News.* Rutledge had been covering late-night police for years. Like our own George Carter, he preferred going to the *News*'s office only to pick up his paycheck. Rutledge, too, was a former *Fort Worth Press* reporter, years before me, but we had many old-timer friends still there. He had started at the *Press* in 1948 as a police reporter and copyeditor. In the early 50s he moved to the *News*, taking over the night police beat.

Johnny and I often talked of days gone by. At 39, he was an intense man who wore a western hat and often was mistaken as a lawman. He enjoyed talking and I enjoyed listening about his days when he had bummed around the country, riding the rails with a friend. They experienced many escapades, covering as much territory as they could on very little money.

I had learned that there seemed to be two types of police reporters: More matures ones, like Rutledge, Carter, Jim Ewell (daytime police reporter at the *News*), and Bob Bain of the *Star-Telegram*, were pleased to stay on the beat as veterans. They were happily among friends, counting especially the detectives who were key contacts. These reporters, it seemed to me, were highly competent, but not busting their butts for further promotion. The other type, younger and more adventurous with higher ambitions, also enjoyed the camaraderie among detectives, but they used the beat as a temporary assignment.

As much as I enjoyed my work on police, I had no intention of spending my career there, and my thoughts of developing exclusive stories on the Kennedy assassination this night seemed exhausted.

AT APPROXIMATELY MIDNIGHT city desk called. Someone had gotten wind of a story out of New York City. A radio station there, WCBS, part of the CBS network, had reported that an eyewitness who positively identified Oswald as the shooter had been found. Police were said to be holding him in protective custody. He was understood to have been interviewed by Dan Rather.

CBS-TV hired Rather in February 1962 after his outstanding work in covering Hurricane Carla, the most severe storm ever to reach landfall in Texas. Rather, anticipating a plush promotion to CBS news headquarters in New York City, was promoted instead to head the Dallas news bureau—consisting of one man, himself—in charge of covering a twenty-three-state area, especially Gulf Coast states where hurricanes were most prevalent. He now was among other CBS newsmen covering the president's tour of Texas, and he was among the first to report his death from Parkland Hospital.[1]

If Rather had this eyewitness story, it would be an exclusive report. Details were lacking, though, for no one on our city desk had heard the broadcast. But if true and further confirmation by police revealed the individual's identity, it would be a sensational story for next morning's paper. Being tonight's on-duty police reporter, it was basically up to me at this late hour to confirm it with detail. The eyewitness might be under protective custody here at the police station. The follow-up had to be done this night, before our last deadline. City desk, probably Carl Burgen, said they would work on the possible story, too, querying the wire services or calling the radio station in New York City. Worst case, the *News* and Rutledge himself may already have this news for their Sunday edition.

I hung up somewhat frustrated. The police station press room, except for Rutledge and me, was deserted. Only a night police crew and a handful of reporters, perhaps two or three, were still around. I felt certain that none of those still here had any idea about such an important development.

Rutledge, alone with me in the press room, had listened with interest to my guarded conversations with the city desk. The press room was so small that he couldn't avoid hearing even my whispers. He looked my way with undisguised curiosity, wondering, I supposed, if I would share with him what I had learned. I didn't. He couldn't expect that from me, and he wouldn't have had the temerity to ask what it was about.

Suddenly I remembered an interesting incident that evening involving the CBS-TV crew. I had seen them—possibly including Rather—whispering in a corner of the press room, seemingly eager that no one overhear them. I watched, though, pretending to be otherwise occupied.

The small group rushed off after I overheard one of them mention a telephone number. As soon as they departed, I had jotted down the number and put it in my notebook. (It's still there!) I thought it might be tied to someone connected to the assassination, perhaps the eyewitness in protective custody, I now surmised. Such an uncertain blind call at this hour seemed awfully foolish, I realized, but I held on to the number, just in case. If the *Times Herald* could be scooped by this network news team or especially by the *News*, I had little desire to be the victim.

I edged out of the press room as discreetly as I could, searching for the best way to pursue the possible existence of a witness in protective custody here in the police station. Meandering along the empty hall, I encountered someone I didn't know—the night police chief, Jack Tanner.

When I explained my situation to him, finding him to be a friendly, down-to-earth individual, he said he knew nothing about an eyewitness in protective custody. I believed him. If he had known about it but didn't want to say so, he would have answered in a different way. A detective cannot tell everything he knows about a case. Usually, he'll hedge a bit to protect himself. I asked Tanner if he had Chief Curry's home telephone number.

"Yes, but I sure don't want to give it to you," he answered.

I didn't blame him, but I had a job to do, too.

"I'm not asking for it yet," I said, "but I may have to."

Tanner shook his head sadly. He could tell I was determined to get a response from someone in higher authority, including, even at this late hour, the weary police chief. By now it was after midnight.

"I won't press you for it unless it's absolutely necessary," I told him. "I can understand how you feel, but this is something big." A friendly approach with Tanner seemed best. If I absolutely had to get that number, I couldn't afford to antagonize him now. So I sympathized with him. Then I walked back toward the press room, stopping at the next-door juvenile bureau to use a telephone out of Rutledge's hearing range to call the city desk.

"Anything new on your end?" I asked.

They had heard a bit more. The story now was that the radio station was saying that prior to 10:00 p.m. the witness had been in protective custody. The man, we assumed, must have been on the depository's

sixth floor to see Oswald fire his rifle. The station was said to be holding up an interview with the man until next day.

I went back to Tanner, buttressed with my new information. It was
pitifully sparse, but I had to try.

"If we're holding such a man, I don't know it," he said lamely.

"Is that report false, then?" I asked.

"I couldn't say it was false," he said, desperately.

It was no use. Tanner still didn't know, but he couldn't deny something he simply didn't know. I reminded him that I still might need
Curry's number.

Rutledge had grown curious. He approached me quizzically,
having caught the import of what I was seeking.

A new concern arose, one that had been lurking beneath the surface.
What if Rutledge and the *News* already had this story, wrapped up and
ready for its Sunday morning edition a few hours away?

By now the first editions of both our Sunday morning papers were
already on the street. No mention of such an eyewitness was in the
News, but it sometimes was the practice to withhold exclusive stories
from earliest editions to prevent the opposition from catching up.
Could the *News* be doing that tonight?

I tried politely to ignore Rutledge and returned to the press room.
I did have the unlisted telephone number for Captain Fritz. As much as
I hated to wake him up in the middle of the night after these past tough
days, I dialed his number first.

But there was no answer. Rutledge, by now at my side, volunteered that Fritz might be at a motel for an uninterrupted night's sleep.
Rutledge knew the police well.

By now he had a good idea of what I was up to. Frankly, at this
point I didn't care. I was watching him closely to see his reaction to the
pieces of information he had been overhearing. If the *News* did have
the story and Rutledge had written it or knew about it, I thought I might
be able to tell from his expressions. But from what I gathered, the
News didn't have the story. If it had, he would have acted like a typical
reporter who knows he has an exclusive story over his opposition and

buries his nose in a magazine. But Rutledge was interested. He wanted to know what I could find out, no doubt about that.

Again, I consulted with the city desk. A rewriteman, I believe Burgen, had managed to call a CBS-TV reporter—perhaps even Rather—at his hotel to see if he could give us a clue as to our information. But the reporter understandably was reluctant to say anything. It did appear, though, that CBS-TV had something. Our night city editor, Tom LePere, talked the problem over with the acting news editor, top man at this early Sunday hour, possibly Charles Dameron. A decision was made for me: I must call the police chief and ask him. I earlier had told the desk that I could get his number by persistent efforts. Now they were taking me up on it.

So I waltzed down the hall one more time to see Tanner. He moaned and groaned, hating so much to give me the number. But he did. I almost wished he had refused. I was reluctant to call the chief at home with a question he probably wouldn't answer. He surely would be asleep. I expected him to thoroughly chew me out. If so, that was not too great a hazard. Reporters get used to being cussed. There had been a number of newsmakers I called as early as 7:00 a.m. for a first-edition story. Doing that was something I never enjoyed. Moreover, it seemed unlikely that the chief would reveal this information to a single reporter.

On the other hand, we possibly stood to gain a tremendous jump on the *News* and maybe the world press—that is, except for the brief radio report. I slipped into the empty bureau office next to the press room to use one of its telephones. I didn't want Rutledge to overhear my conversation. The clock read something like 1:00 a.m., no earlier. We could wait no longer if we were to have the story for our Sunday morning home edition.

AFTER PERHAPS THREE rings a woman—obviously Mrs. Curry—answered. Her husky voice indicated interruption of deep sleep. I identified myself, grateful at least to say I was a local reporter and not one of those out-of-town newsmen. The phone must have been at the couple's bedside, for she immediately handed it to Chief Curry.

I could imagine the looks of displeasure they were exchanging. I looked up and saw Rutledge in the room with me. He had heard me ask for Curry.

With the chief of police on the telephone for an exclusive interview that surely would not be followed by anyone else at this hour, I explained why I was calling, using as simple language as I could since he obviously had been sound asleep. I wanted to give him a chance to wake up. However, he couldn't understand what I was saying, and his strange, unconnected responses made no sense. I explained time and time again why I was calling. Give him time to wake up, I told myself, stalling. He sounded as if he were in a dream, trying to wake up from it, rambling on and on with words and phrases without meaning. I tried to write down what he was saying, but it was no use. There were no connecting links to his words. Finally, I began jotting down some of his phrases. (I still have them today, notes on a pink piece of paper instead of my notebook.)

"I don't know who he is. I want to see who he is," said the chief as I tried to get him say whether such an individual was known and being held under protective custody. "I haven't seen him. And they say he's all right. I saw a man . . . I know something . . . who was greeting the president. But there was an upheaval on my left side . . ."

The "upheaval," I felt sure, was the commotion that arose as the shots were fired into the presidential limousine.

Could the chief be playing a game of diversion with me? No, impossible, I decided. Rutledge was watching me and listening to my questions and comments with immense curiosity. I looked back at him and shrugged my shoulders. Over and over I tried for an answer. If I stayed on the line long enough, maybe the chief would wake up. I made my questions as short and direct as possible. The chief's answers at one point sounded as if he might know of such a person. But when I would try to pin him down on something quotable, he sounded just the opposite. After what must have been five full minutes of questioning and an incomprehensible exchange with the chief, I gave up. He evidently couldn't—or wouldn't—wake up.

Possibly, I thought, he had taken sleeping pills to ease his worried mind and give himself a good night's sleep. As an obvious understatement, it had been a nightmarish weekend. Or perhaps he knew all along what he was doing with me. I certainly doubted this. It would have been too dangerous a game to play. A verbatim report of his senseless words would have been disastrous, and possibly for me as well as the paper, if published. This was an exclusive "interview" with the chief that could not be reported. Never in the future would he mention my phone call, even if he had a vague memory of my post-midnight interruption of his sleep. Nor did he ever mention it in his personal accounts of the weekend.

I called the city desk, hating to say that although I had talked with the chief I had been unable to get a single sentence that made any sense at all.

We let it go. What else was there to do? Perhaps the chief was one of those sound sleepers who wakes up only with difficulty. He obviously was talking but awakened from deep sleep. Or perhaps he was feverish. As I thought of it, his words did sound as if he were feverish. Perhaps he had taken sleeping pills, maybe more than usual.

Rutledge had heard only my end of the conversation, but that had been enough for him to see what was going on. We discussed my purpose and the strangeness of the conversation. Would the chief himself remember it the next day or the next time I saw him? Would he be embarrassed? Angry? Furious? I didn't know.

I had met Chief Curry probably only once before. Certainly, he would not be able to associate my name with my face. But, of course, he might remember the name next time I talked to him.

When I told Tanner of the chief's garbled responses, he shook his head and commented sadly that the past two days had been awfully rough on him. Chief Curry, he said, was a good man. Later, as I became more familiar with the chief through my one or two days each week at the police station, I had to agree with that assessment. On the few times later that I had to interview him or discuss something with him, he was a plain-talking, somewhat shy man whose voice sometimes reflected sarcasm. My telephone call was never mentioned by either of us. I doubt that he recalled it with any specificity.

This early Sunday morning was ended. I thought again about calling the strange telephone number I had overheard from the CBS-TV newsman. But it would have been fruitless, I figured, and I never knew what the number was for. Later we learned that our regular police reporter, Carter, had the chief's unlisted number and could have given it to us. Had we been aware of that, we could have asked him instead of having me call the chief whom he knew so well.

Several viewers at ground level that day of November 22 had seen a rifle and a glimpse of a barely discernible figure at the sixth-floor window. This included our own photographer Bob Jackson and a few others, but the best witness by far who had a clear view of the shooter was a 44-year-old steamfitter named Howard L. Brennan. I learned later that this must have been the man who might have been thought to be in police custody for his own safety. Following are summaries and excerpts from his testimony to the Warren Commission four months later and from his memoir, written twenty-five years later.

BRENNAN HAD TAKEN a noon break that day from his nearby worksite to watch the president's motorcade. He found a good place at the Houston and Elm intersection directly opposite the School Book Depository's entrance and below its upper windows. While waiting, more than once he observed an anxious, unsmiling man occasionally sticking his head out of the sixth-floor window, presumably anticipating the motorcade's arrival.

When the lead motorcycles approached, he saw the same young man reappear at the window. As the president's limousine turned onto Elm Street in front of Brennan, he heard what he thought was a motorcycle backfire. Then, as he testified to the Warren Commission, he saw him again before the third shot was fired, "standing up and resting against the left window sill, with gun shouldered to his right shoulder, holding the gun with his left hand and taking positive aim and firing his last shot. . . . He drew the gun back from the window as though he was drawing it back to his side and maybe paused for another second as though to assure hisself [*sic*] that he hit his mark, and then he disappeared."[2]

Certain that he had seen the man who had fired at the president and surely had hit him, Brennan raced to the nearest police officer not far away and told him what he had just seen, giving a brief description of the shooter. It appeared to Brennan that most officers were running in the wrong direction, and he pointed up to the window near the top of the depository where he had seen the strange-looking man fire toward the president with apparently disastrous results.[3]

Twenty-four years later, recalling those vivid moments in his own memoir, Brennan had a more graphic description: "I saw a sight that made my whole being sink in despair. A spray of red came from around the President's head. I knew the bullet had struck its intended target. . . . To my amazement the man still stood there in the window! He didn't appear to be rushed. There was no particular emotion visible on his face except for a slight smirk. It was a look of satisfaction, as if he had accomplished what he had set out to do."[4]

At home that same day, his wife and grandson exclaimed that they had seen him interviewed on television. "I was there," Brennan responded. "I saw him do it. I saw the man shoot President Kennedy. It was the most terrible thing I've ever seen in my life." Brennan and his wife worried about possible dangers he and the family might face as an important eyewitness. At about 6:30 p.m. that day, Sorrels, alerted to his presence and his advantage as a critically needed eyewitness, sent Secret Service agents to the Brennan home and brought him downtown to see if he could identify Oswald from a lineup of seven or eight men as the person he had seen. Without hesitation Brennan selected Oswald as the one who "most closely resembled" the man he had seen. Sorrels and homicide captain Fritz pressed him, wanting the more positive identification he earlier had made. Now, however, the troubled Brennan declined to be so positive, giving security concerns as his reason because he believed the assassination was a "Communist activity" and that he and his family would not be safe.[5]

Years later in his memoir he said Sorrels told him that "for a while we feel that we should put you in protective custody as a precautionary measure."[6] Another FBI agent, Robert C. Lish, was said to use the same phrase, "protective custody," as he and another agent visited Brennan and his wife at their modest home in Southeast Dallas. "You'll continue to be under protective custody for the time being," Brennan recalled them saying as they insisted that there was no evidence he was in danger but it was merely a precautionary measure.[7] Brennan described how Lish and the other FBI agent spent that night outside his home in their cars. Next day they trailed him and his wife as they drove to Kaufman County for a visit. The FBI and Dallas police "watch" over Brennan and family, Brennan said, continued for "about three weeks," even after Jack Ruby shot and killed Oswald, which had eliminated the possibility of a trial and Brennan's testimony.[8]

The term *protective custody* is usually defined as the confinement, voluntary or involuntary, of a person who government authorities believe will be threatened without such confinement. It was likely that Brennan alone used this phrase, perhaps repeated by the media, such as in the broadcast in New York City.

Another individual near Brennan was considered to be an eyewitness, but he lacked Brennan's more specific descriptions. This was Amos Euins, a 15-year-old Dallas schoolboy who vaguely saw a man firing a rifle from the window. Euins told the Warren Commission that at first he had seen a pipelike object at the window before he realized it was a rifle and saw a man firing it. Euins's best description was that he had a "bald spot" on his head.[9]

It must have been 2:00 a.m. Saturday when we shut down the paper and I went home. I slept uneasily, fearing that next morning the *News* would have a huge banner headline about the supposed individual under protective custody. But there was no story.

Pat awoke as I slipped under the covers and told her of my night with hordes of reporters, glimpses of Oswald, and my telephone call to the chief. Television had given her and millions of television watchers a sense of what it was like to be there. She even said she had seen me as we reporters gathered around police spokespersons for their latest reports. I later heard from a few friends from around the nation that they had recognized me too.

IN THOSE DAYS SO long ago, I was in the middle of a story that the entire nation—even the world—was following with horror, and we were all wondering what could come next. What would be its implications, especially for our nation? I and others were covering an event of dimensions that we had never expected. Somehow, though, we were not overwhelmed by that realization. We were worried about immediate problems, all of us having immediate objectives—both our own and those directed by editors who were away from the scenes yet still intimately involved.

Months later, looking through the Warren Commission's exhaustive twenty-six-volume reports, I saw that my post-midnight call to Chief Curry must have caused the chief and his wife to take their telephone off the hook to avoid further interruptions. Several officers afterward tried without success to reach him that night with what they believed was critical information about threats to murder Oswald during his transfer.

Patrol Captain W. B. Frazier, ranking police officer on duty after Tanner, told the Warren Commission that FBI agent Milton L. Newsom called him at 3:00 a.m. and asked him to alert Chief Curry about a mysterious call from an anonymous man. The man, speaking in a calm way, wished the police to know that an anonymous but organized group of men, numbering from a hundred to two hundred persons, would kill Oswald during his transfer.

These men, the caller said, had no intention of injuring any police officer, deputy sheriff, or other lawman as they carried out their own illegal plan for the sake of the city and nation. The implication was that this act would save the city from harmful publicity inevitably accompanying Oswald's trial, especially if held in Dallas. The caller seemed to suggest that officers might discreetly step aside as these unofficial committee members carried out their mission.

Frazier attempted to alert Curry with this information, but he could not reach him by telephone. After several failed attempts, he asked an operator to check the telephone line. She reported that the line "was out of order."

Deputy Sheriff C. C. McCoy also received the anonymous midnight call, evidently from the same individual. McCoy then called Sheriff Decker to tell him about it, sharing that Newsom had said this boy was going to be killed.[10] Decker asked McCoy to contact the chief to tell him that he thought Oswald should be transferred immediately. Frazier, also unable to reach Curry by telephone, was finally advised by a special operator that the Curry telephone was out of order.

A third similar and anonymous call, evidently from the same individual, was also made to the FBI office. This time the caller used the phrase, "A hundred of us will see that he is dead."[11] Assistant Chief of Police Charles Batchelor and Captain Cecil E. Talbert, advised of these warnings, tried to reach the chief but with the same result.

Not until about 6:30 a.m. did a squad car go to Curry's house and inform him of the threats. Curry, seemingly unalarmed, said he would be in the office between 8:00 and 9:00 a.m. Talbert, asked about Curry's feelings concerning an earlier transfer, doubted that the chief would have agreed to sneak Oswald out of the city jail after having already said that nothing would happen before ten o'clock.[12]

The 65-year-old Decker was far better experienced, known, and respected than Curry. If Curry, police chief for less than three years, had been reached earlier, he might have followed the sheriff's wishes. After Oswald's transfer to the county jail, he would have been Decker's responsibility.

Veteran Dallas County Sheriff Bill Decker, who was to take over custody of
Oswald upon his transfer to the more permanent Dallas County jail, was a
well-respected elected official. Bill Winfrey Collection, *Dallas Morning News*,
the Sixth Floor Museum at Dealey Plaza.

If indeed, improbably, such a vigilante group had organized,
questions about it and its threats were left unexamined. Who was
the smooth-talking individual who had called to alert the police,
sheriff, and FBI of their intentions? How could a committee of
so many have been organized so quickly? And by whom? What
plan might they have conceived to kill Oswald while he was in
custody? Did they intend to halt the vehicle carrying Oswald?
By what means would they have killed him? All this was doubtful,

but there did exist great fear among Dallas citizens that additional publicity during a trial would bring even further harm to the already-troubled city.

The FBI, ranking Dallas police officials, and the sheriff's office certainly did not discount the death threat. Their efforts to advise the police chief, whose responsibility it was to arrange for Oswald's transfer to the sheriff's custody, were foiled, I feared, because my post-midnight call likely caused him and his wife to leave the telephone off its connection.

Chapter 11

"Absolute Panic, Absolute Panic . . ."

N EXT MORNING, SUNDAY, Pat and I slept late. We had closed the drapes to keep out the morning light. Despite my anxiety, it must have been nearly 9:30 a.m. when I got up and found our *Dallas Morning News* in front of our apartment door. Seeing nothing about an eyewitness in protective custody, I relaxed. Today, I thought, would be easier.

On television we saw a crowd of journalists, uniformed officers, detectives, and others in the place where hours before I had tried to interview the inebriated man. Police guards stood at both side entrances of the vehicle ramps. The television showed a moderate-sized crowd behind rope barriers outside the county jail on Houston Street, with a nearer space reserved for reporters, broadcasters, sheriff's deputies, police officers, and probably federal agents.

Since I had no assignment, Pat and I had intended to watch from Houston Street for Oswald's arrival. But ten o'clock was so near we decided to stay and watch on television instead of taking the chance of arriving too late. Television coverage was switching back and forth from the police basement for Oswald's departure to the county jail for his arrival.

I later learned that the effort to prevent outsiders from being any closer, basically neglected until now, had been intensified after the anonymous threats on Oswald's life. This was discussed when Curry arrived at the police station shortly after 8:00 a.m. He, with Assistant Chief Batchelor and Assistant Chief Stevenson, strategized about ways to counter any such threat. One was to summons an armored truck for a safe transfer, but when it arrived it was too tall to pass under the exit. Other tactics included the possible use of decoy police cars.[1]

The press's naïve assumption that Curry intended to start the transfer at 10:00 a.m. was wrong. When Postal Inspector Harry D. Holmes dropped in at the station at about 9:30 a.m. without an appointment, Captain Fritz, in no special hurry, said that he and others were about to have a final interrogation of Oswald before the transfer. If Holmes wanted to take part in it he could. Holmes had questions about Oswald's rental of his post office box under a false name, so he stayed. Interviewing Oswald would be not only Fritz but also Secret Service agents Sorrels and Thomas J. Kelley. Three more detectives would be present to guard the handcuffed Oswald.[2]

Not until about 11:15 a.m. did Fritz finish the interrogation and initiate the transfer. Seeing Oswald wearing a white T-shirt, the homicide captain asked if he needed something better. Oswald said he did. "If it's all the same to you," he said, seeing two choices, "I'd rather wear that black sweater. That might be a little warmer."

Donning the sweater required some maneuvering, since both Oswald's hands were handcuffed. Leavelle was connected to him with another handcuff. Leavelle laughed, "Lee, if anybody shoots at you, I hope they're as good as you are."

Oswald returned the laugh. "Aw, there ain't going to be anybody shooting at me. You're just being melodramatic."

"Well, if there's any trouble you know what to do?" said Leavelle. "Hit the floor." Leavelle would later describe Oswald to the Warren Commission as "cocky," "in control of himself at all times," "enjoying his situation immensely," and having "a lot better education than his formal education indicated."[3]

At 11:21 a.m. Oswald and his police escorts came into view. The prisoner was still handcuffed to Leavelle, with detectives L. C. Graves and L. D. Montgomery providing additional protection.[4]

But no sooner had Oswald appeared than we saw a dark figure move across our TV screen with a pistol pointed directly at him. Detective Billy Combest recognized him and shouted, "Jack, you son of a bitch."[5]

Too late for anyone to stop him, nightclub owner Jack Ruby fired a single shot at Oswald. His face contorted in sudden pain, Oswald clutched his stomach and fell to the floor, pulling Leavelle halfway down. Montgomery and homicide detective W. J. "Blackie" Harrison, who had been standing next to Ruby seconds before, grabbed him and knocked his pistol to the floor. "I've got it," Montgomery shouted.[6]

Standing a few away, live microphone in hand, NBC-TV's shocked Tom Pettit shrieked, "He's been shot. He's been shot. Lee Oswald has been shot. A man in a dark suit and a hat stepped out front and shot him. There is absolute panic, absolute panic here in the basement of Dallas police headquarters. Detectives have their guns drawn. Oswald has been shot. There is no question about it, Oswald has been shot. Pandemonium has broken loose." NBC-TV and Pettit were live, but ABC-TV and CBS-TV quickly joined with live coverage a minute or so later.[7]

WATCHING FROM HOME, I wondered if the gunman might have been a police officer or detective. There were many journalists in the room, too, but I never suspected one of them to be the shooter. Minutes after the shot hit Oswald and he was taken away, I put on my suit and headed for work. Pat needed no explanation. What else might happen? A president had been slain, our governor seriously wounded, a police officer shot and killed by the accused assassin, and now the accused assassin shot by a man on live television in a police basement crowded with armed officers. Nothing else in life could ever come as such a surprise. The assassination of our president had been so shocking, but a follow-up such as this was perhaps even more unbelievable. What else could happen? Was this part of a conspiracy? Quite possibly. Nothing seemed out of the question now.

As order finally prevailed, Montgomery asked FBI agent S. A. Bookhout where he had gone after the two of them handcuffed Oswald. Bookhout said he had gone to listen to the "squawk box."

"Why?" Montgomery asked.

Bookhout responded, "Didn't you know that the chief had received a call during the night that Oswald was going to be shot?"[8]

Totally shocked myself, I now definitely hoped that Oswald would survive. Surely he would; he had only a single bullet wound. If barroom brawl victims with several shots could be saved in emergency rooms, so could he. Parkland Hospital was only a few minutes away.

But upon the 11:30 a.m. hospital arrival of this already unconscious patient, Dr. Malcolm O. Perry realized the worst: "I could tell he was lethally injured when he came in."[9]

Marina Oswald departs from Parkland Hospital with her infant child, Rachel, after learning that her husband has been fatally wounded by Ruby's single pistol shot. *Dallas Times Herald* Collection, the Sixth Floor Museum at Dealey Plaza.

Doctors in Emergency Room 2, across the hall from where President Kennedy had been treated, immediately went to work. The entrance wound was visible over the left lower side of his chest, but the bullet itself was on the opposite side, having injured the spleen, pancreas, aorta, vena cava, right kidney, and liver as it passed through his body. Oswald was rushed immediately to the operating room, where an excessive loss of blood was evident. Massive transfusions, nearly fifteen pints of blood, were given, but there was no heartbeat. At 1:07 p.m. Oswald, never having regained consciousness, was pronounced dead. Dr. Tom Shires, Parkland's chief of surgery, said there would have been an outside chance of survival, but he had lost too much blood in the twenty minutes to reach the hospital.[10]

Unknown to me, our excellent medical reporter, Bill Burrus, who happened already to be in the hospital, sought an exclusive on Oswald's emergency room treatment. Through his friendship with hospital administrator Jack Price, Burrus had been sleeping on a cot in the hospital since Friday, not to miss further medical announcements concerning President Kennedy's death and the continuing treatment of Connally. As soon as he learned of Oswald's approaching arrival, he hid behind a curtain in the emergency room, intending to have an exclusive story about efforts to save him, but Burrus was seen and ejected before treatment began.[11]

Two days earlier I had felt that only Oswald's trial lay ahead. I wanted him to stand trial so we might discover the full story. Everyone I knew, not just members of the press, had been desperate to know how this unintimidated man planned and executed a president's assassination. If we were to learn this, his safety was imperative. He needed be tried in a court of law, his every motive found, his conspirators, if any, identified.

KRLD-TV's Wes Wise, standing outside the county jail with onlookers, saw a surprising public response that was different. When Sheriff Decker announced that Oswald had been shot, people reacted with "a blood-curdling cheer and resounding applause." Wise, in the street with his microphone in hand, shook his head in disbelief.[12]

When Decker announced outside the county jail and courthouse that Oswald
had been shot, the crowd appeared to be jubilant with satisfaction. *Dallas Times
Herald* Collection, the Sixth Floor Museum at Dealey Plaza.

District Attorney Wade was at church. As soon as he was notified,
he found fellow church member Jim Lehrer to tell him about this unset-
tling and unexpected news. There was much to cover. I called city desk
before leaving home, not knowing where I might be needed. It again
would be all hands on deck, every reporter required. The newsroom
normally had few if any staff on Sunday mornings, and except for those
covering the transfer, today was no exception. John Schoellkopf was
working alone on the city desk. At my call he asked me to come to the
office as quickly as possible, as did others.

TEN OR FIFTEEN MINUTES LATER I was there, especially eager
to learn the shooter's identity. If he was known to Dallas police, someone at the paper—perhaps even me—might know him or know of
him. I wasn't the first to arrive. Others were ahead of me. Jim Chambers was there, too, talking to a couple of others about the man who
had shot Oswald.

I moved in to listen. Except for my telephone conversation with him about Zapruder's film, I had never spoken to our *Times Herald* president. That Friday afternoon only two days removed seemed years away. "Who was it?" I asked him at first chance about today's shooter.

"Old Jack Ruby," he said, using an inflection that meant every man in the room must know about him. I didn't, but his name had a familiar ring to it. Ruby, as I learned, owned and operated the Carousel Club, a downtown nightclub featuring strippers. Ruby was a familiar visitor to our newsroom as he sought publicity.

My assignment, soon given and potentially a good one, was to find Marina Oswald. She and her young daughter and infant baby girl probably were with Oswald's mother, Marguerite. Someone thought they had spent the night at the Executive Inn, a large, multistoried hotel close to Love Field.

As I pondered my assignment, I realized it was more difficult than I had imagined. The family probably had already checked out of the hotel. Even if still there, it was highly unlikely that they would be available for a reporter, especially if the FBI or police were protecting them.

Anyway, with a fresh notebook from the supply cabinet, I drove as a starter to the Executive Inn. Its large parking lot was nearly empty. I saw no journalists anywhere. The lobby was virtually empty too. I opened the front glass doors and walked to the registration desk. Only one clerk was on duty. I identified myself and told him that I was trying to locate the Oswald family. They had spent the night there, I believed.

"I'm sorry, we have no one here registered by that name," he said, unconvincingly.

I wasn't surprised. He surely knew, but he had to be following his orders. This 30- something man may well have been telling the truth by saying no one by *that name* was registered. I hadn't expected that the family would be registered under the Oswald name.

Jack Ruby, a known figure to a number of law enforcement officials through
the years as owner of the Carousel Club, was arrested immediately after
shooting Oswald. Bill Winfrey Collection, *Dallas Morning News,*
the Sixth Floor Museum at Dealey Plaza.

I elaborated, telling him, as if he didn't know, that there would be
two women, one older and the other a young mother with a small child
and an infant. Possibly they had been accompanied by others who
registered them under another name. Did anyone come in last night
matching such a description?

Again, he professed not to know.

He had to be hedging. He might not have been on duty last night, and likely he had not seen them. But the wife and mother of an accused assassin, now dead himself, could hardly be in a large hotel without word quickly spreading among the staff. Especially, I figured, the person in charge of the desk would be apprised of the situation.

I asked for the manager. He was "unavailable." Exasperated, I asked for a telephone. He directed me to a pay phone outside the entrance.

From there I brought the city desk up to date. We agreed that I should call the FBI and Secret Service, seeking any leads they might offer. I didn't know any individuals at the FBI or Secret Service. I had scant hope that they would say more than three words. If that were the case, I would pursue the matter further at the hotel, trying somehow to determine whether anyone had seen the Oswalds there.

As usual, the FBI wasn't talking. "We don't have anyone in custody," said the agent, N. A. Pinkston. With that answer, of course, he could mean that the FBI were with the Oswalds but they were not considered actually "in custody." What the difference would be, I wasn't sure. Pinkston surprised me, though, by answering my next question.

When I asked him whether Marina Oswald was with the FBI, he responded, "We don't have anyone in custody. She's in seclusion."

So where in seclusion?

Back to the old runaround. "I don't know whether I know where she is," he said instead of simply, "I don't know where she is." I wrote it down. He wouldn't go any further than that, and I decided to try elsewhere.

Before I could make another call, though, a well-dressed man emerged from the hotel. He identified himself as Chris Ross, hotel manager. He asked politely what he could do for me. He spoke with a French accent and I had some difficulty in understanding him.

He told me that two women matching my description had registered the night before with the name of Allen Grant. Not

understanding him, he took my notebook and wrote down the name
in big letters. Continuing, he said, "He was an FBI man and he had
two ladies—one old and one young. Both were covered up so you
couldn't see them. They had one youngster about two years old with
them," he said, evidently not noting the very young Rachel.

"What do you mean by 'covered up'?" I asked.

"It was cold and they had their coats on."

Earlier this morning, he said, another man, different from the
one who had registered them the night before, arrived. "He asked
me if I was the manager and he said he wanted to pick up the Allen
Grant family. I called the FBI," Ross said, "and the man there said
to go ahead and turn them over." The hotel bill had been paid and
the two women and children were taken to a car outside and driven
away, he said.

It sounded mysterious. I believed, though, that those who had
handled the affair were from *Life* magazine instead of FBI agents.
There were several puzzling aspects. Why would the FBI or Secret
Service check with the desk before announcing that they were there
to pick up the Allen Grant family? It would have seemed normal for
them simply to go straight to the room.

Ross, the manager, insisted, however, that he never was told the
identity of these people. He had figured it out himself.

I called the city desk, gave this information, then returned to the
paper. There was no way I could determine just where Marina and
Marguerite Oswald and the two children had gone. If they were in the
hands of the FBI or *Life* magazine, it was certain that I wouldn't be
able to take them away or even approach them for an interview.

Later, it turned out, my suspicions were correct. Allen Grant was a
photographer from *Life*. His *Life* companion was Tommy Thompson,
a Fort Worth native, University of Texas journalism graduate, former
Houston Press city editor, and soon-to-be famous novelist. Thompson somehow had managed to corral the family—Marina and her two
daughters; Oswald's mother, Marguerite; Oswald's brother, Robert;
and Priscilla McMillan, the journalist who had interviewed Oswald

in Moscow and now was in Dallas as Marina's friend and interpreter. Thompson and Richard Stolley of *Life* had placed the group in the hotel with instructions not to leave but to order from room service anything they wanted.[13]

IT WAS STILL EARLY afternoon when I returned to the paper. Smart had taken over as city editor. It seemed to be a repeat of Friday afternoon. Crisis could be sensed as typewriters clacked. Information newly gained over the telephones was being shouted across the room.

I didn't really have a story. At most I had a single paragraph to insert into another story.

Smart, who normally showed little emotion, again seemed excited when he handed me a slip of paper with a Rawlins Street address. This, he told me, was where Ruby lived. I should make telephone calls there to find out everything possible about Ruby from anyone who knew him. "Talk to neighbors, friends, anybody. What kind of guy he is, what his politics are, what his hobbies are, everything. We need to know every little detail about him."

I found the address, names, and telephone numbers in the familiar crisscross directory. The address represented an apartment house. Of the thirteen individuals living there, I reached seven. None professed to know anything about Ruby.

I drove there anyway. Ruby lived there, all right, but police had sealed his apartment. Journalists were milling around outside. I found one resident who knew Ruby and was willing to talk. What Lowell Gaylor told me was interesting but nonpolitical, failing to hint at why Ruby shot Oswald. Ruby, he allowed, "was a regular old guy, who would ask you to come down to his club. When we'd go down, everything would be free." A man who worked late hours, Ruby frequently sat at the apartment swimming pool talking to everyone. He exercised a lot because he spent late hours at his Carousel Club, which caused him to worry about his health. One special concern for him was his loss of hair. "He was always telling me how he was going to get his hair to grow back. He even wore a ladies' bathing cap when he went in swimming." He had two dachshund dogs, one named Sheba, and he talked to them like they were kids.[14]

Afterward, back at the office, I called every Ruby listed in the telephone directory. There were only three or four in the directory. None knew him.

Smart interrupted me as I typed my notes. Someone—I believe the *Time Herald*'s nightclub writer, Don Safran (yes, we had a designated nightclub writer)— had given him the name of an old-time impresario of small-time stripper talent, C. A. "Pappy" Dolsen, who might be willing to talk about Ruby. I had never met Dolsen, but I recognized his name. During the 1940s and into the 1950s, he had operated a nightclub and restaurant known as Pappy's Showland, where entertainers as prominent as a young Bob Hope and Henny Youngman had performed. In 1956, when the Oak Cliff area where Showland was located banned alcohol sales, Dolsen closed the club. For a while he had been a casino partner with the gambler Benny Binion. Since then he had been involved in several enterprises, especially representing strippers who performed at various clubs, the most prominent being the downtown Colony Club, the Theatre Lounge in South Dallas, and Ruby's downtown Carousel Club.[15]

I reached Dolsen by telephone. He knew Ruby and agreed to talk to me about him if I met him at his office on the fifth floor of the old Interurban Building. But he didn't want me to use his name in a story. Like so many, Pappy didn't want to "get involved." I agreed half-heartedly to his proviso, assuming that he later would change his mind. And if he didn't, that would be all right, too, if not preferable. Anyway, I didn't expect any bombshells.

As I drove across downtown to the Interurban Building, I crossed Joe Sherman, our education reporter, driving in the opposite direction. We already had reporters all over the city, pursuing different possibilities. (Jim Lehrer was so preoccupied that he ran out of gas twice over this long weekend.) This second story in three all-encompassing days found us already capable, I thought, of handling a story of such magnitude.

I got there before Pappy. His office door was locked. I walked up and down the deserted hallway, thinking of questions. This was an interview where I would follow my interviewee down paths he knew best. My job was to search for those paths.

Finally, Pappy arrived, walking down the hallway in measured steps without an ounce of hurry. For now, though, he would be Mr. Dolsen, not Pappy. He was a large, heavyset man, (64, I learned), a perfect match as a movie character running a booking agency. The office, though comfortable enough, looked untouched for years. Miscellaneous papers were scattered about.

Pappy rambled on at first about how he couldn't afford to be linked with Ruby because it might hurt his business. He asked again for me not to use his name. But the matter of whether or not to use his name was dropped, not to be brought up again. I plugged away, seeking for some key that might open the door into Ruby's mind and what possibly could have led him to shoot the president's assassin. How closely did he know Ruby?

"The last time I talked to him was eight or ten days ago. He wanted to buy an act from New York. He was supposed to call me on Friday, but he didn't. Busy, I guess. Jack is the kind that if you ask him a question, he'll answer quickly and walk away. I didn't fool with him. I've never been anywhere with him. If he didn't answer quickly, he'd just walk away without a word. He's the kind of man who won't sit down and talk with you."

Pappy knew Ruby to be "quick-tempered." He once had seen him grab a misbehaving customer at one of his clubs and throw him out onto the street. Another time, he said, "I happened to be passing down Akard and Commerce and he was fighting on the street. Ruby popped the man two or three times and it ended before the police came."

I didn't have much, but Pappy's portrait of Ruby would stand the test of time. Before I left he gave me the telephone number of a man who had known Ruby for eight to ten years. Jack Cole was owner of a theatrical agency that had been supplying acts (well, strippers) for Ruby. Cole agreed to talk by telephone. His comments were less guarded than Pappy's even as they reinforced what Pappy Dolsen had told me, as my notes reveal:

> He [Ruby] was explosive with a tendency to be violent at times. He can be a close friend or a violent enemy. There was no in between. People are intimidated by him often. Physically, he's a strong man. I saw him fight on one occasion and heard of numerous times when he had fought. He was almost a pro fighter, I'd say. He handled himself that well. Once he had difficulty with a man in his place of business. He didn't want to accept the abuse the man was giving so Jack bodily took him out. There was quite a bit of fist-swinging, but Jack didn't get hit a single time. . . . I've heard that he has knocked people out. Other people besides his employees were frightened of him. What he did [shooting Oswald] surprised me, but then it didn't. I was startled but I know him to have very definite feelings. I know he is a violent enough man to do something if his convictions were so. I've also heard him make chance remarks that would lead me to believe he was a strong Kennedy supporter. And I knew he owned a pistol, a .38, which he kept at the club, presumably for protection.

Returning to the office, I turned in the information I had gained from Dolsen and Cole under the heading "Notes on Ruby personality." Some of these notes were incorporated into stories written by other reporters. As the days passed, the characterizations I had learned of the mercurial Ruby were confirmed.

DISPLAYED OVER THE ENTIRE front page of Monday's edition of the *Morning News* was Ira (Jack) Beers's sensational photograph of Ruby pointing his .38-caliber pistol toward an unsuspecting Oswald. Captured here was a dramatic historical moment. Surely no photograph in the newspaper's history had been rewarded with such display, nor would it ever—or so I thought. Beers had snapped his photo perhaps a half second before Ruby pulled his trigger. Oswald, not realizing that a fatal bullet was about to be fired, showed no recognition of that salient fact. Such a timeless photo undoubtedly would win many prizes.

Former *Times Herald* photographer Bob Jackson displays his world-famous photograph taken five decades earlier when Oswald was shot fatally by nightclub owner Jack Ruby in the Dallas police station. The pain of that distant weekend seems etched even then in Jackson's face. Allison V. Smith, photographer.

Aware of Beers's remarkable photograph, our photographer Bob Jackson, who had been on assignment in the police basement, called to me as I headed toward my desk after my visit with Dolsen. "Darwin, come and see this." This was not unusual. Bob and I were friendly. Pat and I occasionally played bridge with him and his wife. He had been assigned as photographer for Oswald's transfer.

He led me to the darkroom. There, swimming in the wash, was his own photograph of the stricken Oswald. It was instantly and unmistakably a sensational photo that made me and others in the newsroom who had already seen it gasp in astonishment. It was far more remarkable than even Beers's photo. Taken a nanosecond later, it showed Oswald's contorted face when the single bullet hit him, revealing his instant shock and pain. "This will win the Pulitzer Prize," I remarked. Others, already in the newsroom, had said the same, for there was universal recognition of its historic value. Bob's photo covered half our front page on our Monday afternoon paper, following the *News*'s earlier edition. It would be and still is one of the most memorable photographs taken in American history.

Bob, a sports car enthusiast who had been assigned to cover President Kennedy's Trade Mart luncheon, told me had chosen a good place in the police basement and was waiting for just the right moment to take the picture. He was using his Nikon S3 camera and 35 mm wide-angle lens. He admitted that he had snapped his camera button an instant earlier than he intended because he thought someone was about to step in front of him and block his view.[16]

Chapter 12

Ruby Did Not Lunge from a Cluster of Newsmen

M ONDAY MORNING, NOVEMBER 25, I returned to the police station to help George Carter in an anticipated full day of news. Most out-of-town reporters, after being away from their home offices for so many days, were gone. But important news remained, the most immediate being a rumor that Chief Curry, under growing criticism, would resign. Reporters and their broadcast compatriots waited outside the third-floor elevator door, anticipating his arrival. Maybe he would confirm or deny the rumor.

Wearing a businessman's suit and fedora hat, the police chief emerged from the elevator, walking past us without glancing our way. The others didn't even recognize him, but I did. I followed him to his office door and asked about the rumor. He emphatically denied it, then shut the door before the others, realizing now that they had missed him, appeared. They wanted to know what he said. I told them. It seemed only fair.

Later that morning in a brief appearance, Curry firmly denied rumors about resigning. City Manager Elgin Crull emphasized later that even if Curry offered to resign, he wouldn't accept it. He already

Questioned severely by the broadcast press after Oswald's death while in
police custody, Chief Curry responds while his public relations representative,
Captain Glen King, watches. Tom C. Dillard Collection, *Dallas Morning News*,
the Sixth Floor Museum at Dealey Plaza.

had assured his chief of police that his job was not in danger. Security obviously had broken down, the city manager acknowledged, but
the chief himself would conduct the investigations about it. Curry was
"discouraged and worn," said Crull, the same as anyone would be.

American citizens across the country, still shocked and dismayed,
were sending mostly hateful telegrams. I asked Glen King, assistant
police chief in charge of public relations, if I could see them. No problem, he said. I followed him into his office.

I counted fifty telegrams or letters using negative variations of "shame" in condemning Dallas. A writer from New Jersey thought the city should change its name to Kennedy. One from Columbus, Ohio, thought Love Field should adopt the new name of John F. Kennedy Memorial Airport. A Philadelphian urged Dallas police to "relinquish control to the Girl Scouts." A missive from Lafayette, California, harshly proclaimed, "Your town is dead. What will you do about it?" From Los Angeles came this telegram: "Why don't you take your filthy city off the map?"

Eighteen messages expressed sympathy. One, identified as "a friend from Colorado," sent these words: "We cry with you the ungodly crime that has blackened your city and our country [and could] happen in any city in the world. . . . This is not real Dallas and this is not true Texas." The mayor of Goldsboro, North Carolina, remembered serving in 1918 at Camp Dick, a temporary military aviation training center at Fair Park. "This love for Dallas will not be shaken by the tragedy that fate visited upon her today," he wrote. A man from Plainview, New York, sent this message to Mayor Cabell: "Please add my name to those who continue to believe in you, Mr. Mayor, the city of Dallas and the state of Texas at this time of terrible trial and mourning." A woman from Miami urged Dallas citizens not to be ashamed. "Always remember he was waving and smiling in Dallas, Texas. You were good to him and made him happy to the end."

Across the nation strong complaints and suspicions persisted, frequently directed toward Curry. To me they seemed unfair and uninformed, but I understood how those far from the scene would have criticisms. How could a known Communist and one-time defector to the Soviet Union be free to shoot the president from a sixth-floor window directly above the motorcade route? How could the suspect charged with the assassination be killed himself in the police department's own basement?

Especially noted were questions as to why Curry announced in advance the time of Oswald's Sunday morning transfer. Dallas City

Councilman Joe G. Moody said he was considering a request to inves-
tigate why Ruby was permitted to be so near to Oswald.

UNDERSTANDABLY, THERE WAS little to cheer in the now
meaningless fact that an overlooked goal had been achieved. The city's
ultraright element, under such strong encouragement, had been silent,
with one generally unseen exception. This was the arrest of six ultraright
demonstrators waiting two blocks from the Trade Mart for the president.
Their signs were harmless enough: "Kan the Kennedy Klan," "Yankees
Go Home," and "Hail Caesar."

When Police Captain Pat Gannaway heard that shots had been fired
at Dealey Plaza, he instructed detectives to arrest this group for possible
conspiracy to commit murder. Police arrested four of the five adults, four
of them related, and took them to the city jail. A sixth person, a juvenile,
was delivered to the Dallas County Juvenile Home. One of the adults was
Bobby Joiner, notorious as the racist who wore the Uncle Sam suit on
the evening of Adlai Stevenson's speech. Even though the case against
Oswald was said to be "cinched" with charges filed late Friday, police
continued to hold the demonstrators in the city jail until Monday.

A couple of weeks after the assassination, a friendly detective,
evidently surprised himself at the charge, stopped by the press room
and asked if we knew that this small group, now released, had been
confined Friday through Monday on this charge of possible conspiracy to commit murder. Since the demonstrators now were released,
none of the one or two other reporters saw much to this story, even
though it indirectly suggested that they had been arrested as possible
conspirators in the assassination. Yet police continued to hold them in
jail after concluding that Oswald had worked alone.[1]

As much as I disapproved of extremist actions in Dallas, I was
surprised that police had continued to hold this small group for
"possible conspiracy." Were they still suspected of conspiracy?
I went down the hall and asked to see the arrest report, a routine
procedure. My request was denied, but my appeal to City Manager
Crull succeeded. The words of "possible conspiracy" were removed

and replaced with the charge of "trespassing." After interviews with Chief Curry and Captain Pat Gannaway, who had ordered their arrests, my eight-paragraph story appeared on Dec. 5, 1963. "As soon as I heard the news of the assassination," Captain Gannaway told me, he instructed detectives to arrest them "since they were protesting Kennedy's visit." And on that particular day in Dallas, such an act was verboten.

On this day—Monday, November 25—three funeral services were held. Overshadowing entirely the other two, and compelling the nation's full attention, was that of John Fitzgerald Kennedy. It climaxed three days of official state services witnessed in the nation's capital city by three hundred thousand or more mourners, watched on television by millions of Americans, and concluded with burial beneath an eternal flame at the hallowed Arlington National Cemetery. The second service, in Fort Worth after being first rejected by a Dallas funeral home, was for Lee Harvey Oswald

Only a few attended Oswald's funeral and burial at Rose Hill Cemetery in Fort Worth. Volunteering journalists helped carry his casket to the gravesite for burial. Gene Gordon Collection, the Sixth Floor Museum at Dealey Plaza.

before a handful of individuals including only his close family members (wife, two children, mother, and brother). There were several funeral home attendants, some officers for security, and reporters (a few of whom volunteered to help carry Oswald's coffin to his grave). The third service, this one at Officer J. D. Tippit's Baptist church, had a packed crowd, including more than seven hundred law enforcement officers.

IN THE WEEKS AND MONTHS that followed, we local journalists, and I'm sure others elsewhere, continued to ponder the assassination and Oswald's death at the hands of a nightclub owner. Our own friends excitedly advised us of possible conspiracies, most of them easily dismissed. We still had to cover routine local news, but what we all discussed and tried to do as best we could—sometimes in tandem, other times individually—was to find an angle that might lead to missing information and Oswald's cohorts or Ruby's unusual connection.

Was Oswald holding secrets that Ruby needed to silence? Did Ruby's alleged mob connections have anything to do with it? Were gunmen behind the wooden fence at Dealey Plaza? Exactly how many shots were fired? Why had Oswald made a recent visit to Mexico City with stops at the Cuban and Soviet embassies? The press, especially reporters from our local newspapers, continued their quests for new information, as did major newspapers such as the *New York Times* and news magazines such as *Time*.

Most important, and of lasting note, only a week after the assassination, President Johnson created by executive order on November 29 a high-powered commission to be headed by no less than Chief Justice Earl Warren. He charged it with investigating all aspects of the assassination, the murder of Officer Tippit, and Ruby's fatal shooting of Oswald. The commission began its work right away. Before its year-long effort was completed, it had held private interviews with more than five hundred individuals and found more than three thousand exhibits of photographs, copies of official documents, letters, diagrams, and more.

The US Government Printing Office published 235,000 copies of the single volume, named as the *Report of the Warren Commission on the Assassination of President Kennedy*, and 5,600 copies of the twenty-six-volume set entitled *Hearings before the President's Commission on the Assassination of President Kennedy*. The original price for the volumes was seventy-six dollars. Despite the expense, I purchased both the single volume and the twenty-six volumes.

The single summary book was excellent, written in narrative format and filled with names and details that I'm sure none of us had been fully aware of. Individual staff members immediately read the report and originated many follow-up stories. It held little-known information on Oswald's childhood in a sixty-three-page biographical portrait, and twenty-eight pages were devoted to his limited financial resources.

The first fifteen volumes of the set contained complete transcripts of some 550 witnesses' sworn testimony. The remaining eleven volumes showed copies of documents, photographs, letters, diagrams, and other evidence. These volumes were above the interest level or pocketbooks of most citizens, but their important information made them essential acquisitions for major libraries and serious students, scholars, and writers. Finally, the commission concluded that Oswald alone had assassinated the president and wounded Governor Connally, and that Ruby had acted alone in murdering Oswald.

Unfortunately, it also declared that Jack Ruby was able to shoot Oswald because "the presence of a great mass of press representatives created an extraordinary security problem," and furthermore that "a swarm of news people in the basement substantially limited" police ability to detect the presence of unauthorized persons. So many sources, including the official report of the Dallas Police Department, declared that Ruby had broken unnoticed from "a crowd of news reporters and television men." Dallas Police public relations chief Glen King told the American Society of Newspaper Editors that there was "no question" but that the newsmen had made it possible for Ruby to commit the crime. The *New York Times* flatly observed that Ruby "lunged from a cluster of newsmen" to shoot Oswald. These descriptions, critical to an understanding of what happened that morning, were not just overstated; they were wrong, creating a false impression lasting to this day.[2]

Ruby did not break from "a crowd of news reporters and television men." The police department's own study showed that 110 persons were in the basement and only 36 of them were journalists. Seventy-four were law officers of some kind—some wearing police uniforms, some detectives in civilian clothing, some uniformed or plain-clothed sheriff's deputies, and others representing law enforcement. Many of them were there from mere curiosity. At the time Ruby burst forward with his pistol, he was standing next to Detective Blackie Harrison, an officer he had known for twelve years, not from "a cluster of newsmen."[3]

The greater question is, How did Ruby gain entrance? Why was he not challenged on the third floor on Friday and Saturday or at the midnight press conference, where his proximity to Oswald perhaps was closer than on Sunday morning? Moreover, did the presence of the press permit Ruby to enter the basement without question, or did he walk down that auto ramp because security precautions were inadequate?

Ruby, as we have seen, was there out of curiosity, the same curiosity that had compelled him to be present for the Friday midnight press conference for Oswald at which he interacted with a number of detectives and District Attorney Henry Wade. Ruby was among the newsmen at the police station's third floor Friday and Saturday. (I may have seen him in the Saturday crowd, but I wouldn't have recognized him.)

There remained in the minds of some conspiracy speculators the idea that Ruby had secret connections—perhaps with mob elements—that gave him inside knowledge for the time of Oswald's transfer. If he had gone to the basement with the notion of shooting Oswald, he surely would have arrived before 10:00 a.m. instead of more than an hour later. It was the third consecutive day he had been in the police station within shooting range of Oswald. The conclusive evidence was that he had impulsively shot Oswald very soon after he walked into the police basement.

ONE OF MY POST-ASSASSINATION stories was to interview Oswald's one-time fellow workers at the Jaggars-Chiles-Stovall printing firm, where he worked in its photography department from October 1962 to May 1963. My story appeared on November 29 under a three-column headline, "Co-Worker Calls Oswald Intelligent but Obnoxious," with a small kicker: "A Real Kookie Guy."

The company required one important condition. I could identify neither the firm by name nor the names of those interviewed. The company did "classified work" for the federal government, but never involving Oswald. My interviews included Oswald's immediate supervisor, John Graef, head of the photography department.

A nearly unanimous opinion of Oswald's fellow workers was that he was obnoxious. One employee said there "must have been three or four persons he had run-ins with." Another said nearly three-fourths of his fellow workers had threatened to "knock his block off." Oswald, one person said, seldom smiled or laughed or talked with others. "He was definitely a loner." An example of rude behavior occurred when he would barge into a small space for two darkroom developing sinks with barely enough space for one person. He paid no attention to their complaints. On some days he brought Russian magazines and copies of the *Daily Worker* to work. Finally, the company fired Oswald for incompetence. His next job was at the Texas School Book Depository.

Far more explosive were reports in both local papers and across the nation that some Dallas elementary schoolchildren, inured by hearing grown-ups or parents express their hatred of Kennedy, had cheered upon hearing the news that he had been killed. School officials in both the Dallas and suburban Richardson districts vehemently denied this, contending that the students cheered when told they would be released from school for the rest of the day. Without knowing for sure, I thought both explanations contained elements of truth.

Other stories generally failed to arouse such emotions. Governor Connally's interview from the hospital on November 28 brought full coverage. Some news stories arose from the always publicity-minded assassin's mother, Marguerite Oswald. My National Guard friend, Eddie Hughes, wrote an interesting story in which she claimed unconvincingly that her son had wanted to be a writer. Many stories dealt with fundraising efforts for police officer Tippit's widow and family, a principal one sponsored by the *Times Herald* and its family of KRLD television and radio stations. Less than a few days after his death, the fund reached $30,000 with $15,000 more pledged. Still other stories appearing by December 1 involved discussions of what sort of monument, if any, should be erected for the slain president. On Sunday, December 1, Jim Lehrer wrote that Oswald's post office box application listed just two names—Fair Play for Cuba and the American Civil Liberties Union.

Still the stories continued: Oswald as a schoolboy truant in New York City and a "pleasant little boy" in Fort Worth; unfounded claims that a man resembling Oswald had been practicing at a gun range near Grand Prairie; names of individuals in a small notebook found in his room at 1026 North Beckley; Ruth Paine's attempts to teach him how to drive a car; and Marina Oswald, without her husband's knowledge, secretly having had their daughter, June, baptized at an Eastern Orthodox Church.

ONE OF THE FRONT-PAGE stories came on December 6, 1964, revealing that Oswald was the person who took the unsuccessful shot at Edwin A. Walker. Marina confirmed this when on February 3, 1964, she was the first person to testify to the Warren Commission. When she had asked Oswald why he wanted to kill Walker, he told her because he was "a very bad man, that he was a fascist, that he was the leader of a fascist organization . . . [and that] if someone had killed Hitler in time it would have saved many lives."[4]

I was surprised the first week in December when Pat came home from school and told me that her friend, fellow fourth-grade teacher Eleanor Cowan, had been suspended by the crotchety, dictatorial, and long-time school superintendent W. T. White because of a letter she wrote that appeared in *Time* magazine's December 6 issue. Eleanor, a quiet but strong-minded person with avowed Democratic persuasions, expressed what seldom was said in these early post-assassination days, reminding readers of the city's conservative viewpoints that earlier had been so critical of President Kennedy. Dallas was not entirely guilt free, she contended, but many of the city's leaders were falsely stressing that Oswald was an "outsider," ignoring his ties to Dallas and Fort Worth.

Eleanor asserted that "Dallas is as responsible as anyone, if not through action through apathy" because of its right-wing absolutism. No matter what President Kennedy had favored, she wrote, Dallas's leaders and its daily newspapers had been obstinate in criticizing him and his policies. "I have tried to instill in my students a respect for the leaders of our country," she wrote. "How can they ever grow up to be good citizens when the newspapers, their parents, and the leaders of their own city preach dissension?"[5] For these observations the superintendent suspended her.

I approached Ken Smart next morning with that information. I wanted to write a story about it. Did teachers in Dallas not have free speech? Ken listened carefully, agreeing that White's action was unpardonable. He concluded, though, that breaking this story might bring further harm to Eleanor. Why not wait a few days, he said, to see what might happen next? I argued briefly for prompt publication, but to no avail.

Just as I had feared, our delay cost us an exclusive story. The *Morning News* published the news under the byline of Carlos Conde, a journalism friend of mine at the University of Texas now covering education for the *News*.[6] Eleanor's suspension was not merely a local story; it became national news. Official Dallas had taken yet another step to repress free speech.

The Associated Press's lengthy story quoted Greg Olds as declaring that her suspension violated her First Amendment rights and must be lifted immediately. School board president R. B. Gilmore, justifying

White's action, complained that Eleanor had identified herself as a teacher in the letter rather than acting as "a plain citizen."[7]

White commented that her suspension was effective until "an investigation" was completed. Obviously chagrined over the wide amount of critical nationwide attention, he next issued this statement: "Mrs. Eleanor Cowan came by this afternoon. We had a very pleasant informal conference. We are pleased that she will return to the classroom tomorrow." The suspension had lasted two days. So much for the "investigation."[8]

An explosion of support for her arose afterward through a series of letters to the editor, especially in the *Times Herald*, all expressing support for her and condemnation of the superintendent's actions. One came from a prominent and wealthy Dallas citizen, Everett L. DeGolyer Jr., whose letter bore the headline "Another Horror." DeGolyer, a liberal-minded oilman, said White's suspension of his teacher was "an immensely foolish action."

The *Times Herald*'s timid editorial support of Eleanor declared her reinstatement to be "merited." A spirited reply by a reader begged to differ with its understated tone. The situation had called out for "a fearless pronouncement that the suspension WAS WRONG," said the writer, Kim Carpenter. Another letter writer, Elsie Wik Johnson, declared that "again I'm ashamed of my city." In a harsh but justifiable letter, Jim Piles declared that it was about time that "we 'average citizens' speak up against what has been going on in the city that we love, and there was nothing in her letter [that] was not the truth as the majority of us see it."[9]

One result was that a group of prominent Presbyterian ministers voted to establish a nine-member committee to study freedom of speech in the school system. Thomas Fry, pastor of the First Presbyterian Church, met within the week with Superintendent White to discuss the situation. The committee's purpose, he said, was to know the facts and issues of Eleanor Cowan's suspension. While the committee's purpose was short-lived, the actions of these Presbyterian ministers surely made a strong statement.[10]

Dallas's conservative leaders continued to defend the city. Oswald was an outsider, so many asserted, failing to acknowledge his past ties to our city with periodic residences in both Dallas and Fort Worth, that our ultraconservative city had been a haven for zealots who had attacked Stevenson only a month earlier, and that our city had feared so much about the president's safety here.

As the New Year arrived, though, Stanley Marcus, the rare liberal member of the Dallas Citizens Council and president of Neiman Marcus bought half-page advertisements in both the *Times Herald* and *Dallas Morning News* under the retail store's logo with his comments entitled "What's Right With Dallas?" Acknowledging the city's strengths, Marcus pointed to its unfortunate smugness, concluding, "Let's have more 'fair play' for legitimate differences of opinion, less coverup for our obvious deficiencies, less boasting about our attainments, more moral indignation by all of us when we see human rights infringed upon. Then we won't have to worry about the 'Dallas Image'—it will take care of itself."[11]

IN MARCH 1964, TOWARD the end of the Warren Commission's exhaustive work, a young Dallas man named James Richard Worrell Jr. was scheduled to testify as an eyewitness. Few of us knew anything of him or what he might say, but any eyewitness could be important.

Smart asked me to interview him. Worrell, easily located, met me in the newsroom shortly before his interview in the nation's capital. A clean-looking 20-year-old youth and recent local high school student, Worrell sat alongside my desk as we talked. He would tell the Warren Commission, he said, that immediately after shots were fired, he saw a man run from the rear entrance of the depository and disappear.[12]

Worrell had skipped school to see the president, first going to Love Field but finding it so crowded that he decided instead to try downtown. He said he was standing directly beneath the depository's sixth floor when he heard the first shot. "I heard four shots, I don't care what they say," he told me. He said he looked directly above and saw a rifle extending from the high building window. "I looked up real quick and saw the barrel fire again. I looked to see where it hit and saw President Kennedy hit in the back of the head. Then I looked up again and saw it fire a third time." By that short period of time, though, he was fearfully "moving out." He thought he heard a fourth shot as he ran around to the back of the building.

He crossed Houston Street and, out of breath, leaned against a building. "I saw somebody strike out of the back door . . . I just saw his back and couldn't say who it was. He came out and bolted alongside the building parallel to Elm and then he cut to his right [toward Pacific Avenue]. . . . He was sure running like everything." Worrell thought he was about two hundred feet from the man. He saw no one else leave.

I asked why he had felt compelled to run behind the building. "Because everybody was hitting the ground and you never know how many might have been up there or how many were to get it." He said the man had "dark hair" and wore a dark sports coat. He carried nothing, and he wasn't looking behind him in his mad dash.

The next day he called Farmers Branch police to tell his story. Afterward he contacted the Dallas police. "The police came out and got me and took me downtown. I told the FBI and another policeman what I had seen." Since then he had heard no more from any of these or other law enforcement agencies.

I was certainly intrigued by Worrell's story, and I believed him to be telling the truth as he saw it. The Warren Commission, however, discounted his testimony. Its one-volume summary described it this way: "One witness, James R. Worrell, Jr., claims to have seen a man running from the rear of the building shortly after the assassination, but in testimony before the Commission he stated that he could not see his face." Worrell is still mentioned in some assassination conspiracy sites existing on the internet.

His recollections would feed the appetites of the growing number of conspiracy seekers, although as far as I knew he personally took no part in doubting the Warren Commission's eventual findings.

My interview with him was published on March 6, 1964, under the headline, "Dallasite Says Man Fled from Assassination Site."

On November 5, 1966, Worrell, employed as a driver for a local retail store, died from a severe head injury when his motorcycle went out of control. His death became fodder for the increasing number of conspiracy theorists.

Another premature death, still mentioned by conspiracy theorists, included my 30-year-old fellow *Times Herald* reporter Jim Koethe, whom I relieved at the police station that Saturday after the assassination. On September 21, 1964, he was found dead in his East Dallas apartment. His death, police said, was caused by an unknown assailant who must have used a "karate chop" to break his neck. Koethe's case was never solved, although Dallas police came to believe that an individual named Larry Earl Reno was guilty. To the disbelief of *Times Herald* reporters who knew Koethe very well, the police homicide detectives contended unofficially that there must have been a homosexual relationship between the two. Since they had Reno in custody for burglary with more conclusive evidence, Reno was convicted of that crime. Reported missing from Koethe's apartment were his notes for a book he had been writing about the assassination. Koethe's official death certificate stated that his cause of death was pending autopsy results.

THREE DAYS AFTER MY Worrell interview, I reported to work as usual at 7:00 or so on the early Saturday morning of March 7, 1964. Once again my city editor, Smart, greeted me with a slip of paper bearing an address: 629 Belt Line Road, in suburban Richardson. This, Ken said, was where Marina Oswald now lived with her small daughter, June, and five-month-old Rachel. Go there and see if you can interview her, he told me.

Gulp. With no appointment, this seemed doubtful. This early in the morning? Was she living alone? Wasn't her security with her? Until now, the only sit-down interviews she had given were to Dallas police, the FBI, and Secret Service; lengthy sessions with the Warren Commission in early February (aided by two interpreters); and a rare television interview by Eddie Barker, news director for Dallas's KRLD-TV.

I had no idea that weeks earlier, Chief Justice Warren, speaking on behalf of the Warren Commission, assured her at her own request that she now was "perfectly free" to live a normal life "without any interference from anyone." Her attorney John M. Thorne said that "at this time she can walk among people with her head held high. She has nothing to hide. She is not afraid."[13]

How Ken found her address he didn't say, and I didn't ask, but I was both nervous and pleased. I imagined that she would be surrounded by attorneys or friends, even now. But I'd make a try. Her testimony to the Warren Commission was not yet released.

I drove to Belt Line Road to her address and easily found her modest brick house. Parking in front, I gathered my courage and rang the doorbell twice before the door opened. There stood Marina— Marina without a doubt. "Excuse me, I'm not awake yet," she said, looking as pretty as so many photographs had revealed.

I explained my mission. She responded politely that her lawyer insisted that she not be interviewed without his knowledge and presence. I understood that; it was what I had expected. It had become obvious to America and the world that she was innocent of her husband's brutal murders, and now she had been left to raise two small children.

She deserved, I felt, all the privacy she could gain. It had been only three months since her husband had assassinated the nation's president. Now she was fending alone for herself and her children, choosing to stay here while still a citizen of the Soviet Union. (She became an American citizen in 1989.)

Here I was, though, an inquisitive reporter. I would not push too hard, although at this point it would have been awkward for me to simply apologize and leave. I told her that I understood her position, but would she please permit me to come inside to use her telephone to inform my office. She could have said no, but she readily agreed, leading me into her kitchen through her unfurnished living room with a highly polished hardwood floor. She explained that she had been up until about two-thirty in the morning working on that floor. "The furniture is out," she said, explaining the empty living room and seeming to be a bit embarrassed about it. Her children were still asleep in a bedroom.

Marina spoke in a soft, accented voice. I couldn't understand all her words, but without prodding she said she was so tired of publicity and just wanted a normal life. As I sat down at her kitchen table, she excused herself to go to the bathroom, where she obviously dabbed her face with water. She returned visibly refreshed, an attractive lady.

When I took out my pencil—prematurely, it now seems obvious— she anticipated my need. "You need paper?" she asked. Without waiting for my response, she tore off a half sheet of white paper for me.

I assured her that I would not reveal her address. She tossed up her arm. "Oh, everybody knows where I live," she said, exasperated. I said I would not push her further, and as I began thanking her she walked to the front door with me, still chatting amiably. Opening the door for me, she said a final farewell as I walked away without even having called the office.

It had not really been an interview, but I had seen her, conversed pleasantly with her, and walked through part of her house. I could do something with that.

Back at the office I wrote a brief story, published on the front page of next day's Sunday edition. The editors displayed it with a border around three columns, a stock single-column photo of her, and a simple headline, "A Visit With Marina."[14] I was happy that I had managed to make something out of so few minutes with her. My story earned a lot of undeserved praise.

Looking back, I think I could have and should have engaged her longer. I believe she would have responded. I should have asked, "How about the children?" "Do you want to stay in this country?" "What sort of job do you want to find?" Simple things like that.

I was alarmed, though, to see that she, confronted by an unknown visitor such as me, would invite a stranger into her house. Was there no security for her? I might have been a "patriot" out for revenge for this Soviet woman who had been married to the president's assassin. After finishing my short feature, I called one of her attorneys,

William A. McKenzie, and stressed how dangerous it was for her to let a stranger into her house. McKenzie thanked me and assured me that she would be further assisted with security. He also told me that he knew she had been up until 2:30 a.m. polishing that living room floor.

A year or so later Marina married Kenneth Porter. They had two additional children, both boys. Marina's two daughters and the new sons would grow up in the suburban town of Rockwall, northeast of Dallas, living like any other American youngsters. For a time Marina worked as a retail salesperson in the Army/Navy store near the SMU campus, where I had become a journalism professor. I saw her there a couple of times cheerfully waiting on customers. As far as I could tell, they had no idea who this attractive woman was. I was discreet on these occasions, not calling attention to her and never speaking to her.

GENE GUINN, ONE OF THE demonstrators at Adlai Stevenson's speech and one of the six men arrested for holding anti-JFK signs along the motorcade route near the Trade Mart prior to the assassination, called me in September 1964. He had filed a civil suit seeking damages of $150 against the Dallas Police Department. He said he had been suffering from a stomach ulcer during his three-day confinement in jail. Police offered him only two aspirins for relief. When finally released, he contended he was in such bad shape that doctors had to administer whole blood and other medication "in order to preserve" his life. He wanted me to attend the trial and write a story about it. The courthouse was now my beat, so I was happy to say I would.

At the hearing, without an attorney to represent him, Guinn presented his case. At one point he mentioned a fact from my earlier story about his arrest. Justice of the Peace Charles Davis, presiding, declared that this was hearsay and inadmissible.

Guinn quickly retorted. "But your honor, the reporter who wrote it is here in the courtroom and he could testify." That was me. So Davis told me to take the witness stand and he swore me in. I answered a few of Guinn's questions and some from the police's attorney. Finally, after not much ado, Justice of the Peace Davis ruled that Guinn had failed to present sufficient evidence of malice and dismissed the case.[15]

I congratulated Guinn for having the courage to file suit and represent himself without attorney, no matter how much I disagreed with his anti-JFK picketing. Guinn, a Korean War veteran, would appear in the news no more. My stories about him, placed on the inside of the paper under a one-column headline, didn't arouse much interest.

Journalists' involvement, a considerable factor in the assassination and its investigation, took on an extra dimension shortly before Jack Ruby stood trial. Melvin Belli, the flamboyant attorney from California, assumed Ruby's defense from Ruby's first attorney, Tom Howard, a man who knew his way around the courthouse, but Ruby's scattered family members wanted more than that. In early December they arranged for Belli to take over.

Belli, starting quickly with a great deal of Hollywood flair, must have looked for possible help from every individual even remotely involved in the pending case. He issued a wide range of subpoenas, including for many of our reporters "to personally appear" in Ruby's upcoming murder trial in Judge Joe B. Brown's Criminal District Court. This included me, based surely on my bylines. Most of us were notified by a sheriff's deputy who visited the newsroom to pass out our subpoenas. (I still have mine as a souvenir.) I had not witnessed Oswald's death, had not met Ruby, nor had I ever been in Ruby's Carousel nightclub, so I was puzzled as to what might be expected of me. But I was ordered with other journalists to appear at the courthouse on Monday, February 10, 1964. As it happened, neither I nor any of the other reporters went or were called upon to testify.

As the world soon came to know, Belli's unsuccessful defense was based on his unusual claim that Ruby had shot Oswald while under a psychomotor epileptic seizure. The claim was torn to shreds by District Attorney Wade and prosecutor Bill Alexander. The jury's verdict, returned on March 14 after deliberating for just more than two hours, declared Ruby guilty of murder and sentenced him to death in the electric chair.

I later saw Ruby for the first time when he was permitted to hold a news conference at the courthouse. During this brief exposure,

I became convinced, as I had heard others often speculate, that he had lost his mind during confinement. His rambling comments, one uninterrupted sentence following another, were incoherent. Ruby died in 1967 of cancer before a final jurisdictional decision on his appeals.

ONE MORNING, PROBABLY in early March, as I got off the newsroom elevator, several of my journalism mates rushed to tell me that my picture was in a new book about the assassination. An advance copy had been sent to the paper. I had no idea I would be in one of the pictures. *Four Days: The Historical Record of the Death of President Kennedy* was, as I remember, the first significant book about the assassination weekend. My photo, without identification, showed me taking notes as I stood next to homicide detectives Marvin Johnson and L. D. Montgomery outside the depository entrance. The book was a handsome, oversized joint effort by United Press International and American Heritage, and as the title indicated, it was dedicated to the four days beginning with the Kennedys' visit to Fort Worth.

I had no idea that the picture had been taken, but news photographers had been at every critical site during that awful weekend. As I thumbed through *Four Days*, I saw my good friend Jack Moseley (wearing glasses) standing just behind the president's side outside Hotel Texas before leaving for Dallas. (I soon would be best man in Jack's wedding to Margaret Burris, whom I also knew at the *Press*.) I could see in the photo of the police station's crowded third floor my friend and television newsman Michael Whittaker standing just under the outstretched arms of a plainclothes officer holding aloft Oswald's rifle. And just to the right of the detective was Peggy Simpson of the Associated Press, the only female reporter visible (and one of only two or three women to be directly involved in covering the assassination). Bob Jackson's famous Oswald's photograph was closely cropped and expanded to two full pages. (*Four Days* would not become a collector's invaluable item. So many thousands were printed that today one can be bought for a few dollars.)

In the days to come, many of our reporters' images or quotes would appear in other books. Three more images of me would appear, usually without identification. Similar to the photograph in *Four Days*, one showed me in front of the depository interviewing Detective Montgomery holding the lengthy paper bag that Oswald had used to conceal his rifle.

As the Pulitzer Prizes were being considered, some thought that both the *Times Herald* and *Morning News* might be nominated for best team effort in 1963. As finally realized, there was no such category, but if there had been, the *Times Herald* brass concluded that they should have won such an award. As a morning newspaper, the *News* had more than half a day to gather and polish its stories and photographs before press time. This was an advantage of twelve hours or so before its home edition deadline at midnight or so. We at the *Times Herald* had worked under so much greater pressure with an immediate deadline rather than a late-night deadline.

In fact, only two Pulitzer Prizes were awarded for journalistic work in the assassination. One in the photography category went to Bob Jackson, for his dramatic photo of Ruby shooting Oswald, and the other in national reporting to UPI reporter Merriman Smith for his exclusive report from the press car about shots being fired at the president.

Chapter 13

What Motivated the Assassin?

I N THE APPENDIX I will attempt to briefly ascribe motives of the nation's first three assassins, Booth, Guiteau, and Czolgosz, for killing presidents Lincoln, Garfield, and McKinley, respectively. Now, however, I turn more fully to the background of the fourth assassin, Lee Harvey Oswald, emphasizing the formative years of this young man who used his cheap Italian-made rifle to shock the nation and world. What possible factors, we wonder, may have combined to prompt a self-proclaimed Marxist such as Oswald to commit an act of such consequence against his own nation and the world? He had no significant political experience, no social status, no educational credentials, not even a high school diploma. Why would he assassinate a president for whom, unlike his three motivated predecessors, he had not expressed personal anger or hatred?

His older brother, Robert Lee Oswald, believed that to understand why Lee assassinated John F. Kennedy one needed "to look at what transpired before that, everything from childhood on up."[1] I hope to help in that assignment in the following pages, based primarily on the Warren Commission's often neglected but extensive interviews of family members and psychologists who best knew young Oswald and his family life.

The outbreak of mass shootings by maladjusted young individuals in recent years has led to significant research into their backgrounds and formative years. These recently angered perpetrators invariably share unfortunate childhoods, as demonstrated by their inability to make social adjustments, victimization by bullies (verbal and/or physical), failure to make friends, loneliness, school problems (notably excessive truancy), poor school grades, depression, and fascination with violent topics. Oswald's formative years include all these.[2]

Instead of shooting large numbers of unknown individuals in specific places such as schools, shopping malls, or churches, Oswald chose to kill the chief executive of our nation's democratic society. President Kennedy's death, Oswald rationalized, would be an eventual step toward the adoption one day of a Marxist society, a system that he believed, if properly instituted, would offer great advantages to millions of ordinary individuals. His target was the elimination of the democratic capitalistic system, led by its president. As an early and heroic proponent of a worldwide transition to Marxism, Oswald fantasized that future histories might proclaim him as one of the heroes who helped bring about its eventual adoption.

Unlike the weeks he spent making plans to shoot the "fascist" former general Edwin A. Walker, at best he had only a short notice to know specifically that President Kennedy would pass below his place of employment. A map of the motorcade's route with street names was published on the front page of the *Times Herald* on Thursday, November 21. A written description was published in the *Morning News* on Tuesday, November 19. The *Times Herald* put a map of the route on its front page on the morning of the twenty-second. To take advantage of his situation at the conveniently located Texas School Book Depository, Oswald had to decide quickly and move fast. Thus, he visited Marina in Irving that Thursday evening, November 21, one day earlier than his normal Friday routine. This gave him time to retrieve his rifle from Mrs. Paine's garage and next morning bring it, concealed in a large paper bag, to his sixth-floor vantage point above the motorcade's route to the Trade Mart.

Lee Harvey Oswald began life in New Orleans on October 18, 1939. He was the youngest of three sons of his widowed and self-indulgent mother, Marguerite Frances Claverie Oswald. He had an older half brother, John Edward Pic, born in 1932, not long before Marguerite and her first husband divorced. Marguerite's second husband, Robert Oswald, was father of Lee's other brother, Robert Lee Oswald, born in 1934. Five years later came Lee, unfortunately born two months after his father had died of natural causes. In his early childhood Lee was never close to his older brothers, both of whom left their mother, Marguerite, at their first opportunity.

In his first years, Lee's mother usually left her youngest son to the care of others during her long working hours. He lived for long sequences with Marguerite's older sister, Lillian Claverie Murret, who with her husband already had five of their own children. Testifying at length (sixty-five pages) to the Warren Commission, Mrs. Murret generously described three-year-old Lee as "really a cute child, very friendly. . . . I would take him to town, and when I would he would have on one of these little sailor suits, and he really looked cute, and he would holler, 'Hi,' to everybody, and people in town would stop him and say, 'What an adorable child he is.'"[3] Cute as he was, even in these early years while his aunt got her own children ready for school, Lee developed a habit of "slipping out of the house in his nightclothes and sitting down in somebody's kitchen" just a few doors away.[4]

Hard times and little money, a lifelong problem for his mother Marguerite, also prompted her to place Lee, age three, and his brothers as so-called half orphans at the Evangelical Lutheran Bethlehem Orphan Asylum in New Orleans. ("Half-orphans" referred to those with single parents who worked full-time.)

In 1944 Marguerite, anticipating a marriage to a well-paid traveling industrial engineer, briefly withdrew all three sons from the orphanage. She soon changed her mind, though, asking it to take back all three children on a full-time basis because she wanted to travel with her soon-to-be husband, Edwin Ekdahl, on his job. "Under the circum-stances," she rationalized, "it is impossible for us to take the children traveling, living at hotels and attempting to arrange for their schooling. For this reason I think you will understand better why I wish to have the boys return to the house." The orphanage rejected her request.[5]

In 1945 Lee, now six, the two older boys, and Marguerite and her husband moved to Dallas, where Ekdahl expected to be transferred. Marital problems had emerged, though. Following another move in 1946 to Benbrook, a Fort Worth suburb, the couple alternately sepa-rated, then reconciled, then separated again, and divorced finally in 1948. Lee's brothers departed as soon as they were old enough: John enlisted in the Coast Guard at 17 and Robert soon after joined the Marine Corps. Both had determined to leave home as soon as possible.[6] Asked why by a Warren Commission inquisitor, John replied, "The yoke of depression from my mother."[7]

John's continuing anger toward his mother, shared by Robert and Lee, was amply attested in his Warren Commission interview. "She didn't have many friends and usually the new friends she made she didn't keep very long. . . . I remember every time we moved she always had fights with the neighbors or something or another."[8] He also believed that anything Lee had done—referring to the assassination—"was aided with a little extra push from his mother in the living conditions that she presented to him."[9]

In 1964 the commission interviewed Oswald's relatives, neigh-bors, and a few of his earlier junior high school associates. One of his few friends at New Orleans's Beauregard Junior High, Edward Voebel, said Oswald "was living in his own world,"[10] not interested in making other friends. Bennierita Smith, who knew of him at school but was not a friend, said her best recollection of him was that the only friend he had was Voebel. "As far as mixing with other people, he didn't," she said.[11]

Lee was frequently apart from his too-busy mother, who through-out her life would hold one after another short-term sales jobs requiring long hours. In the fourth grade, Oswald's IQ was recorded at 103. His grades were below average. His teacher described him as a lonely boy, quiet, shy, and unable to make friends. He was smart enough, but he often stayed home alone while his mother worked. (He did suffer from one academic disability—dyslexia, a difficulty in identifying proper letter sequence in spelling, evident later in his handwritten letters, such as his frequent mistake in spelling "etc." as "ect.")

NOW CAME ANOTHER change. After three years in Fort Worth, Lee's mother moved with him to the Bronx in New York City. There, Lee also failed at making friends. Classmates taunted him for his Texas accent and unfamiliar blue jeans. More and more he stayed home instead of going to school. He preferred to be alone at the apartment, watching television and reading books and magazines. His unconcerned mother, busy with work, paid little concern to his truancy.

His school absences, a growing problem, caught the attention of authorities. At the age of 13, he underwent interviews and studies for three weeks at the school district's Youth House. On the Wechsler Intelligence Scale for Children, he scored an IQ of 118. Social worker Evelyn Strickland noted in her assessment that young Oswald stayed at home by himself most of the time, that he read books (selected by himself from the public library), watched television, and usually made his own meals. Sometimes he argued with his mother because there wasn't enough food in the house for him to make his own supper.

In her lengthy study Strickland described Lee as a "seriously detached, withdrawn youngster" . . . [who] spent all his time alone because he didn't make friends with the boys in his neighborhood. He withdrew into a completely solitary and detached existence where he did as he wanted and he didn't have to live by any rules or come into contact with people. He stayed in bed until eleven or twelve [in the morning], got up and made himself something to eat and then sat and looked at magazines. . . . He just felt his mother 'never gave a damn' for him."[12]

When Strickland asked him to talk about his "fantasy life," he refused, saying this was his "own business." But finally, he answered

Oswald, about 15 years old, poses at the Bronx Zoo. His mother and he moved
from Texas to live in New York City. Oswald was about this age when he
privately declared himself to be a Marxist. AP photo.

certain questions. He acknowledged that his fantasies sometimes involved being powerful and sometimes about "hurting or killing people."[13] When asked for further details, he refused.

"He feels almost as if there is a veil between him and other people through which they cannot reach him, but he prefers this veil to remain intact," Strickland wrote. "He admitted, however, the tearing aside of the veil in talking to a social worker was not as painfel [sic] as he would have anticipated."[14]

Strickland summarized: "Despite the fact that he is very hard to reach, Lee seems to have some ability to relate which in view of the solitary existence he has been leading, is somewhat surprising. There is a rather pleasant, appealing quality about this emotionally starved, affectionless youngster which grows as one speaks to him, and it seems fairly clear that he has detached himself from the world around him because no one in it ever met any of his needs for love."[15] There were indications, Strickland thought, "that he has suffered serious personality damage but if he can receive help quickly this might be repaired to some extent." His mother, Strickland concluded after talking with her, was "a very self-possessed . . . superficially affable . . . defensive, rigid, self-involved person."[16]

The Youth House's chief psychiatrist, Dr. Renatus Hartogs, reflected similar thoughts in his assessment on May 1, 1953. He wrote, "Lee has to be diagnosed as [having] personality pattern disturbance with schizoid features and passive-aggressive tendencies."[17] He described him "as an emotionally, quite disturbed youngster who suffers under the impact of really emotional isolation and deprivation, lack of affection, absence of family life and rejection by a self-involved and conflicted mother." Nine years later (after the assassination) the Warren Commission interviewed Hartogs, who still remembered Oswald. "When I examined him I found him to have definite traits of dangerousness. In other words, this child had a potential for explosive, aggressive, assaultive acting out which was rather unusual to find in a child who was sent to Youth House on such a mild charge of truancy from a school."[18] Hartogs had recommended that he be placed at the Youth

House for an indefinite period, treated preferably under the supervision of a male clinician who would act as a "father figure."[19]

But his mother refused to permit him to stay at Youth House for the recommended treatment. Lee returned to his Bronx school under probation. More intransigent now, he refused to salute the American flag, did as little schoolwork as he could, angered easily, and sailed paper airplanes around the classroom. Marguerite Oswald decided to take her troubled son back to New Orleans.

We know that as an adolescent, having encountered Marxism's idealistic doctrines in his random but somewhat intensive reading, he sought to escape his difficult and lonely life, proclaiming at the age of 15 to be a follower of Marxism, presumably as practiced in the Soviet Union. In his solitary existence, he found refuge through his dreams that Marxism one day would prevail as the governing body of the nation—perhaps the world—and that he himself possibly could become recognized as a pioneer in bringing about such a dramatic transition.

It was during this turbulent time in the Bronx that young Oswald, through his own independent reading at this young age, made a life-long decision. "I am a Marxist and have been studying socialist principles for well over fifteen months," he declared in October 1956 in a letter to *The Socialist Call* magazine. He said as a new subscriber he wanted information about its Youth League. "I would like to know if there is a branch in my area, how to join."[20]

Much of Oswald's following years are more familiar—especially his surprising enlistment in the Marine Corps in 1956 following that of his brother Robert. Up to this point Lee had moved to a different location with his mother some twenty times.[21]

In the marine barracks he did not conceal his radical political views despite his military enlistment. He became the butt of jokes. His open efforts to learn Russian brought derision and nicknames— Oswaldskovich and Ozzie Rabbit. Military assignments in Japan and the Philippines as a radar operator failed to make a dent in his continuing interest in the Soviet Union. He enjoyed enticing marine

As soon as he turned 17, Oswald, despite his political beliefs, enlisted in the US Marine Corps. There, though, he continued to profess his Marxist viewpoints. Gary Cornwell Collection, the Sixth Floor Museum at Dealey Plaza.

officers into arguments about foreign affairs and then showing them his superior knowledge of the subject. He dropped his solitary habits in the Far East, often joining others in visits to nightclubs. He even had dates with Japanese women (and contracted gonorrhea). Finally, though, as a result of blows exchanged in a fight with another Marine, he was court-martialed and spent forty-five days in the brig.

He had had enough of marine life. Claiming falsely that his mother now needed his support, he managed to obtain an early discharge in 1959. Three days later, having rejected his US citizenship with accompanying publicity for this unusual move, he made his way to the Soviet Union with the intention of gaining citizenship there. He was yet a teenager, 19 years old.

A NEW LIFE BEGAN in the Soviet Union for the young refugee (celebrating his twentieth birthday two days after reaching Moscow). The American journalist Priscilla Johnson (later Priscilla Johnson McMillan), a correspondent for the North American Newspaper Alliance, interviewed this unusual American who had rejected his life in the United States for the Soviet Union. To her surprise, not only did Oswald agree to an interview, but the two enjoyed hot tea from a burner in his hotel room as they talked from 9:00 p.m. until 2:00 or 3:00 a.m. "Here," she soon wrote, "was a boy of twenty who, with only the money he had been able to save in less than three years as a Marine Corps private, had come six thousand miles with no thought but to live out his life in a country he had never seen, whose language he knew only slightly, and whose people he knew not at all."[22]

Among the many details Oswald shared had been his discovery at the age of 15 of *Das Kapital*. In her article the journalist described his knowledge of Marxist principles as superficial. "I saw him as a little lost boy and, as such boys often are, rather lonely and proud," she wrote.[23] But Oswald insisted that his decision was "not an emotional one." He was acting solely from an intellectual conviction that Marxism was the only proper way of life.[24]

But in his pursuit of Soviet citizenship, there were interminable delays. When his request was denied (the government feared that he might be an American spy), his expiring visa required him to leave the country immediately, and he slashed his left wrist in an apparent suicide attempt. After a weeklong stay in a Moscow hospital, he was released and told that he could remain there without citizenship. Pleased, he went to the American embassy in Moscow and turned in a note: "I Lee Harvey Oswald do hereby request that my present citizenship in the United States of America, be revoked." His request for Soviet citizenship, he said, was pending.[25]

Uncertain how to handle him but now concluding that Oswald was not an American spy, the government assigned him a job as a metal worker in Minsk. Here, the one-time loner with his own government-assigned apartment entered into an active social life with fellow workers and others, dancing and enjoying rock music, dating various women, and finally meeting and marrying Marina Prusakova in June 1962.

Fascinated with the United States' reputation, Marina agreed to return there with him and their young daughter, June. The principal advantages for the return, he told her, was the far greater availability and variety of goods. However, his two and a half years in the Soviet Union had not altered his convictions about the superiority of a true Marxist or Communist way of life. The Soviet problem, he was convinced, was its failure to properly apply Marxist principles.

Both Marina and even Oswald had to gain the government's permission to leave the country, which they ultimately achieved, and with their newborn daughter the family came to Texas. Various funds such as unemployment benefits supported the young family in their efforts to make a living in Texas or Louisiana. Oswald's occasional jobs were short-lived. He showed little interest in them, but they quickened when he found a job at the Dallas graphics and printing firm Jaggars-Chiles-Stovall. Even there, though, he was fired after several months in the spring of 1963 when, as had become the norm, he failed to have a good relationship with his fellow workers.

Other familiar interests had taken over his mind. While in New Orleans, where he was being helped by surprised relatives to look for work there, he wrote to the *Worker* to ask a favor. "I have formed a 'Fair Play for Cuba Committee here in New Orleans. . . . I ask that you give me as much literature as you judge possible since I think it would be very nice to have your literature among the 'Fair Play' leaflets."[26] He included a leaflet he had had printed with the headline "HANDS OFF CUBA!" which requested interested persons to join his charter branch of the existing national committee in New York. His branch would offer free literature and lectures. He sent a letter and leaflet to the *Worker*, which was forwarded to Arnold Johnson, an executive with the Communist Party USA. Johnson responded that the party had no organizational ties with the struggling "Fair Play" committee, but he sent Oswald some literature under separate cover.[27]

IN EARLY 1963 OSWALD ordered by mail a .38 revolver from one sporting goods company and a rifle from another, using a fake name, A. Hidell. With their arrival he strapped the pistol around his waist, held the rifle across his body, stuck visible copies of the *Militant* and the *Worker* in his pockets, and had the quizzical Marina take his picture under the outdoor stairway to their duplex rental on West Neely Street in Dallas's Oak Cliff area. He told her to keep a copy for daughter June. It would prove his early efforts to win the battle for Marxism, he said. Perhaps June, or maybe her grandchildren, would be alive to witness the nation's conversion to a Marxist or Communist way of life. The photo would show his dedication as a warrior to that cause.

Now he was prepared to take a definite action against fascism, and he chose a target—Edwin A. Walker, whose vehement, ultrarightism has become so extreme that even conservative Republicans were dismayed. Walker reminded Oswald of Hitler.

With Marina unaware of his intentions, he recorded elaborate plans in a special notebook to assassinate Walker. On a dark evening in early March 1963, he went to the alley behind Walker's house and took photographs. He drew a map of the surrounding area, noting the best escape route by public bus and time schedules. (Oswald had no car and could not drive.) He decided to make his attempt on a late Wednesday evening, timing it to coincide with the conclusion of a church meeting adjacent to Walker when departing members' noise and chatter would help obscure his escape. On the Tuesday evening before the planned assassination, he returned to the alley with his disassembled rifle and hid it among leaves and bushes for his use. He recognized that even his careful plans might not permit him to escape. With his recognition of such an eventuality, he composed a careful list of helpful information (in Russian) for Marina to use if he unexpectedly failed to return home one evening, leaving it at a place where she would be certain to find it. (Its translation to English follows.)

1. This is the key to the mailbox which is located in the main post office in the city on Ervay Street. This is the same street where the drugstore, in which you always waited is located. You will find the mailbox in the post office which is located 4 blocks from the drugstore on that street. I paid for the box last month so don't worry about it.

2. Send the information as to what has happened to me to the Embassy and include newspaper clippings (should there be anything about me in the newspapers). I believe that the Embassy will come quickly to your assistance on learning everything.

3. I paid the house rent on the 2d so don't worry about it.

4. Recently I also paid for water and gas.

5. The money from work will possibly be coming. The money will be sent to our post office box. Go to the bank and cash the check.

6. You can either throw out or give my clothing, etc. away. Do not keep these. However, I prefer that you hold on to my personal papers (military, civil, etc.).

7. Certain of my documents are in the small blue valise.

8. The address book can be found on my table in the study should need same.

9. We have friends here. The Red Cross also will help you.

10. I left you as much money as I could, $60 on the second of the month. You and the baby [apparently] can live for another 2 months using $10 per week.

11. If I am alive and taken prisoner, the city jail is located at the end
of the bridge through which we always passed on going to the city
(right in the beginning of the city after crossing the bridge).[28]

On his chosen dark night, retrieving his rifle from its hiding place in the
alley, Oswald could see Walker sitting alone at his desk, an easy target.
Oswald fired a single shot, hurriedly returning his rifle to its hiding
place (later to recover it) and returned home safely. As it happened,
Oswald's shot had been deflected by the window frame, and although
he was hit by minor window glass debris, Walker was not injured.
Oswald returned home breathless, but admitted to Marina what he
had attempted, not yet knowing if he was successful. (He would learn
the next day from news accounts that the window frame deflected his
bullet.) But why, Marina asked, did he try such a thing? Walker, he
answered, was a dreaded fascist, and if Hitler had been killed, millions
of lives would have been saved.[29]

OSWALD STILL WAS DETERMINED, somehow, to be a factor in
bringing about his dreams of a Marxist society, no matter how tiny or far
away in time his role would be. In August 1963 he wrote to the American Central Committee of the Communist Party for its opinion on how
he should conduct himself. "Comrades," he began his letter, he wanted
their advice for a "problem of personal tactics." His question: Would it
be best for him to continue an "open fight" against capitalistic forces, as
he had done, or better for him to remain "in the background" as a quiet
supporter of Communism?[30] The letter was referred to the same Arnold
Johnson, a prominent Communist who in 1953 had been convicted and
sentenced to a three-year term for advocating the violent overthrow of
the government, who discreetly replied that "often it is advisable for
some people to remain in the background."[31]

By the next month, September, Oswald had made his decision. Cuba,
with its still-young Marxist/Communist system, was a place where he
might be welcomed as a fellow comrade, even valued because of his
dedication to the cause and his experience in the Soviet Union. Even

Fidel Castro, he thought, might welcome him as a comrade. He decided to go to Mexico City, where a Cuban embassy—as well as Soviet—might appreciate his past actions and help him get there.

Telling Marina of his trip, he arrived in Mexico on September 26, 1963, and began a round of visits to the Cuban, Mexican, and Soviet embassies to obtain a visa for Cuba. He had with him documents to prove his friendship for Cuba ("Fair Play for Cuba"), his lengthy time in the Soviet Union (nearly three years), and his allegiance to Marxism since a teenager.

Again, though, he encountered disappointment. Mexican and Soviet authorities finally advised him that he could not depart for Cuba unless he first obtained a visa from the Soviet Union. That, he was told, could be issued no sooner than a wait of four months. Once more thwarted, Oswald returned to Dallas on October 3 after difficult bus rides through Mexico and into Texas.

In mid-October Ruth Paine, Marina's new friend, arranged an afternoon interview for Oswald as an order-filler at the Texas School Book Depository. Oswald was hired and began work the next day.

IN NOVEMBER PRESIDENT Kennedy announced that he would make a visit to Texas that would include Dallas on Friday, November 22. On November 5 the site for the luncheon was announced as the Women's Building at Fair Park. The other site considered was the Trade Mart, which had been determined to pose greater security risks. Nine days later, on November 14, that decision was reversed. Despite security concerns, the Trade Mart had other advantages.

On November 15 the *Morning News* reported that it was unlikely that a motorcade would be held for the president and party. On the following day, November 16, the newspaper reported that a motorcade would pass through parts of the city, but its route had not yet been determined. Not until November 21 would Oswald and readers of the *Times Herald* see on its front-page map that the motorcade would pass alongside the depository.

Here was a sudden and unexpected opportunity to strike a blow against capitalism, a moment in history in which his name would forever be remembered. But there was no time to make the same elaborate plans as he had done for his attempt on Walker. In fact, the motorcade's passage alongside the depository was to occur the next day. Nor would there be time to write a new note to Marina with instructions on what to do if he was captured or killed. His previous note would have to do.

But the rifle used in his attempt to kill Walker was in Ruth Paine's garage, hidden under a blanket. Normally, he visited and spent the weekend with Marina and the two girls beginning after work each Friday. But now, with Kennedy planning to pass the depository on Friday noon the very next day, he changed his routine. He would visit Marina and their daughters on Thursday evening, November 21, giving him the opportunity to bring his disassembled rifle to work in a large paper sack the next morning. Such improvisation would be necessary.

In his lengthy note of careful instructions for Marina before his attempt on Walker, he had acknowledged that he might be captured or killed. Surely he could feel even less certain now about his escape from a sixth-floor site with so many spectators and law enforcement officers just below. He could die himself in a shootout with police or face his capture and following trial that would result in a sentence of death or lifelong imprisonment. But the chance of being a history-maker for generations to come would be worth it.

Marina, dissatisfied with her unreliable, often hostile husband, had left him six weeks earlier to stay in the Paine house with June, 2, and one-month-old Rachel, whose birth had brought Oswald to tears. Oswald loved his children, and despite his rough treatment of Marina, he also often expressed to her his love. Marina, though, was planning on a divorce.

Perhaps, it may have seemed to him, an alternative to an attempt at assassination existed. Without telling Marina of an attempted assassination, that night in Irving he implored her to return to him so they could be united once more as a family. If so, he promised, he would buy the washing machine she had wanted and so badly needed. If she agreed, it is likely that he would forget his possibly impossible plan to shoot the president. But Marina rejected him. It was too late for that. No, she would not return to him. She would divorce him as planned.

Oswald, disappointed, spent the night there, presumably in bed next to her. Awakening early on this morning of November 22—while our *Times Herald* journalists, including me, were getting ready for the Kennedy visit—Oswald kissed his two sleeping children good-bye, took off his wedding ring, placed it in Marina's favorite china cup on the bedroom dresser, and left $170 of his money on the dresser, keeping for himself only the remaining $13.87.[32]

Before catching a ride with a friendly neighbor to go downtown for work, he grabbed his disassembled rifle from the garage and concealed its parts and barrel in a lengthy paper sack. When the driver asked what that was in that big brown sack, Oswald's answer was window curtain rods.

Oswald's rejection of the American democratic and capitalistic way of life, prompted by his untutored reading of Karl Marx and Marxism, led to his conviction that its aims were superior in attending to the needs of the general population, including himself. Capitalism would be replaced at some point, he thought, by a Marxist society. He might be recognized in history as an early activist in that transition. His defection to the Communist Soviet Union might be, in his opinion, an early step. But disappointed in finding that its cumbersome form of Marxism was intolerable for its general population, he returned to the United States with his allegiance to idealistic Marxism intact. Thus, he continued in his dreams to achieve a historic part in creating a proper form of Marxism.

He had thought he might achieve that recognition if he became known as the Marxist who killed the ultrarightist fascist Edwin A. Walker. Then came his wish to join Castro in Cuba in his efforts there to create a proper Marxist society, superior to what he had experienced in the Soviet Union. But both efforts failed. Now, surprisingly presented with the possibility of assassinating President Kennedy from a window, a feat he had never considered possible until now, he would make his own single-handed statement as a major figure in history.

The question now is what, if anything, in his short life led Oswald to beliefs so opposite to the established American culture in which he had failed? Extensive material about his formative childhood and teenage years has existed, much of it existing but being overshadowed in the Warren Commission's extensive ten-million-word, 19,200-page, and twenty-six-volume report. Priscilla Johnson McMillan's *Marina and Lee*, published in 1977, Norman Mailer's *Oswald's Tale*, published in 1995, and Vincent Bugliosi's *Reclaiming History*, published in 2007, are among the books offering more personal information.

A question that soon possessed so many, including me, was what had Oswald anticipated? Did he believe he would be able to flee unnoticed from the building's sixth-floor? He must have recognized the possibility of being caught or killed. In either case he might forever be remembered as a hero for the Marxist cause. We know of his first stop at his Oak Cliff rooming house to pick up his pistol and jacket. But then where would he go?

We recall that he had less than fourteen dollars in his pocket. That amount of money would not take him far.

My own opinion is that he didn't know what to do. It is likely that he didn't expect to escape. And if he did escape, he obviously realized that he would be identified almost immediately as the only worker who left the building. His mission at the depository, he may have thought, was suicidal. Anything less than arrest or possibly a shootout with arresting police officers, such as J. D. Tippit, was imminent. There were no major transportation outlets in Oak Cliff—no bus station, no train depot, no commercial airport for a quick getaway. He had no friends or associates there. Other facts, and so many documents, would point to his culpability. He had tried to shoot the nearest arresting police officer at the Texas Theatre rather than beg innocence.

Chapter 14

Reinventing Dallas

V ISITING JOURNALISTS NOW were arriving to examine more closely the ways Dallas worked. The powerful influence of the Dallas Citizens Council became widely known. In the journalists' words, it became the oligarchy.

Without question the city must construct a memorial for the martyred president. On December 3 Erik Jonsson and other familiar Dallas leaders held the first meeting of their self-appointed group as the John F. Kennedy Citizens Memorial Committee. After many delays, the famous architect Philip Johnson was hired. He designed a cenotaph, or open tomb, for a county-owned property behind the old red courthouse, a block from Dealey Plaza. It was completed in 1970. The unadorned thirty-foot high structure, open at the top, suggested visitors look into the sky as they contemplated visions of the nation's beloved president.[1]

Other changes, surely more meaningful as the city's future was concerned, came much faster. At least one prominent business leader I interviewed, Mayor Earle Cabell, was loath to say that the city needed to change anything. His family had been prominent in

Dallas for a century. Leaning back in his comfortable office chair at his family-owned Cabell's Dairy, he said, "The inference keeps creeping on that there was something here that made the assassination happen." There was no need to change anything now because "there was nothing that needed to be changed." To say anything else would deny his family's important role in the city's history. Cabell's own grandfather, William Lewis Cabell, was Dallas's three-term mayor in the 1870s and 1880s; his father, Ben Cabell, served as mayor from 1900 to 1904; Earle won election to the mayor's seat in 1961, a position he now continued to hold.

Despite Cabell's posture, obvious changes that even involved Cabell himself already had occurred when I interviewed him. Prominent individuals now felt little hesitation in criticizing the past conservative atmosphere, unchecked by the Dallas Citizens Council, that had dominated the city. Two days after the assassination, the Rev. William A. Holmes, pastor of the well-known liberal Northaven United Methodist Church, asked from his pulpit: "In the name of God, what kind of city have we become?"[2]

Dallas's previously positive image had virtually disappeared. Now it was widely recognized as being dominated by an unelected contingent of businessmen, the Dallas Citizens Council, who directed major changes from behind the scenes. Indeed, as we have seen, the organization was the official host for the president's visit. After Oswald's untimely murder in the police basement, vicious letters from throughout the nation redoubled. Critical newspaper and magazine assessments became the norm. Football fans elsewhere were calling the Dallas Cowboys football team "the assassins." Dallas itself was "a city of hate" dominated by the unelected group of businessmen. *Fortune*, the magazine of business, titled its story, "How Business Failed Dallas." A *New York Times* headline described the Council as a "Group of Businessmen Rules Dallas Without a Mandate From the Voters," criticizing it as an organization without representation from the fields of law, medicine, education, and religion.[3]

It could not be denied that Dallas needed an upgrade, not only in image but also in the reality of its local politics. As we have seen,

Dallas's voters had preferred Nixon over Kennedy in the 1960 presidential election. Change quickly followed, though. For instance,
Dallas County's nine-member delegation to the Texas Legislature
had consisted of eight Republicans and one Democrat. In the 1964
election, Dallas County Democrats captured all nine seats. Lyndon
Johnson carried the county's vote for president over Republican Barry
Goldwater, whereas Kennedy had failed to win the county despite his
overall majority in Texas.

New strategizing by the city's leaders brought an attitude that had
not prevailed since Franklin D. Roosevelt. Despite Cabell's comments
that nothing needed changing, he participated in a complicated
upheaval that brought significant changes. As part of an agreed-upon
strategy, Cabell resigned as mayor and announced his candidacy as
a Democrat to campaign against the ten-year reign of Republican
congressman Bruce Alger. As part of the strategy, J. Erik Jonsson,
outgoing president of the Dallas Citizens Council, would be appointed
by the elected city council to fill Cabell's vacant seat.

As the returns came in, it was obvious that Alger was a clear loser.
Cabell, winner as a moderate Democrat, billed his victory as "a return
to sanity on the part of the people of Dallas County."[4] Cabell easily
toppled Alger by 44,000 votes out of some 200,000 cast. The *Times
Herald* had boosted Cabell's campaign with what even I considered
an unfair and one-sided series of articles opposing Alger's effort for
a sixth term.

On election night my assignment was to interview the obviously
losing Alger at his election headquarters. I don't believe I had ever met
Alger, but I felt certain that as a *Times Herald* representative I would
encounter a bitter man resentful of our paper's one-sided campaign
against him. I didn't look forward to interviewing him, but I need not
have worried. I was astonished that he offered warm cordiality, not
a hint of resentment over the *Times Herald*. Undeterred in his own
political thought, though, he believed that Dallas was "moving into a
socialist dictatorship."

Lyndon Johnson, also on the ballot seeking his full term as
president, was a big winner in Dallas and Texas, as well as the nation.

The last telephone call Johnson made on election night was to Cabell, in which the two mutually expressed the large majorities both had enjoyed. "You'll have to come up the next week or so . . . and we'll have to start gettin' some stuff [earmarked for Dallas] in this budget and start movin'," Johnson told him.[5]

A major part of that "stuff" was a new federal building for Dallas, which was constructed and named for Cabell in 1971. Previously, Alger as congressman had refused to support such an initiative on the grounds that it would be too expensive and was not needed. Cabell would go on to serve four terms in Congress as its Democratic representative.

With Cabell taking on his new assignment, the new mayor—the conservative businessman Jonsson with progressive ideals—took over as planned. Brooklyn-born J. Erik Jonsson had moved to Dallas in the mid-1930s, a few years later becoming a founder of Texas Instruments. Jonsson, who was born on the same day in 1901 that McKinley was assassinated and was the man who announced to the shocked Trade Mart crowd that the president had been seriously wounded, was different from the former homegrown mayors such as Cabell. He was a Republican of the Rockefeller type, not a person to stand still.[6]

In this period when Dallas's image needed repair, Jonsson, no penny pincher, wanted the finest for the city. His authoritative influence took priority with members of his familiar Dallas Citizens Council and the elected city council, over which he presided as mayor. One ambition in 1964 was to establish a bold program called Goals for Dallas. It brought together some 100,000 Dallasites representing a wide sector of citizens (including a few Blacks and Latinos) to meet and establish new goals in local government, in the design of the city, and in transportation, health and welfare, education, culture, recreation, and public safety. On this basis, *Look* magazine declared Dallas its "All-American City" for 1970, a coveted honor in those years when the magazine was in its prime. Goals for Dallas endured into the 1990s, with regular updates and revisions.

In his most productive move, Jonsson managed to end what had been a serious and litigious fight with Fort Worth for aviation superiority. He persuaded the two cities to unite in creating the huge Dallas Fort Worth Regional Airport (now the Dallas-Fort Worth International Airport). When its construction was completed after ten years, it was the largest airport in the world in acreage and soon one of its busiest. Jonsson was chosen for the first five two-year terms to be chairman of its board of directors. Ross Perot had persuaded even the Fort Worth members of the board to name the airport for Jonsson, but Jonsson absolutely refused to accept it.[7]

Realizing the need for a new city hall, instead of another unattractive add-on attachment as preferred by City Manager Crull, Jonsson arranged for I. M. Pei to design an entirely new and ultramodern building. While Jonsson introduced the idea of Pei's design and made many presentations with an impressive model, it was his successor, journalist Wes Wise, who managed to win final support for its completion at a cost of nearly $70 million. Architecture critic Ada Louise Huxtable declared it to be one of the most important public buildings in the nation. Four years later a modernistic new central public library replaced the outgrown Carnegie library. It was named the J. Erik Jonsson Central Library.

Also deemed of great importance was what to do with the Texas School Book Depository, especially after its ownership changed, the depository moved elsewhere, and the building was empty. Should the building, constructed in 1901, be demolished as a sad reminder of its past? A strong core of prominent individuals favored its destruction.

Others, led by civic leader and preservationist Lindalyn Adams, committed to saving it as an important if ignoble part of Dallas and American history. Finally, Adams and her supporters prevailed when the Dallas City Council, to end the squabble, passed an ordinance that temporarily froze demolition permits. In 1977 Dallas County purchased the structure, placed county offices on floors one through five, and left the sixth floor open for the creation of the Sixth Floor Museum at Dealey Plaza.[8]

AS 1963 MOVED INTO 1964, Dallas journalists continued to seek additional information about the assassination, always looking for new details and especially hints of a conspiracy. Rarely did we find anything of unusual significance. But some young journalists who covered the assassination that weekend in Dallas became national figures.

A few years later Jim Lehrer left the *Times Herald*, started a Dallas evening news program called *Newsroom* (for which I was a reporter), and then went to Washington, DC, joining MacNeil on PBS-TV for evening wrap-ups of the Watergate hearings. Upon MacNeil's retirement Lehrer became sole anchor for the evening *NewsHour* program. He also gained special distinction in becoming the most frequent moderator of presidential debates in broadcast history.

For years to come, Lehrer worried about the impact on that early November 22 morning of his push for an early decision on the bubbletop. If he hadn't pressed for a quick answer, would it have been left on? Although not bulletproof, it would have offered a degree of protection for its passengers. Perhaps a potential assassin holding a cheap Italian rifle on the sixth floor of the Texas School Book Depository, seeing the bubbletop, would have decided not to shoot. If not, though, would the bubbletop at least have deflected the bullets' paths? His target certainly would have lacked clarity. Would the unhappy history we remember today have taken place? Lehrer's continuing concern prompted him fifty years later to write an imaginative novel about the decision's impact: *Top Down: A Novel of the Kennedy Assassination*, published in 2013 by Random House. "*Top Down* is fiction," he wrote in his author's note, "but there are some autobiographical elements that deserve attention." The novel would be one of more than two dozen Lehrer wrote during a prominent television career that overshadowed his literary achievements.

Dan Rather was promoted to be CBS-TV's White House correspondent in 1964 and afterward the network's news anchor for twenty-four years. Bob Schieffer of the *Fort Worth Star-Telegram* also went to CBS-TV and covered the White House, Pentagon, Department of State, and Congress. From 1991 to 2015 he hosted *Face the Nation*.

Robert MacNeil, already a national figure on NBC-TV, gained further fame as a commentator and news host on PBS-TV.

My friend Hugh Aynesworth of the *News* went to work for *Newsweek* and the *20/20* television news program, wrote books, and earned a national representation before returning to Dallas, where he continues to live. Aynesworth had been present at Dealey Plaza at the time of the assassination, was also present inside the Texas Theatre to witness Oswald's capture, and was in the police underground parking lot to see Ruby shoot Oswald. But it was in April 1964 that he scored the most sensational scoop yet on Oswald's life in the Soviet Union. Now, incredibly, Hugh had gained access to the heretofore unknown diary Oswald kept during his nearly three years in the Soviet Union. It contained intimate details about his disillusionment with the Soviet Union's brand of Communism, his failed attempt at suicide, his marriage to Marina, and much more. No reporter had been more successful or dogged than Hugh in his perseverance.

I stayed in Dallas, where I was flattered when City Editor Smart gave me an important assignment to write our one-year anniversary story of the assassination and its impact on the city. I briefly repeat, immodestly, the city editor's opening sentences in his note: "If you didn't write so well, we wouldn't ask you to do so much. But you do—and we do. Your editors have unanimously chosen you to write our piece on the anniversary of the assassination."[9]

My story, under the headline, "JFK Death Left Deep City Imprint," was accompanied on the front page by a large pen and ink drawing by the *Times Herald*'s fine illustrator, Bob Taylor. My article, printed on November 22, 1964, was slightly more than two thousand words long. Taylor's lovely drawing showed a weary Kennedy-like figure trudging up a showy hill in the wilderness alongside poet Robert Frost's words, referring to John Kennedy's humanitarian spirit:

The woods are lovely, dark and deep
But I have promises to keep
And miles to go before I sleep
And miles to go before I sleep.[10]

As the thirtieth anniversary approached in 1993, a handful of those journalists still living or working in Dallas had an idea. Although earlier we journalists sometimes found ourselves in small groups to discuss our adventures at the new Sixth Floor Museum or Press Club, it had never happened on a large scale. One day Alex Burton and Jim Ewell dropped by my office at SMU. Why not have a reunion in which we—that is, those who were still alive—could share our fading memories? Southern Methodist University (where I had become chairman of the journalism department) might provide a convenient site. Eddie Barker, Hugh Aynesworth, Alex Burton, Jim Ewell, Bert Shipp, Bob Porter, Gary Schultz, Tony Zoppi, and I, especially aided by Farris Rookstool III, were the principal organizers. SMU provided the student union ballroom for the event. We located more than eighty-one journalists who had participated in the Dallas coverage from November 22 to 25. They came from as far away as Finland.

Attending and available for comments were a number of involved local public officials, attorneys, police officers, and detectives. It was an all-day event, open to the public, in which our discussions attracted national and international news coverage. We named the event "Reporters Who Remember: 11/22/63." Small panels of journalists discussed their own firsthand experiences at the places where they had been involved—Love Field, the motorcade, the assassination site at Dealey Plaza, Oswald's capture at the Texas Theatre, Ruby's dramatic shooting of Oswald, and more. Television coverage from many cities, even international, covered our event.

Then, as is true today, conspiracy theories abounded. We conducted a poll of participating journalists, asking them to respond in writing to the question, "Do you believe Lee Harvey Oswald acted alone in assassinating President Kennedy?" Seventy-five thought he acted alone and six said no. A colleague of mine in the SMU journalism division, Laura Hlavach, and I published a full transcript of our event entitled *Reporting the Kennedy Assassination: Journalists Who Were There Recall Their Experiences* (Dallas: Three Forks Press, 1996).

Despite the journalists' well-founded opinions that Oswald acted alone, individuals throughout the nation who believed that he was part of a conspiracy continued to grow in numbers. By the 1970s a number of vociferous conspiratorial groups went so far as to believe that Oswald was not even the person buried under the marker bearing his name. Some thought the casket might be empty. After their persistence the grave was opened in 1981. His deteriorated body was examined by a panel of medical examiners who concluded without a doubt that the body inside the casket was that of Oswald.[11]

At the date of this writing, six decades after the crime, an untold number of conspiracy groups—perhaps growing in number—continue to dedicate themselves to proving that Oswald did not act alone or that he was not even guilty of firing the fatal shots. Forty years after the assassination, a Gallup poll found that about three-quarters of Americans still believed that Oswald did not act alone. In what has been perhaps the most lengthy and substantive history of the assassination, author Vincent Bugliosi devoted two chapters to address and correct these mistaken beliefs.[12]

AFTER A FEW YEARS, though, citizens across the nation and often elsewhere had thought of things other than the assassination on mentions of Dallas. One was the highly popular weekly television series *Dallas*, which dealt with a fictitious oil-rich family and especially its lead character, Larry Hagman, surrounded by an excellent cast. It was a CBS-TV weekly drama that lasted for thirteen years. Also, starting in 1966 with its first football divisional championship followed by four National Football League championships, the Dallas Cowboys' frequent appearances on national television brought wide recognition as "America's Team."

Nowadays hardly any American citizens are unaware of the incredible growth of the Dallas–Fort Worth–Arlington metropolitan statistical area. With Dallas leading the way, the area constitutes a continuous urban area with some 7.7 million citizens, the fourth most populous of the nation's metropolitan districts. Demographers calculate that the DFW metroplex will surpass Chicago in size in the 2030s to be the nation's third largest metropolitan district. It now trails only New York City in number of Fortune 500 company head-quarters. The city's elected city council now has had two Black mayors and a city council in which minorities at times have outnumbered the once-dominant white members.[13]

Although these decades have passed and the nation's currently complex problems are acute, distracting, and frightening, my haunting memories of that fateful November 22–25 weekend remain vivid. My wife and I often routinely drive past Dealey Plaza on our way to my sister June's house in Oak Cliff. To this day the plaza offers a pleasant green relief to adjacent downtown buildings, remarkably unchanged from 1963.

One immediate and continuing change in the city is the arrival of so many locals and visitors who visit Dealey Plaza. The visitors are easily identifiable as they walk up and down its green grass slope toward the Triple Underpass, looking up to the sixth-floor window where Oswald fired his rifle down Elm Street. Especially on weekends we inevitably see them calculating the distance from where he was shooting, examining the fading mark of the X on Elm Street where the fatal shot hit its target and finding the place where Abraham Zapruder stood with his Bell & Howell camera. An inevitable visit for these visitors to the Sixth Floor Museum in the former Texas School Book Depository is a few steps away.

From Dealey Plaza we pass under the Triple Underpass as my wife, Phyllis, and I sometimes drive across the Trinity River and its wide floodplain to Oak Cliff, turn left on Beckley, and glance at Oswald's rooming house at 1026 North Beckley. A couple of blocks later we inevitably turn our heads to the right at Neely Street, where the Oswalds lived in the upstairs duplex. It's where Marina took a now-famous picture of her husband as he stood beneath the outdoor stairway displaying his rifle, pistol, and two Marxist publications. Only a few seem to know of the house's existence. A few blocks away is Jefferson Boulevard, where Oswald sought to hide, and the Texas movie theater where police found and arrested him.

Only a handful of Dallas journalists who covered the assassination are still alive. Our city gives daily reminders of so many places where history was made. Their powerful impact remains. None of us who are able can resist occasional returns to those places where we covered the most unforgettable story of our lives.

Acknowledgments

It required far more than my six-decade memory and notes from my two reporters' notebooks to show how we journalists worked so desperately hard on those earth-shattering days. We, of course, never before had faced such a challenge. I could not be everywhere at once in such a fast-paced and changing story, and it seemed important to include not just my own experiences but also summaries of those important events of which I quickly became aware. At the time Police Officer J. D. Tippit was shot to death in Oak Cliff and Oswald was captured at the Texas movie theater, I was at the School Book Depository interviewing detectives and going upstairs to the assassin's sixth-floor window. And when Jack Ruby shot Oswald on Sunday morning, November 24, I was waking up in my apartment, having been at the police station until about 2:00 a.m. to see detectives escorting Oswald back and forth for interrogations and reporters pressuring Chief Jesse Curry for the time of Oswald's transfer next morning to the county jail. I have sought to make the differences clear between what I was experiencing personally and what I later learned from fellow reporters and editors, through extensive research and especially sworn testimony from those interviewed by the Warren Commission Report research, as well as other reliable resources.

Following me through this writing process with corrections, additional information, and literary suggestions was my good friend Max Holland, perhaps the foremost scholar of the Kennedy assassination. Max is the author of *The Kennedy Assassination Tapes* and nearing completion of what will be a monumental history of the Warren Commission. Other early first readers included Michael V. Hazel, Dallas historian and founder and editor of *Legacies: A History Journal for Dallas & North Central Texas*. So many others read all or parts of the book with encouraging and critical eyes: Thomas H. Smith, Scott Spreier, Roger Summers, Bob Schieffer, and Scott Payne.

Ronald Chrisman, director of the University of North Texas Press, who quickly responded to my questions throughout the publication process, surprised me with the generous offer that I could use thirty-five illustrations in the book—fine news indeed. A huge number of remarkable black-and-white photos taken principally by professional photojournalist were available especially through the extensive collections of the Sixth Floor Museum at Dealey Plaza. Choosing them and arranging them for display was a fascinating and personally rewarding experience.

Allison V. Smith, a professional freelance photographer, formerly of the *Dallas Morning News*, whose works appear often on the *New York Times*, *Washington Post*, and other media (in addition to this book), became my very excellent photo editor. With a team consisting of Allison, photo specialist Michael Thomas, and myself, we scanned scores and scores of photos and chose what we thought best to accompany key events. Evans Caglage used his technical magic to bring out the best on so many of the images.

And how wonderful it was to work through the graces and special generosity of the Sixth Floor Museum at Dealey Plaza, including especially Megan Bryant, director of collections and interpretation; Nicola Longford, chief executive officer; and Stephen Fagin, curator. What a beacon of light the Sixth Floor Museum has been for Dealey Plaza, Dallas, and the entire nation and world in its careful attention to one of the most tragic and significant events in our history.

I am grateful especially to the fine staff of the University of North Texas Press who worked diligently and professionally in bringing this work into a book also available through electronic means. I refer to Director Chrisman, Managing Editor Amy Maddox, and Marketing Manager Elizabeth Whitby. Many others at the University of North Texas Press, yet unknown to me, deserve my sincere thanks.

Just a telephone call away was the excellent assistance of Southern Methodist University's computer help office, whose experts pulled me out of my frequent computer difficulties with their special knowledge. Thankfully, the university provides this service for emeritus professors such as me and for retired staff such as my wife, Phyllis.

Still others who must be mentioned regarding past and recent help include Eleanor Cowan, Martin Frost, Keith Shelton, Doug Stanglin, Michael Granberry, Jim Schutze and Mariana Greene, Helene Schwartz Harrison, Farris Rookstool III, Roger Summers, Albert Mallard, Greg Olds, Spencer Bevis, Erin Sood, Tricia Gesner, Cecil Floyd, Bob Jackson, Lissa Johnston, John Slate, Carol Toler, Kate Lehrer, Michael Beschloss, and Bob Schieffer.

Instead of hours spent at research libraries examining letters and documents important to my previous books, my "office" for writing this memoir was home. When my visiting son, Scott, saw the small computer screen on which I was editing, he saw a need that would simplify my work. My Christmas gift from him and his family (his wife, Brandy; son, Grant; and daughter, Caroline) thus was a new wide screen that could display at one time four very readable pages—a boon for anyone dealing with lengthy documents.

All family members have been helpful with their encouragement in this lengthy period of work (starting with the pandemic several years ago)—especially my sister, June Payne Marco, a lifelong resident of Dallas. My younger sister, Sally Ann Estes Payne, and her husband, Jim, who live way out in West Texas, have been supportive and eager to hear more as I progressed. Closer to home in Dallas my daughter Hannah Payne St. Romaine, mother of our newest granddaughter, Zadie Claire, along with her husband, Darnell, are on my list of interested encouragers. In Colorado our first daughter, Sarah, her husband, Bryan, and their daughters, Georgia and Rebecca, supported me from afar. Most of all, I must thank my amazing wife, Phyllis. Without her service as the "office manager" who offered her constant love and saw to my daily needs of all kinds with affection, this book simply could not have been completed.

As far as sources used to help confirm my own memories or provide needed further information for events occurring outside my eyesight, I encourage readers to examine my bibliography. As hard as I tried to be correct in all things, any errors are mine alone.

Darwin Payne

Appendix: Review of the Earlier Presidential Assassinations

TO PLACE THE NATION'S fourth presidential assassination in a broad context, we review the first three, beginning with a tragedy familiar to all—the death of President Abraham Lincoln, occurring in 1865 only five days after the conclusion of the War between the States. Of course, Lincoln's death had little effect in Dallas, which had a population at the time of less than two thousand residents. News traveled slow then, and its impact on such a small and far-removed place as Dallas was not considerable.

Surely all of today's citizens—even newly arrived ones from across the seas—have at least a smattering of information that Honest Abe was shot to death while he and his wife, Mary, attended a play at Ford's Theater. Almost all might even know that the play they attended was a comedy entitled *Our American Cousin* and that the assassin was a handsome 26-year-old actor and Shakespearean tragedian named John Wilkes Booth, member of the famous Booth theatrical family.

Less familiar, most likely, is the ironic fact that Lincoln greatly enjoyed young Booth's theatrical works. He had seen him perform numerous times with admiration for his histrionic skills. In fact, so impressed was Lincoln that he had invited Booth to the White House several times. But Booth, a racist from Maryland and ardent supporter of the Southern cause, despised Lincoln. He declined every invitation, explaining to others that he "would rather be applauded by a negro."[1]

Booth and eight fellow conspirators whom he had rounded up as help, at first plotted to kidnap Lincoln and exchange him for Confederate prisoners. Various circumstances intervened, however, and by war's end Booth decided to assassinate the president himself while his compatriots tried to murder Vice President Andrew Johnson and Secretary of State William Seward.

When Booth learned that Lincoln and his wife, Mary, would attend the play at Ford's Theater, a place both he and Lincoln knew well, he secretly fixed the back door to the presidential box so it would remain ajar. When the Washington police officer left his assigned post there, Booth saw his opportunity. Familiar with the play, Booth anticipated that the audience would roar with laughter at a certain point. He chose that time to open the door, shoot the president, jump to the stage with dagger in hand, and before fleeing make his famous utterance: "Sic simper tyrannis" (thus always to tyrants). His concurrent plan for his colleagues to attack Vice President Andrew Johnson failed to materialize, but another of his conspirators severely wounded Seward at home with a knife. Booth fled to a farm in Maryland. Days later he was found there and shot to death. Eight of his associates were eventually captured; four of them were hanged.[2]

Perhaps the best indication of public interest in Lincoln's death was indicated by the fact that the *New York Herald*, beginning with its 2:00 a.m. edition on the morning of April 15, 1865, did not finish covering the breaking news until six more updated editions concluded at 3:30 p.m. the next day. Across the nation the news was distributed by the Associated Press via the latest media device, the telegraph. (Associated Press had been founded in 1846 by five New York City newspapers to share in the cost of transmitting news of the War with Mexico.)

Sixteen years after Lincoln's death and four months after James A. Garfield assumed the presidency in 1881, Garfield, an Ohio-born former Union general, an eighteen-year veteran of the House of Representatives, and the nation's last president born in a log cabin, was shot to death by Charles Guiteau.

A 40-year-old office-seeker, lawyer, former utopian, and lately mere loiterer, Guiteau was furious because he believed that without crediting him, the president had used a speech he had sent him. Although the two were not acquainted and he had little reason to expect a political appointment, Guiteau foolishly wanted to be rewarded with a diplomatic post, perhaps to France. Anguished, he had been stalking Garfield for several weeks with his recently purchased and powerful British Bulldog revolver.

His best chance came at the Baltimore and Potomac train station. The 50-year-old new president was waiting for a train. A small group stood with him before his intended departure for a summer vacation. Those with him included Robert Todd Lincoln, Lincoln's firstborn son and now Garfield's secretary of war. At the station Guiteau approached the unsuspecting Garfield from behind and fired two shots, one penetrating the president's back and the other grazing his shoulder. "My God, what is this?" the collapsing president exclaimed.[3] A police officer outside heard the shots and grabbed Guiteau before he could reach the cab he had engaged to wait outside.

Garfield lived for another seventy-nine days, suffering intense pain while dying from infections caused by his wound and his doctor's futile probing by hand to extract the bullet deep in his body. Alexander Graham Bell, recent inventor of the telephone, used an improvised electrical device that might specifically locate the bullet in Garfield's body, but his effort failed. Guiteau expressed no regrets for his act. He claimed that God had prompted him to kill the president. A jury quickly convicted Guiteau, and he was hanged in September 19, 1881.[4]

Two decades later, in early September 1901, William McKinley became the nation's third president to be assassinated. This occurred at a reception for him at the Pan-American Exposition in Buffalo, New York. The assassin was Michigan-born Leon Frank Czolgosz, a 28-year-old unemployed Polish-American steelworker and self-proclaimed anarchist. (His last name is pronounced "Chol-guh.") Czolgosz, having recently purchased a short-barreled .32 revolver pistol, stood innocently in a receiving line, ostensibly waiting to greet President McKinley. Concealing his pistol with a handkerchief, when his turn came he twice shot McKinley instead of shaking his proffered hand. The first bullet ricocheted off McKinley's coat button. The second went into his stomach. The injured but still conscious McKinley, seeing that crowd members quickly had caught and were pummeling his attacker, shouted, "Go easy on him, boys." To his close aide, George L. Cortelyou, he whispered, "My wife, be careful, Cortelyou, how you tell her—oh, be careful."[5]

Eight days later, growing weaker by the day, the president died from infections caused by his wound. Czolgosz, found guilty by a jury despite his plea of insanity, was sentenced to death by the electric chair. The sentence, executed with three shocks of 1,800 volts, was carried out on October 29, 1901. Before his death, Czolgosz said, "I killed the president because he was the enemy of the good people—the good working people." In 1906 Congress passed legislation officially designating the US Secret Service to be in charge of presidential security.[6]

Sixty-two years later the assassination of our fourth president by Lee Harvey Oswald occurred at Dealey Plaza. Oswald, uniquely among the assassins, used a rifle to shoot President Kennedy. His hiding place was on the sixth floor of the Texas School Book Depository. The president was passing below in a motorcade whose route was planned and announced in advance. Since this book concerns itself primarily with Oswald and the Kennedy assassination, I devote greater detail about his formative years in chapter thirteen. But a few observations about all four of the assassins follow.

Three of the four assassinations occurred within a forty-year period, 1865 to 1905. All four assassins were men; three were in their 20s; three were bachelors; four acted alone; all were spurred by strong if varied political feelings; all used a firearm. Two of the four—Czolgosz and Oswald—were motivated particularly by their hatred of the nation's capitalistic economic system. Booth was a racist who hated Lincoln. Czolgosz was a proclaimed anarchist influenced by Emma Goldman. Guiteau, possibly insane, had a far-fetched notion that McKinley had failed to acknowledge his submitted speech.

Oswald was a self-proclaimed Marxist who had hope in a future Marxist system of government.

Despite overwhelming and virtually incontrovertible facts that Oswald was a lone assailant, there remain large numbers of skeptics who, six decades later, have convinced themselves otherwise. I delay until chapter thirteen the possible factors in his childhood and early adult years that brought him to assassinate a president for whom he had no personal animosity.

We remind ourselves that there indeed could have been other presidential assassinations, for several presidents barely escaped attempts. My descriptions here are limited to the most recent attempts, beginning with Harry S. Truman in 1950 when I was 13 years old, a *Dallas Times Herald* paperboy.

President Truman, living with his wife, Bess, at the Blair House while the nearby White House underwent major renovations, was targeted for death by two Puerto Rican activists promoting independence for this island territory of the United States. The pair, 25 and 36 years of age, were neatly dressed New York City residents. Between them they carried sixty-nine rounds of ammunition for their two pistols. Thus armed, they approached the Blair House from opposite directions, strategically timing their arrival for the same moment.

When security officers sought to stop the pair, a torrent of gunfire from all sides broke out (twenty-seven shots fired in about two minutes). On this unseasonably warm day, Truman was taking an early afternoon nap. When Bess heard the outside fusillade, she looked out, saw what was happening, and alerted her husband: "Harry, someone's shooting our policemen." The president hurried to his wife at the second-floor windows until a Secret Service agent saw them and shouted: "Get back! Get back!"[7] One of the activists, Oscar Collazo, who never before had fired a pistol, was wounded. The other, Griselio Torresola, was killed, but not before one White House officer, Leslie Coffelt, was slain and two others wounded in the shooting frenzy. Collazo was sentenced to life in prison. (President Jimmy Carter commuted him in 1979.)[8]

Moving to 1975, a scheme similar to Czolgosz's plan to kill President McKinley was attempted by Lynnette "Squeaky" Fromme. She was a 25-year-old Manson Family cult member who, like Czolgosz, rejected President Gerald Ford's offer to shake her hand in Sacramento, California. She intended to shoot him with a .45-caliber pistol, but it failed to fire. A Secret Service agent quickly arrested her. She was sentenced to life in prison and released from custody in 2009.

Seventeen days later, in September 1975, shortly after Fromme's aborted attempt, Sara Jane Moore fired a pistol at President Ford. A bystander in the crowd grabbed her arm and her shot missed. Moore, sentenced to life in prison, was paroled on the last day of 2007 after thirty-one years in prison.

In 1981, eighteen years after the JFK assassination, we note the serious wounding of President Ronald Reagan by an armed assailant as the president approached his limousine after an engagement in a Washington, DC, hotel. His assailant, John Hinckley, a fan of movie actress Jodie Foster, said he wanted to impress her with his actions. Press Secretary James Brady was wounded by a shot in his head and three other officers also were wounded. Brady's wound permanently disabled him. Reagan's wounds put him close to death before he recovered at a hospital in the nation's capital city.

Endnotes

Chapter 1

1. "Teddy's '05 Dallas Visit Presidential Pacesetter," *Dallas Times Herald*, Nov. 17, 1963; "Guest of Dallas," *Dallas Morning News*, Apr. 5, 1905; Douglas Brinkley, *The Wilderness Warrior: Theodore Roosevelt and the Crusade for America* (New York: Harper Perennial, 2010), 597; Michael V. Hazel, "Hail to the Chief: Two Early Presidential Visits," in *Dallas Reconsidered: Essays in Local History* (Dallas: Three Forks Press, 1995), 294–304.
2. "J. D. Manley Hearing Is Begun," *Dallas Morning News*, Nov. 3, 1909.
3. "50,000 Pack Bowl, Cheering Roosevelt at Every Pause," *Dallas Morning News*, June 13, 1936; Kenneth B. Ragsdale, *The Year America Discovered Texas: Centennial '36* (College Station: Texas A&M University Press, 1987), 246–48.
4. Margaret Truman, *Harry S. Truman* (New York: William Morrow, 1973), 31–33.
5. Dwight D. Eisenhower, *Mandate for Change, 1953–1956: The White House Years* (Garden City, NY: Doubleday, 1963), 71.

Chapter 2

1. In 1966 the Tower was where ex-marine Charles Whitman, after killing his wife and mother, went to the twenty-eighth floor with a rifle and shot to death fourteen others and wounded thirty-one on the campus grounds.
2. Gary Cartwright, "Stop the Press," *Texas Monthly*, Sept. 1975, https://www.texasmonthly.com/articles/stop-the-press/.
3. Bob Schieffer, *This Just In: What I Couldn't Tell You on TV* (New York: G. P. Putnam's Sons, 2003), 1.
4. Chandler Davidson, *Race and Class in Texas Politics* (Princeton: Princeton University Press, 1990), 213–14.
5. Darwin Payne, *Big D: Triumphs and Troubles of an American Supercity in the 20th Century* (Dallas: Three Forks Press, 1994), 309; "Sen. Kennedy Fails to Shake Ministers," *Dallas Morning News*, Sept. 14, 1960.
6. "'Matinee-Idol' Squeals Greet Jack in Tour Through City," *Fort Worth Star-Telegram*, Sept. 14, 1960.

7. Letter from Hughes to Senator Ralph Yarborough, Mar. 15, 1965, folder 12, box 1893, STH Papers, University of North Texas Archives, quoted by Darwin Payne in *Indomitable Sarah: The Life of Judge Sarah T. Hughes* (Dallas: SMU Press, 2004) 198–99. Two years after this experience, President Kennedy appointed Hughes as judge of the US District Court in Dallas and Sanders as the area's US district attorney. On Nov. 22, 1963, Hughes and Johnson would stand together on Air Force One as Hughes gave the presidential oath of office to Johnson.
8. "Jack Gets Record Welcome," *Fort Worth Star-Telegram*, Sept. 14, 1960.
9. Recently I sent birthday greetings to Martin Frost. He responded that everything else had been easy after his summer internships at the *Press*.

Chapter 3

1. Robert A. Caro, *The Passage of Power: The Years of Lyndon Johnson* (New York: Alfred A. Knopf, 2012), 149.
2. Oral History of Bruce Alger, Bruce Alger Collection, Dallas History and Archives, Dallas Public Library.
3. Payne, *Big D*, 306.
4. Stephen Fagin, *Assassination and Commemoration: JFK, Dallas, and The Sixth Floor Museum at Dealey Plaza* (Norman: University of Oklahoma Press, 2013) 21–23; Payne, *Big D*, 279–83, 306–7.
5. Rowland Evans and Robert Novak, *Lyndon B. Johnson: The Exercise of Power* (New York: New American Library, 1966), 302.
6. *Dallas Times Herald*, Nov. 7, 1960.
7. *Abilene Reporter-News*, Nov. 6, 1960
8. Caro, *Passage of Power*, 150.
9. Payne, *Big D*, 306–7. See also *Dallas Times Herald*, Nov. 6 , 1964; *Dallas Morning News*, Nov. 5, 1960.
10. During his long tenure, Senator Tower played a prominent role in Republican politics. On Apr. 15, 1991, he and his daughter died in a commuter plane crash.
11. *Hearings before the President's Commission on the Assassination of President John F. Kennedy*, 26 vols. (Washington, DC: Government Printing Office, 1964), I:9 (hereafter cited simply as *Hearings* with volume and page numbers).
12. A few years later Sloan would be the author of popular books on World War II battles in the Pacific.

13. Jim would become a national figure as moderator of PBS's evening news show after experience in Dallas as news director of a ground-breaking, five-day-a-week show entitled *Newsroom*.

Chapter 4

1. Payne, *Big D*, 309, and "Kennedy Fails to Shake Ministers," *Dallas Morning News*, Sept. 14, 1960.
2. Edward H. Miller, *Nut Country: Right-Wing Dallas and the Birth of the Southern Strategy* (Chicago: University of Chicago Press, 2015), 56–58.
3. Miller, *Nut Country*, 104–10. In 1964 Morris revived his hopes in Texas for a Senate seat but lost in the Republican primary to future president George Herbert Walker Bush.
4. Payne, *Big D*, 307.
5. Miller, *Nut Country*, 92–93.
6. Miller, *Nut Country*, 146–47; Payne, *Big D*, 308.
7. Payne, *Big D*, 307–8; David M. Hardy, Section Chief, Records Management Division, FBI, memo re: National Indignation Convention, to Ernie Lazar, Mar. 10, 2004, https://archive.org/details/nationalindignationconventiondallas1051264.
8. "Foreign Relations, Trouble for Tito," *Time*, Oct. 27, 1961.
9. Payne, *Big D*, 308, 310–11.
10. Gallagher's iconic photo changed Stevenson's campaign narrative to one that showed him as a symbol of hard work and frugality. When Gallagher won the Pulitzer Prize, Stevenson sent him a telegram: "Glad to hear you won with a hole in one."
11. "Taunting Signs Fail to Faze Stevenson," *Dallas Morning News*, Oct. 18, 1952.
12. Miller, *Nut Country*, 72.
13. Payne, *Big D*, 310; "Walker Says U.S. Main Battleground," *Dallas Morning News*, Oct. 24,1963. But as a self-proclaimed Marxist, Oswald was no supporter of the ultraright. Hiding on the evening of Apr. 10, 1963, in the alley behind Walker's house on Turtle Creek Boulevard, Oswald had tried to kill him with a rifle shot, but it glanced off the windowsill (the same rifle he would use on Nov. 22).
14. Bill Minutaglio and Steven L. Davis, *Dallas 1963* (New York: Twelve, 2013), 242–43.
15. Bob Huffaker et al., *When the News Went Live: Dallas 1963* (New York: Taylor Trade, 2004), 111; see also 112.

16. Huffaker et al., *When the News Went Live*, 111.

17. Huffaker et al., *When the News Went Live*, 111.

18. Warren Leslie, *Dallas Public and Private: Aspects of an American City* (Dallas: SMU Press, 1996), 188–212.

19. The conversation between Stevenson and Frederickson was reported by AP and UPI wire services. The UPI report of the conversation, along with a close photograph, appeared in the *New York Times*, "Stevenson Booed and Hit By Dallas Demonstrators," Oct. 25, 1963. See also Minutaglio and Davis, *Dallas 1963*, 247.

20. Arthur M. Schlesinger Jr., *A Thousand Days: John F. Kennedy in the White House* (Boston: Houghton Mifflin, 1965), 1020.

21. Wise recalled this evening in *When the News Went Live*, 116; see also 111–16.

22. "Chief Hits Critics of Adlai Escort," *Dallas Morning News*, Oct. 26, 1963.

23. Payne, *Big D*, 312.

24. "Cabell Appeals for Sanity," *Dallas Morning News*, Oct. 27, 1963: "When the Ku Klux Klan in the early twenties barreled through the South, Dallas was the Southwest hate capital of Dixie." Payne, *Big D*, ch. 5 ("Embracing the Ku Klux Klan," 67–96) describe the Klan's activities in which Dallas Klan No. 66 consistently refers to itself as the nation's largest Klan chapter (p. 75).

25. I summarized these reactions in *Big D*, pages 312–13. The quotes appear in news stories from *Dallas Morning News*, Oct. 26, 1963, and *Dallas Times Herald*, Oct. 27, 1963.

26. Marcus to Dealey, Oct. 27, 1963, Stanley Marcus Papers, DeGolyer Library, Southern Methodist University, cited by Minutaglio and Davis, *Dallas 1963*, 253.

27. Payne, *Big D*, 313.

28. Payne, *Big D*, 313.

29. Payne, *Big D*, 313–14.

30. William Manchester, *The Death of a President: November 1963* (New York: Harper & Row, 1967), 22–25.

31. Epilogue in Ragsdale, *America Discovered Texas*, 294–306.

32. Huffaker et al., *When the News Went Live*, 117.

33. Minutaglio and Davis, *Dallas 1963*, 280.

34. Payne, *Big D*, 315.

35. Payne, *Big D*, 316.

Chapter 5

1. Phenix described the affair in Huffaker et al., *When the News Went Live*, 83–84. News director Eddie Barker, he said, chewed him out for his failure to take film of Walker pummeling him. Phenix said that later in the year he was involved in two more altercations but managed both times to get film.
2. Laura Hlavach and Darwin Payne, eds., *Reporting the Kennedy Assassination: Journalists Who Were There Recall Their Experiences* (Dallas: Three Forks Press, 2013), 23.
3. In his 1964 testimony before the Warren Commission, on the basis of the Fifth Amendment, Surrey declined to answer persistent questions about his involvement in printing the handbills. *Hearings*, V:420–49. But as years passed his involvement became confirmed by federal investigators.
4. The ad was delivered at the last minute. A part-time young employee accepted a cash payment and sent it to the back shop without manage-ment review. William Manchester later would quote publisher Ted Dealey as saying that "the ad reflected the editorial position of the paper." Judith Garrett Segura, *Belo: From Newspapers to New Media* (Austin: University of Texas Press, 2008), 114.
5. Read revealed the "cue" for Jackie's arrival in his *JFK's Final Hours in Texas: An Eyewitness Remembers the Tragedy and Its Aftermath* (Austin: Dolph Briscoe Center for American History, 2013), 33.
6. Miller, *Nut Country*, 7.
7. Vincent Bugliosi, *Reclaiming History: The Assassination of President John F. Kennedy* (New York: W.W. Norton & Co., 2007), 4, 14. Chief Curry's summary of assignments is in *Retired Dallas Police Chief Jesse Curry Reveals His Personal JFK Assassination File* (Dallas: American Poster and Printing, 1969), 23.
8. Lehrer's Dallas contact, possibly Sorrels, might have called Winston G. Lawson, the advance Special Secret Service Agent in Dallas. Lawson had been advised to take off the bubbletop if the weather was clear but to leave it on if not; *Hearings*, IV:349.
9. Mary Barelli Gallagher, Jackie Kennedy's personal secretary, described her as a reluctant campaigner who "did not take to politics as the other Kennedy women did." *My Life with Jacqueline Kennedy* (New York: Paperback Library, 1970), 53.
10. Cathy Trost and Susan Bennett, *President Kennedy Has Been Shot* (Naperville, IL: Sourcebooks, 2003), 16.

11. Roberts recalled her comment for Trost and Bennett, *President Kennedy Has Been Shot*, 15–16.
12. The motorcade route was established Monday, Nov. 18, by Dallas's deputy chief R. H. Lunday, Assistant Chief Charles Batchelor, and Secret Service agents Winston G. Lawson and Forrest Sorrels. Curry, *JFK Assassination File*, 11–12.
13. Robert Hollingsworth oral history, Mar. 18, 2011, Oral History Collection, the Sixth Floor Museum at Dealey Plaza, https://emuseum. jfk.org/objects/33016/robert-hollingsworth-oral-history?ctx=0eae-ec121da5ac5ec5a9469d6169331bdabccdda&idx=0.
14. Carter's use of the word "hit" occurred when he heard the police dispatcher use "hit" at 12:31 p.m., saying, "It looks like the President has been hit." Curry, *JFK Assassination File*, 31.

Chapter 6

1. The *Times Herald* ceased publication in 1991.
2. I thought for years that it probably took about fifteen minutes to get there. Six decades later, I tried duplicating our pace from the newspaper's site, 1101 Pacific Avenue. I was astonished to reach Dealey Plaza in just under eight minutes.
3. Bugliosi, *Reclaiming History*, 69.
4. Kellerman testimony, *Hearings*, II:73. This injury was so severe that medical experts concluded that Kellerman couldn't have heard the president say anything at that point; Bugliosi, *Reclaiming History*, 472–82
5. *Hearings*, III:243–70.
6. Zapruder told me he heard only two shots, and reiterated that in his testimony before the Warren Commission. Investigators soon determined, however, that a total of three shots had been fired. A mast arm holding a traffic signal deflected the first of the three shots; Zapruder heard and filmed the next two. The second shot hit the president in the upper back and exited his throat; the third and final shot struck the back of the president's head with catastrophic results. See Max Holland, "The Truth Behind Kennedy's Assassination," *Newsweek*, Nov. 28, 2014, https://www.newsweek.com/2014/11/28/truth-behind-jfks-assassination-285653.html.
7. Cronkite, *A Reporter's Life* (New York: Alfred A. Knopf, 1996), 304–8, gives a good account of his work this day. More details are in Douglas

Brinkley's biography, *Cronkite* (New York: HarperCollins, 2012), 264–84.

8. The Sixth Floor Museum has a copy of at least one page of Bates's notes.

9. Alexandra Zapruder, *Twenty-Six Seconds: A Personal History of the Zapruder Film* (New York: Twelve, 2016), 37. The author was Zapruder's granddaughter.

10. Eight months later, interviewed by the Warren Commission, Zapruder again broke into tears as he described what he had seen; *Hearings*, VII:571.

11. Bugliosi, *Reclaiming History*, 42.

12. Trost and Bennett, *President Kennedy Has Been Shot*, 7.

13. Trost and Bennett, *President Kennedy Has Been Shot*, 7.

14. This personal note reminds me of how near many Dallasites were to assassination events. Only upon reading Alexandra Zapruder's *Twenty-Six Seconds* and Richard Trask's *National Nightmare on Six Feet of Film* (Danvers: Yeoman Press, 2005), 98, did I learn that the third man was Erwin Schwartz, Zapruder's partner, later well known to my present wife, Phyllis Schmitz Payne. Schwartz's daughter Helene was one of Phyllis's closest childhood friends. She came to know Schwartz and his family very well at their comfortable home in North Dallas, and he is remembered by her as an unusually cheerful father who interacted closely with her and other visiting friends. Erwin Schwartz would play a major role in assisting Zapruder with the sale of his film and later publication rights.

15. Cronkite, *Reporter's Life*, 49–51.

16. Trost and Bennett, *President Kennedy Has Been Shot*, 103.

Chapter 7

1. City Manager Elgin E. Crull, to whom Chief Curry reported, met with Curry to discuss plans for dealing with the number of reporters arriving from across the nation and world. They agreed that the department should continue its usual policy of cooperating with the press. The unintended consequence of the policy was to enhance the impact of television coverage. Local newspaper reporters were at a disadvantage. Chief Curry later told the Warren Commission that he could not recall giving a single interview to newspaper reporters.

2. Richard B. Trask, *Pictures of the Pain* (Danvers: Yeoman Press, 1994), *553*.

3. See, for example, Frank S. DeRonja and Max Holland, "A Technical Investigation Pertaining to the First Shot Fired in the JFK Assassination," *Journal of the Association for Crime Scene Reconstruction*, no. 20 (May 9, 2016), 9–33.

4. Mrs. Bledsoe's recollections are in *Hearings*, VI:400–27. Her surprising sighting of Oswald on the bus is on pages 408–12.

5. *Hearings*, I:75; Bugliosi, *Reclaiming History*, 5, 179, 955–56; "The Sixth Floor Museum Announces Addition of Lee Harvey Oswald's Wedding Ring to Exhibit," Global News Wire, Oct. 19, 2015, https://www.globenewswire.com/news-release/2015/10/19/777323/37415/en/The-Sixth-Floor-Museum-Announces-Addition-of-Lee-Harvey-Oswald-s-Wedding-Ring-to-Exhibit.html.

6. Payne, *Big D*, 318.

7. She and her husband, George Hughes, came to Dallas in 1922 to begin separate law careers. She had completed her undergraduate studies at Goucher College and earned her law degree through evening studies at George Washington University. She was elected to the Texas legislature in 1931. After three terms, Texas governor James Allred appointed her as the state's first female district judge in history. (Aside from swearing in Lyndon Johnson as president this very day, Hughes would be remembered for presiding over a three-judge panel in *Roe v. Wade* (1970), in which all three agreed that the plaintiff had a right to a legal abortion. I later wrote her biography, *Indomitable Sarah*.

8. Payne, *Indomitable Sarah*, 249.

9. Payne, *Indomitable Sarah*, 249–50.

10. US Const. art. II, § 1, cl. 8, Oath of Office for the Presidency.

11. Payne, *Indomitable Sarah*, 255.

Chapter 8

1. Carter, "PRESIDENT DEAD," *Dallas Times Herald*, Nov. 22, 1963.

2. Trost and Bennett, *President Kennedy Has Been Shot*, 103.

3. "PRESIDENT DEAD," *Dallas Times Herald*, Nov. 22, 1963.

4. Trask, *National Nightmare*, 560.

5. This surely was the man my uncle Gene Payne saw, based on a picture of the innocent man depicted in Trask's *Pictures of the Pain*, 547.

6. As chief prosecutor, the street-smart Alexander was well known to reporters. He was closely involved in many aspects of investigations

into the assassination. He prepared the indictment for Oswald on Friday evening, Nov. 22, and was the chief prosecutor in the murder trial of Jack Ruby. Born in 1920 in Wichita Falls, Texas, he graduated from the University of Arkansas, followed by a law degree from Southern Methodist University.

7. Forty years later, in 2013, Gladys Johnson's granddaughter, Patricia Hall, recalled her different memory of Oswald two or three weeks before the assassination when she was 13 years old. "My brothers were rough-necking outside," she told CBS reporter Tracy Smith, "and Lee was out on the front porch. He pulled them apart from each other and sat them on the stairs, and he says, 'Now, boys, I want y'all to listen to me. You're brothers. You need to love each other. And never, ever do anything that would harm another human being'"; Smith, "A Peek inside Lee Harvey Oswald's Room," *CBS*, Oct. 18, 2013.

8. Oswald's mother, Marguerite Oswald, was driven there from Fort Worth by *Star-Telegram* reporter Bob Schieffer after she told him she was Oswald's mother and needed a ride to see her son. Before departing with her, Schieffer put on his fedora hat so indicative of detectives. Arriving in Dallas, he took her into Captain Fritz's office. Officers assumed he was a Fort Worth detective. When they realized he was a reporter, they turned him out into the crowded hallway.

9. *Hearings*, I:9.

Chapter 9

1. Some years later I looked at microfilm copies of that day's paper in the downtown Dallas Public Library. Alas! My byline was not there. The microfilm copies had been filmed from the earliest papers off the presses. My byline had not yet been inserted. Today, nearly sixty years later, my personal copies with my byline are getting yellower and yellower. My deteriorating copies will be gone, I'm sure, when my great-grandchildren are here.

2. John B. Mayo Jr., *Bulletin from Dallas: The President Is Dead* (New York: Exposition Press, 1967), 65.

3. Darwin Payne, "The Press Corps and the Kennedy Assassination," *Journalism Monographs*, no. 15 (Feb. 1970).

4. The ease of entrance into the police and third floor was confirmed by eleven other reporters in Payne, "Press Corps and the Kennedy Assassination," 41–42; and also *Hearings*, XV:378–79.

5. *Hearings*, IV:159–60.

6. Astonishingly, later in his questions for Captain Fritz, Warren Commission member John J. McCloy mistakenly believed reporters were permitted to stay in the homicide office during Oswald's interrogations. No reporters were ever permitted to witness interrogations. One or two police guards routinely stood at homicide office doors to keep out reporters or other unauthorized persons. Similarly, a month later Assistant Counsel Leon D. Hubert displayed the same erroneous belief in questioning Captain Glen King. Such assumptions surely led to the Warren Commission's exaggerated notions about press interference. See *Hearings*, IV:160, 246–47, and XV:55. Also Payne, "Press Corps and the Kennedy Assassination," 32–33.

7. Mayo, *Bulletin From Dallas*, 131.

8. Oswald also had told Fritz and Judge David Johnston at his 1:35 a.m. Saturday arraignment that he wanted Abt as his attorney. Fritz had assured him that he could make the call to Abt free of charge at the upstairs jail cells. Oswald was unsuccessful in his efforts but managed to get two of Abt's telephone numbers. He also told his brother Robert and Marina on their visits that he was trying to reach Abt. At about 4:20 p.m. he surprised Ruth Paine by calling her and asking her to call Abt in his behalf. She was astonished to hear directly from Oswald. They did not mention Oswald's involvement in the assassination. Oswald must have learned of Abt, a member of the Communist Party of the USA, through his involvement in representing the party.

9. Payne, "Press Corps and the Kennedy Assassination," 20.

10. Kantor later created controversy by claiming that he had been a friend of Jack Ruby's and that Ruby and the "mob" were tied into Oswald's murder in *The Ruby Cover-Up* (New York: Zebra Books, 1980). I regarded his assertion doubtfully. Seth and Ruby had nothing in common, nor would he have spent much time at a place such as Ruby's Carousel Club.

11. Marina Oswald told the Warren Commission that when she talked with him at police headquarters and he denied his guilt, she "could see by his eyes that he was guilty"; *Hearings*, I:78.

12. Curry, born in 1936 in Hamilton, Texas, came to Dallas as an infant with his parents. He attended Dallas Technical High School (later Crozier Tech) and was an all-district tackle on the school football team. He worked his way through the ranks to police chief in 1960. He retired in 1966 and died in 1980 after a heart attack.

13. *Hearings*, VII:268.

14. Wade held the office for nine more terms before retiring in 1986. He was the "Wade" in the famous Roe v. Wade. Wade had nothing against abortion, and his name appeared simply because he was the district attorney in charge of enforcing state laws in Dallas County.

15. Bugliosi, *Reclaiming History*, 169–70.

16. My summary is based primarily from Bugliosi, *Reclaiming History*, 184–89; Payne, "Press Corps and the Kennedy Assassination," 24; *Hearings*, XV:510; and film of the brief session widely available on the internet; one example is "Oswald Holds Press Conference," *CBS*, Nov. 19, 2013, https://www.cbsnews.com/video/oswald-holds-press-conference/.

Chapter 10

1. In the fall of 1962, Rather further distinguished himself by covering rioting in Oxford, Mississippi, where protestors sought to prevent James Meredith's enrollment at Ole Miss as its first Black student. Rather had left Dallas to be bureau chief in New Orleans by the time of the assassination.

2. *Hearings*, III:143–44.

3. *Hearings*, III:145.

4. Howard L. Brennan, *Eyewitness to History: The Kennedy Assassination As Seen by Howard Brennan*, with J. Edward Cherryholmes (Waco: Texian Press, 1987), 13–14. Other information concerning Brennan includes Agent Robert C. Lish's testimony in *Hearings*, III:142–46; and Trask, *Pictures of the Pain*, 502.

5. *Hearings*, III:148; Brennan, *Eyewitness to History*, 20.

6. Brennan, *Eyewitness to History*, 19.

7. Brennan, *Eyewitness to History*, 28.

8. Brennan, *Eyewitness to History*, 42.

9. Some three decades later a prominent researcher on the assassination, Max Holland, found that Euins was living in a Dallas suburb. Holland and I went there, and Euins carefully peeked through his door when we arrived. Finally relaxing, he said he remained suspicious of strangers because of what he saw at Dealey Plaza, and he had never returned there. He reluctantly agreed to meet us at there to show exactly where he had been and what he had seen. He said he had waved to the president and the president had returned his wave. Euins's testimony to the Warren Commission was on Mar. 10, 1964; *Hearings*, II:201–10.

10. The comment that "this boy was going to be killed" was paraphrased by Decker in *Hearings*, XII:48.
11. *Hearings*, XII:4, 110.
12. Information about these calls is in the testimonies of W. B. Frazier, *Hearings*, XII:53–55; Charles Batchelor, XII:4; Decker, XII:48–49; and Cecil E. Talbert, XII:109–10. Bugliosi describes the events in *Reclaiming History*, 242–44; Curry, in his brief work *JFK Assassination File*, does not address these questions.

Chapter 11

1. Bugliosi, *Reclaiming History*, 245–47, 253–54, 256, 260, 262–63.
2. *Hearings*, XVV:296–97.
3. *Hearings*, VII:269. See also "Living History with James 'Jim' Leavelle," Sixth Floor Museum, June 20, 2014, YouTube video, https://www.youtube.com/watch?v=R99EvAveiuU; and Bugliosi's *Reclaiming History*, 269–71. They sometimes differ in minor details but are basically consistent.
4. *Hearings*, VII:268–69.
5. Bugliosi, *Reclaiming History*, 273.
6. Larry A. Sneed, *No More Silence: An Oral History of the Assassination of President Kennedy* (Dallas: Three Forks Press, 1998), 414–15.
7. Mayo, *Bulletin from Dallas*, 72.
8. Montgomery interview in Sneed, *No More Silence*, 416.
9. United Press International archives, Nov. 24, 1963, https://www.upi.com/Archives/1963/11/24/Physician-says-Oswald-lethally-injured-by-time-he-arrived/8181204553842/.
10. Bugliosi, *Reclaiming History*, 281–82.
11. Burrus described his experiences in a Kindle Cloud Reader edition entitled *Bill Burrus, Newspaperman: An Oral History by William M. Burrus* (self pub., Amazon Digital Services, 1994), 63–64.
12. Huffaker et al., *When the News Went Live*, 124.
13. McMillan was surely the only person in America who had known so well both President Kennedy and Oswald. She earlier had been an advisor to Kennedy when he was a US senator. Sam Roberts, "Priscilla McMillan, Who Knew Both Kennedy and Oswald, Dies at 92," *New York Times*, July 15, 2021.
14. Trost and Bennett, *President Kennedy Has Been Shot*, 221.

15. Brandon Murray, "Do It for Pappy: The Legacy of Pappy's Showland and C. A. 'Pappy' Dolsen," *Legacies: A History Journal for Dallas & North Central Texas* 34, no. 1 (Spring 2022): 18–31.

16. Jackson details his photo best in his biography, *The Shot: A Photographer's Story*, written by his son-in-law, James A. Burgess, and published in 2016 by Archway Publishing, Bloomington, Indiana.

Chapter 12

1. "Protestors Arrested, Released," *Dallas Times Herald*, Dec. 5, 1963.

2. Payne, "Press Corps and the Kennedy Assassination," 38.

3. Payne, "Press Corps and the Kennedy Assassination," 39.

4. *Hearings*, I:16–17.

5. Letters to the editor, *Time*, Dec. 6, 1964.

6. Carlos Conde, "Teacher Suspended for Writing Story," *Dallas Morning News*, Dec. 10, 1963.

7. AP nationwide news release, Dec. 9, 1963.

8. "Teacher Gets Job Back," *Dallas Times Herald*, Dec. 12, 1963.

9. Editorial and letters to the editor, *Times Herald*, Dec. 10 and 11, 1963.

10. Payne, *Big D*, 321.

11. "What's Right With Dallas?," *Dallas Times Herald*, Jan. 1, 1964, and *Dallas Morning News*, Jan. 2, 1964.

12. *Hearings*, II:190–201.

13. *Hearings*, I:125–26.

14. Darwin Payne, "A Visit With Marina," *Dallas Times Herald*, Mar. 8, 1964.

15. "Guinn Loses Arrest Suit in JFK Death," *Dallas Times Herald*, Sept. 29, 1964.

Chapter 13

1. Bugliosi, *Reclaiming History*, 513.

2. Numerous examples are found in National Threat Assessment Center, *Protecting America's Schools: A U.S. Secret Service Analysis of Targeted School Violence*, 2019, https://www.secretservice.gov/sites/default/files/2020-04/Protecting_Americas_Schools.pdf. Others are in Pablo Patricio Zarate-Garza et al., "How Well Do We Understand the Long-Term Health Implications of Childhood Bullying?," *Harvard Review of Psychiatry* 25, no. 2 (Mar. 4, 2017): 89–95; Adam Sands et al., "The Long-Term Outcomes of Prepubertal

Depression and Internalizing Problems: A Scoping Review," *Harvard Review of Psychiatry* 30, no. 3 (May–Jun 2022): 163–80, https://pubmed.ncbi.nlm.nih.gov/35576448/; and Douglas Vanderbilt and Marilyn Augustyn, "The Effects of Bullying," *Paediatrics and Child Health* 20, no. 7 (July 2010): 315–20.

3. *Hearings*, VIII:106–7.
4. *Hearings*, VIII:107; see also 91–154, and XI:472–73.
5. *Hearings*, XXI:58–59; see also I:126–264.
6. *Hearings*, XI:1–82.
7. *Hearings*, XI:4.
8. *Hearings*, XI:77.
9. *Hearings*, XI:80.
10. *Hearings*, VIII:7.
11. *Hearings*, VIII:23; see also 1–15 and 21–27.
12. *Hearings*, XXI:485, 487.
13. *Hearings*, XXI:489.
14. *Hearings*, XXI:487.
15. *Hearings*, XXI:485.
16. *Hearings*, XXI:489; see also 485–95; and VIII:224–28.
17. *Hearings*, VIII:224.
18. *Hearings*, VIII:217.
19. *Hearings*, VIII:221; see also XX:89–90; VIII:214–24.
20. *Hearings*, XX:25.
21. Heather Maher, "Why Lee Harvey Oswald Fled to the Soviet Union," *Atlantic Monthly*, Nov. 20, 2013, review of Peter Savodnik's book, *The Interloper: Lee Harvey Oswald Inside the Soviet Union*, (New York: Basic Books, 2013).
22. *Hearings*, XX:307.
23. Priscilla Johnson, "Oswald in Moscow," exhibit no. 6, in *Hearings*, XX:307.
24. *Hearings*, XX:308; see also 307–11.
25. *Report of the Warren Commission on the Assassination of President Kennedy* (New York: McGraw-Hill, 1964), 392.
26. *Hearings*, XX:257.
27. *Hearings*, XX:257–75, 511–33.
28. *Report of the Warren Commission*, 183–84.
29. Police learned that Oswald was the shooter when Marina told the Warren Commission, *Hearings*, I:16–20.

30. *Hearings* XX:262–64.

31. *Hearings* XX:265; see also 257–73.

32. *Hearings*, I:75; Bugliosi, *Reclaiming History*, 5, 179, 955–56.

Chapter 14

1. The square monument, free of excessive adornment, was made of precast concrete columns about thirty feet high and open to reveal the sky above.

2. Payne, *Big D*, 322.

3. Darwin Payne, *No Small Dreams: J. Erik Jonsson—Texas Visionary* (Dallas: DeGolyer Library, 2014), 123; Payne, *Dallas Citizens Council: An Obligation of Leadership*, published in 2008 by the Dallas Citizens Council.

4. Payne, *Big D*, 324.

5. Max Holland, *The Kennedy Assassination Tapes* (New York: Alfred A. Knopf, 2004), 270.

6. Payne, *No Small Dreams*, 128.

7. Darwin Payne and Kathy Fitzpatrick, *From Prairie To Planes: How Dallas and Fort Worth Overcame Politics and Personalities to Build One of the World's Biggest and Busiest Airports* (Dallas: Three Forks Press, 1999).

8. Fagin, *Assassination and Commemoration*, offers a full history of this compelling story. This nonprofit establishment flourished with exhibits, archival items, and documents for the public and researchers.

9. Undated memo from Ken Smart to me in my personal JFK assassination materials.

10. Frost, "Stopping by Woods on a Snowy Evening," in *New Hampshire* (New York: Henry Holt, 1923).

11. "Doctors Identify Body as Oswald: Experts Say Teeth, Scar, Primary Clues," *Fort Worth Star-Telegram*, Oct. 5,1981.

12. Bugliosi, *Reclaiming History*, chapters entitled "Jim Garrison's Prosecution of Clay Shaw and Oliver Stone's movie *JFK*" (1347–436) and "Conclusion of No Conspiracy," (1437–461).

13. Joel Kotkin and Cullum Clark, "Big D Is a Big Deal," *City Journal*, Summer 2021.

Appendix

1. David S. Reynolds, *Abe: Abraham Lincoln in His Times* (New York: Penguin Press, 2020), 742.
2. Reynolds, *Abe*, 741–44, 908–14.
3. Evan Andrews, "The Assassination of President James A. Garfield," *History*, updated March 27, 2023, https://www.history.com/news/the-assassination-of-president-james-a-garfield.
4. Andrews, "Assassination of Garfield."
5. Margaret Leech, *In the Days of McKinley* (New York: Harper and Brothers, 1959), 595–96.
6. Leech, *In the Days of McKinley*, 596; see also 591–96.
7. Truman, *Harry S. Truman*, 487–88.
8. David McCullough, *Truman* (New York: Simon & Schuster, 1992), frontispiece and 809–12. Maureen Dowd's father, an inspector in charge of Senate security at the time, arrived in time to wrest a 38-caliber pistol from one of the shooters. "Rhapsody for a Boy in Blue," *New York Times*, Jan. 30, 2022.

Bibliography

Note: I used two of my reporters' notebooks to record notes during my assassination coverage. These I treated as original sources. I also consulted works listed below in order to add a broader context to this book and describe events at which I was not present.

Government Documents

Hearings before the President's Commission on the Assassination of President John F. Kennedy. 26 vols. Washington, DC: Government Printing Office, 1964. (I have used and cited numerous complete transcripts of interviews with persons of significant interests as well as documents, exhibits, and photographs, all of which are cited with references in footnotes.)

Report of the President's Commission on the Assassination of President John F. Kennedy. New York: McGraw-Hill, 1964.

Books

Aynesworth, Hugh. *JFK: Breaking the News*. Richardson: International Focus Press, 2003.

Aynesworth, Hugh. *Witness to History*. Dallas: Brown Books, 2013.

Barker, Eddie, and John Mark Dempsey. *Eddie Barker's Notebook*. Houston: John M. Hardy, 2006.

Brennan, Howard L. *Eyewitness to History: The Kennedy Assassination As Seen by Howard Brennan*. With J. Edward Cherryholmes. Waco: Texian Press, 1987.

Brinkley, Douglas. *Cronkite*. New York: HarperCollins, 2012.

Brinkley, Douglas. *The Wilderness Warrior: Theodore Roosevelt and the Crusade for America*. New York: Harper Perennial, 2010.

Bugliosi, Vincent. *Reclaiming History: The Assassination of President John F. Kennedy*. New York: W. W. Norton, 2007.

Burgess, James A. *The Shot: A Photographer's Story*. Bloomington, IN: Archway, 2016.

Burrus, William M. *Newspaperman: An Oral History by William M. Burrus*. Self-published, Amazon Digital Services, 1994. Kindle.

Caro, Robert A. *The Passage of Power: The Years of Lyndon Johnson*. New York: Alfred A. Knopf, 2012.

Catton, Bruce, ed. *Four Days: The Historical Record of the Death of President Kennedy*. New York: American Heritage, 1964.

Cronkite, Walter. *A Reporter's Life*. New York: Alfred A. Knopf, 1996.

Curry, Jesse E. *Retired Dallas Police Chief Jesse Curry Reveals His Personal JFK Assassination File*. Dallas: American Poster and Printing, 1969.

Dallek, Robert. *An Unfinished Life*. Boston: Little, Brown, 2003.

Davidson, Chandler. *Race and Class in Texas Politics*. Princeton: Princeton University Press, 1990.

Eisenhower, Dwight D. *Mandate for Change, 1953–1956: The White House Years*. Garden City, NY: Doubleday, 1963.

Evans, Rowland, and Robert Novak. *Lyndon B. Johnson: The Exercise of Power*. New York: New American Library, 1966.

Fagin, Stephen. *Assassination and Commemoration: JFK, Dallas, and The Sixth Floor Museum at Dealey Plaza*. Norman: University of Oklahoma Press, 2013.

Frost, Robert. *New Hampshire*. New York: Henry Holt, 1923.

Gallagher, Mary Barelli. *My Life with Jacqueline Kennedy*. New York: Paperback Library, 1970.

Gregory, Paul R. *The Oswalds: An Untold Account of Marina and Lee*. New York: Diversion Books, 2022.

Hazel, Michael V. *Dallas Reconsidered: Essays in Local History*. Dallas: Three Forks Press, 1995.

Hlavach, Laura, and Darwin Payne, eds. *Reporting the Kennedy Assassination: Journalists Who Were There Recall Their Experiences*. Dallas: Three Forks Press, 2013.

Holland, Max. *The Kennedy Assassination Tapes*. New York: Alfred A. Knopf, 2004.

Huffaker, Bob, Bill Mercer, George Phenix, and Wes Wise. *When the News Went Live: Dallas 1963*. New York: Taylor Trade, 2004.

Kantor, Seth. *The Ruby Cover-Up*. New York: Zebra Books, 1980.

Leech, Margaret. *In the Days of McKinley*. New York: Harper and Brothers, 1959.

Lehrer, Jim. *Top Down: A Novel of the Kennedy Assassination*. New York: Random House, 2013.

Leslie, Warren. *Dallas Public and Private: Aspects of an American City*. Dallas: SMU Press, 1996.

Mailer, Norman. *Oswald's Tale*. New York: Random House, 1995.

Mallon, Thomas. *Mrs. Paine's Garage and the Murder of John F. Kennedy*. New York: Pantheon Books, 2002.

Manchester, William. *The Death of a President: November 1963.* New York: Harper and Row, 1967.

Marcus, Stanley. *Minding the Store.* Boston: Little, Brown, 1974.

Mayo, John B., Jr. *Bulletin from Dallas: The President Is Dead.* New York: Exposition Press, 1967.

McCullough, David. *Truman.* New York: Simon & Schuster, 1992.

McMillan, Priscilla Johnson. *Marina and Lee.* New York: Harper & Lee, 1977.

Miller, Edward H. *Nut Country: Right-Wing Dallas and the Birth of the Southern Strategy.* Chicago: University of Chicago Press, 2015.

Minutaglio, Bill, and Steven L. Davis. *Dallas 1963.* New York: Twelve, 2013.

Payne, Darwin. *Big D: Triumphs and Troubles of an American Supercity in the 20th Century.* Dallas: Three Forks Press, 1994.

Payne, Darwin. *Dallas Citizens Council: An Obligation of Leadership.* Dallas: Dallas Citizens Council, 2008.

Payne, Darwin. *Indomitable Sarah: The Life of Judge Sarah T. Hughes.* Dallas: SMU Press, 2004.

Payne, Darwin. *No Small Dreams: J. Erik Jonsson—Texas Visionary.* Dallas: DeGolyer Library, 2014.

Payne, Darwin, and Kathy Fitzpatrick. *From Prairie to Planes: How Dallas and Fort Worth Overcame Politics and Personalities to Build One of the World's Biggest and Busiest Airports.* Dallas: Three Forks Press, 1999.

Pry, Will, ed. *The Reporters' Notes: JFK Assassination.* Canada: Pediment, 2013.

Ragsdale, Kenneth B. *The Year America Discovered Texas: Centennial '36.* College Station: Texas A&M University Press, 1987.

Read, Julian. *JFK's Final Hours in Texas: An Eyewitness Remembers the Tragedy and Its Aftermath.* Austin: Dolph Briscoe Center for American History, 2013.

Reynolds, David A. *Abe: Abraham Lincoln in His Times.* New York: Penguin Press, 2020.

Russo, Gus, and Harry Moses. *Where Were You? America Remembers the JFK Assassination.* Guilford: Lyons Press, 2013.

Schieffer, Bob. *This Just In: What I Couldn't Tell You on TV.* New York: G. P. Putnam's Sons, 2003.

Schlesinger, Arthur M., Jr. *A Thousand Days: John F. Kennedy in the White House.* Boston: Houghton Mifflin, 1965.

Segura, Judith Garrett. *Belo: From Newspapers to New Media.* Austin: University of Texas Press, 2008.

Sneed, Larry A. *No More Silence: An Oral History of the Assassination of President Kennedy*. Dallas: Three Forks Press, 1998.

Trask, Richard B. *National Nightmare on Six Feet of Film*. Danvers: Yeoman Press, 2005.

Trask, Richard B. *Pictures of the Pain*. Danvers: Yeoman Press, 1994.

Trask, Richard B. *That Day in Dallas*. Danvers: Yeoman Press, 2013.

Trost, Cathy, and Susan Bennett. *President Kennedy Has Been Shot*. Naperville, IL: Sourcebooks, 2003.

Truman, Margaret. *Harry S. Truman*. New York: William Morrow, 1973.

Zapruder, Alexandra. *Twenty-Six Seconds: A Personal History of the Zapruder Film*. New York: Twelve, 2016.

Newspapers and Articles

Dallas Times Herald

Dallas Morning News

Fort Worth Press

Fort Worth Star-Telegram

New York Times

Washington Post

Cloward, Tim. "Conspiracy-A-Go-Go: Dallas at the Fiftieth Anniversary of the Assassination." *Southwest Review* 98, no. 4, (2013): 407–36.

DeRonja, Frank S., and Max Holland. "A Technical Investigation Pertaining to the First Shot Fired in the JFK Assassination." *Journal of the Association for Crime Scene Reconstruction*, no. 20 (May 9, 2016), 9–33.

Holland, Max. "The Truth Behind Kennedy's Assassination." *Newsweek*, Nov. 28, 2014.

Kotkin, Joel, and Cullum Clark. "Big D Is a Big Deal." *City Journal*, Summer 2021.

Maher, Heather. "Why Lee Harvey Oswald Fled to the Soviet Union." *Atlantic Monthly*, Nov. 20, 2013.

Murray, Brandon. "Do It for Pappy: The Legacy of Pappy's Showland and C. A. 'Pappy' Dolsen." *Legacies: A History Journal for Dallas & North Central Texas* 34, no. 1 (Spring 2022): 18–31.

Payne, Darwin. "The Press Corps and the Kennedy Assassination." *Journalism Monographs*, no. 15 (Feb. 1970).

Sands, Adam, M. T. van Dijk, E. Abraham, T. Yangchen, A. Talati, and M. M. Weissman. "The Long-Term Outcomes of Prepubertal Depression and Internalizing Problems: A Scoping Review." *Harvard Review of Psychiatry* 30, no. 3 (May–Jun 2022): 163–80.

Smith, Tracy. "A Peek inside Lee Harvey Oswald's Room." *CBS*, Oct. 18, 2013.

Time. Letters to the editor. Dec. 6, 1964.

Time. "Trouble for Tito." Oct. 27, 1961.

Vanderbilt, Douglas, and Marilyn Augustyn. "The Effects of Bullying." *Paediatrics and Child Health* 20, no. 7 (July 2010): 315–20.

Zarate-Garza, Pablo Patricio, Bridget K. Biggs, Paul Croarkin, Brooke Morath, Jarrod Leffler, Alfredo Cuellar-Barboza, Susannah J. Tye. "How Well Do We Understand the Long-Term Health Implications of Childhood Bullying?" *Harvard Review of Psychiatry* 25, no. 2 (March 4, 2017): 89–95.

Index